Make It Again, Sam

Make It Again, Sam

A Survey of Movie Remakes

Michael B. Druxman

South Brunswick and New York: A. S. Barnes and Company
London: Thomas Yoseloff Ltd

A. S. Barnes and Co., Inc.
Cranbury, New Jersey 08512

Thomas Yoseloff Ltd
108 New Bond Street
London W1Y OQX, England

Library of Congress Cataloging in Publication Data
Druxman, Michael B   1941-
Make it again, Sam.
Includes filmographies.
"Compendium of film remakes": p.
1. Moving-picture remakes. I. Title.
PN1995.9.R45D78   791.43'7   74-19810
ISBN 0-498-01470-3

Also by Michael B. Druxman:

Paul Muni: His Life and His Films
Basil Rathbone: His Life and His Films

PRINTED IN THE UNITED STATES OF AMERICA

Contents

Preface   9
Acknowledgments   11
Introduction   13

1   An American Tragedy   27
2   Ben-Hur   32
3   The Blue Angel   38
4   The Champ   42
5   Destry Rides Again   45
6   Dr. Jekyll and Mr. Hyde   50
7   Four Daughters   59
8   Goodbye, Mr. Chips   63
9   High Sierra   69
10   House of Strangers   75
11   The Hunchback of Notre Dame   81
12   Jesse James   88
13   Les Miserables   94
14   Macbeth   100
15   Madame X   108
16   The Maltese Falcon   114

17   Moby Dick   120
18   The Mummy   125
19   Mutiny on the Bounty   128
20   One Sunday Afternoon   134
21   The Phantom of the Opera   139
22   The Philadelphia Story   145
23   The Prisoner of Zenda   151
24   Rain   157
25   Red Dust   163
26   Rio Bravo   168
27   The Sea Hawk   173
28   The Sea Wolf   176
29   Show Boat   185
30   The Spoilers   192
31   Stagecoach   200
32   The Ten Commandments   205
33   Wuthering Heights   210

Compendium of Film Remakes   215

Preface

Determining the approach and scope of *Make It Again, Sam*[1] was not an easy task. Little has been written about film remakes, so there were no precedents to follow, and it seemed that everybody I discussed the project with had a different idea on how to proceed.

True, I had a basic outline for the work from the beginning. There would be an Introduction, followed by thirty-three chapters detailing the film life of a like number of literary properties—chosen for their illustrative value. Each of these chapters would acknowledge every known version of a particular story—with special emphasis on the major remakes—and attempt, as much as possible, to answer three questions: (1) Why was the picture remade? (2) How was the remake different from the original as far as *important* story changes were concerned? (3) What was the critical reaction to the remake?

Whenever they were available, individuals involved with the production of these films would be consulted.

Finally, the book would have an Compendium—a long, if partial, list of other well-known literary properties and their multiple movie versions.

When executed, this outline would accomplish the book's twofold objective—to provide a comprehensive dissertation on the remake practice, as well as an easy reference for those individuals wanting basic information on a large number of motion pictures and their subsequent renditions.

In defining a "remake" for our purposes, I decided to limit the discussion to those *theatrical* films that were based on a *common literary source* (i.e., story, novel, play, poem, screenplay), but were not a sequel to that material. Still, this seemingly infallible signpost left much room for conjecture, as many pictures that are obviously remakes do not credit their origins. (In cases such as these, the new movie would have had to borrow more than just an element or two from its predecessor to qualify. *Frenchie,* a 1950 Universal flick whose two leading characters were *inspired* by the James Stewart and Marlene Dietrich roles in *Destry Rides Again* would, therefore, *not* be considered a remake because its story is substantially original.)

Nevertheless, the rule solved more problems than it created in that it allowed me to classify nonfiction films in a more concise manner. Jesse James, for instance, has been the subject of numerous pictures, but only the two 20th Century-Fox productions (1939 and 1957) have a common derivation.

On the other hand, historical movies based on the same characters or incidents, but by *different* writers, were labeled as remakes if they dealt with the material in essentially the same manner as a predecessor. Biographies of figures like Cleopatra and Christ, though originating from diverse manuscripts, were similar enough in content to be considered remakes.

Excluded from consideration were the foreign-language versions of early talkies. Although these were basically original productions (made by American studios at the same time as the English version in order to capitalize on the European market), they didn't meet the definition of "remakes." As far as this book is concerned, a film must have been produced *after* and *independently* from its predecessor in order to be included. There were, of course, many marginal situations and I simply used my own discretion in deciding whether or not to embrace them. Also ignored was the relatively recent trend in remaking old theatrical features for television. Indeed, both of these areas would make interesting topics for their own separate books.

---

[1] The title, of course, was inspired by *Casablanca* (1942), a film that has, wisely, never been remade as a theatrical feature, but whose story has served as the basis for two television programs: a March 1955 production on NBC's "Lux Video Theatre," starring Paul Douglas in the Humphrey Bogart role, and as a segment of the short-lived 1955 *Casablanca* series that featured Charles McGraw as Rick.

I have attempted to limit my personal comments on the films as much as possible (there are, again, several exceptions). Artistic criteria have changed so radically during the past few years that it is unfair to judge the earlier pictures, especially, by today's standards. In most cases, I have deferred, at least partially, to critical reviews appearing at the time of a movie's initial release. For similar reasons, I have tried to avoid discussing topics like directorial style, preferring to confine my remarks to the actual story and character changes that are present in the new renditions.

I've dealt with the material in a way that will, hopefully, appeal more to the film "buff," rather than to the serious cinema scholar. My intent is to both amuse and inform the *light* reader of movie memorabilia, but, at the same time, to give him a firm starting point should he wish to research the subject further.

The Compendium, listing films and their remakes *not* covered in the text portion of the work, has had its entries limited to those literary properties that, I feel, would be of greatest interest to the reader for which the volume is intended. Most notably absent from this section are familiar, even classic, stories, which have not been remade since the era of silents or early talkies. Information regarding new remakes that have been announced or that are currently in production is the most recent available at press time.

As far as the longer entries are concerned, I've utilized my personal judgment in editing these to eliminate the less important filmings of a property, as well as those remakes whose existence could not be verified by at least one *substantial* reference material.

Naturally, a work of this sort will foster some complaints with regard to various omissions of one sort or another. Since it is conceivable that a revised and updated edition will be published in the future, any recommendations regarding its content are welcome.

Acknowledgments

Grateful acknowledgment is made to the many individuals and organizations who gave of their time, their knowledge, loaned films for viewing purposes, and/or helped gather stills in preparation of this book:

Mort Abrahams, Academy of Motion Picture Arts and Sciences, Allied Artists, American Film Institute, American-International, Audio-Brandon Films, Rudy Behlmer, Curtis Bernhardt, Henry Blanke, Eddie Brandt, Budget Films, W. R. Burnett, James Cagney, John Carradine, Dane Clark, James B. Clark, Robert Clarke, George Cukor, Bob Cummings, Edward Dmytryk, Gordon Douglas, Paul Ecenia, Julius J. Epstein, Films, Inc., Buddy Freed, Neil Hamilton, Howard Hawks, Paul Henreid, Jesse Hibbs, Jean Holloway, Charlene Holt, Ronnie James, Allan Jones, Howard Keel, KHJ-TV, KTLA, KTTV, Larry Edmunds Bookshop, Kenneth G. Lawrence, Margaret Lindsay, Robert B. Little, Anita Lowe, Arthur Lubin, Ida Lupino, A. C. Lyles, John Lee Mahin, George Marshall, Barbara Massey, Metro-Goldwyn-Mayer, Jack Miller, Movie Star News, Richard Murphy, National Telefilm Associates, John O'Steen, Paramount Pictures, Lindsley Parsons, Joe Pasternak, Stephanie Powers, Martin Rackin, David Lowell Rich, Ruth Roman, Herb Ross, Stanley Rubin, William Sackheim, George Schaefer, Leroy Scott, Randolph Scott, George Sidney, Don Siegel, Sol Siegel, Tony Thomas, Richard Thorpe, Claire Trevor, Twentieth Century-Fox, United Artists Corporation, Universal Pictures, Turnley Walker, Hal B. Wallis, Raoul Walsh, Warner Brothers, William Wellman, and William Wyler.

11

Introduction

Almost from its beginnings, the motion picture industry has made a practice of capitalizing on past successes by remaking them. Few of these later editions have achieved the distinction enjoyed by their predecessors, but, at the very least, the majority of them can be rated as "interesting efforts."

In most instances, the decision to film a new version of a once-popular movie is a voluntary one (i.e., the producer and/or the studio feel that the original story is still viable and has the potential of again becoming a big money-maker). However, during the thirties and forties, when studios had to grind out a certain amount of product each year in order to fill their theaters, staff producers, unable to find fresh material, were forced to revert back to using previously filmed stories as the basis for their B and, sometimes, top-of-the-bill pictures. These old scripts, which had served well before, were retitled, then disguised with a new setting, "original" characters, and some novel incidents. Otherwise, the updated plots were essentially the same, point by point, as the earlier renditions.

Warner Brothers was constantly switching their old stories around. *Hi, Nellie,* a 1934 light-weight newspaper yarn starring Paul Muni, became *Love Is on the Air* with Ronald Reagan in 1937, *You Can't Escape Forever* with George Brent in 1942, and as late as 1949 was utilized as *The House Across the Street* starring Wayne Morris. Another Muni vehicle, *Dr. Socrates* (1935), was remade in 1939 as *King of the Underworld,* with Kay Francis playing the Muni role. (Howard Hawks did something similar when he remade *The Front Page* in 1940 as *His Girl Friday.* In the new film, Cary Grant essayed the part created by Adolphe Menjou in the 1931 version of the Hecht/MacArthur comedy, but the Pat O'Brien part was revamped to accommodate Rosalind Russell. Then, in 1970, Warners refilmed the Alfred Hitchcock suspense classic *Strangers on a Train* as *Once You Kiss a Stranger* and cast pretty Carol Lynley as the homicidal

maniac—played by Robert Walker in the 1951 picture.)

There have been other provocative story switches courtesy of the Burbank lot:

The plot from *Kid Galahad* (1937), a boxing story starring Edward G. Robinson and Bette Davis, was rewritten with a circus background (the fighter became a lion tamer) for the 1941 Humphrey Bogart/Sylvia Sidney film, *The Wagons Roll at Night.*

Five Star Final (1931), an exposé of yellow journalism with Robinson in the lead, had its setting changed from a newspaper office to a radio station when Bogart did it as *Two Against the World* in 1936.

The basic plot from *The Mayor of Hell* (1933), a James Cagney vehicle about crooked politicians running a boys' reformatory, was later used for *Crime School* (1938) with Bogart, and *Hell's Kitchen* (1939) starring Ronald Reagan.

Over at Twentieth Century-Fox, Darryl Zanuck would do pretty much the same thing. Blessed with an astute sense for good story construction, the studio head rationalized that, if a plot worked well once, it would probably do so again. Ergo, he took a property like *Three Blind Mice* (1938) with Loretta Young and used only the bare story line for a Betty Grable musical, *Moon Over Miami* (1941), and later a June Haver picture, *Three Little Girls in Blue* (1946).

Zanuck found that the "old switcheroo" was a good way to supply *all* his musical talent—Alice Faye and the Misses Grable and Haver—with stories for their films. *King of Burlesque* (1936) with Faye later served as the basis for her *Hello, Frisco, Hello* (1943), and the actress's *Tin Pan Alley* (1940) provided June Haver with a plot for the 1950 musical *I'll Get By.* Zanuck had his writers do little more than switch locales when Betty Grable's *Coney Island* (1943) was turned into a subsequent vehicle for her, *Wabash Avenue* (1950).

A 1937 Tyrone Power movie, *Love Is News,* was a

13

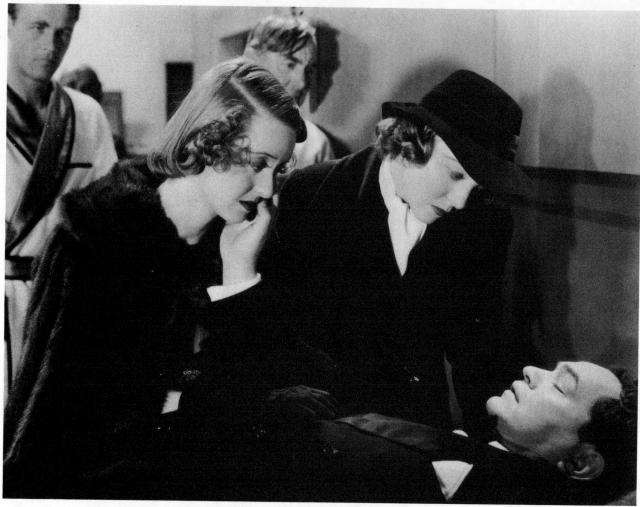

Kid Galahad (1937): Bette Davis, Jane Bryan, and Edward G. Robinson. In background: Wayne Morris and Harry Carey.

The Wagons Roll at Night: Humphrey Bogart, Sylvia Sidney, and Joan Leslie.

particular favorite of Zanuck's, so in 1943, he ordered that its tale be borrowed for Grable's *Sweet Rosie O'Grady,* then used the property again with Power in *That Wonderful Urge* (1949).

Executives like Jack Warner and Zanuck reasoned that the public wouldn't notice or wouldn't care that they were paying to see the same story over again every few years. After all, movies were better than radio, which was about the only *home* entertainment that was then available.

Aside from supplying ready material to meet their production schedules, there was another valid reason for regularly resurrecting these old stories—economics. Until relatively recently, studios would usually purchase the rights to novels, plays, and stories *in perpetuity.* They were, therefore, able to remake them as many times as they wished—without an additional payment to the original author. This made the new version's only story expense the cost of revamping the plot, a task usually accomplished by a staff writer.[1]

On the other side of the coin, there is the *direct remake*—a film that doesn't try to hide the fact that it is based on an earlier production. Such projects *may* have a new title (to avoid confusion with the original), updated dialogue, and some "minor" alterations in detail (these can range from simply changing the names of the characters to having the hero/heroine survive, where he/she may have died in a former version), but it essentially is the same film as its predecessor—with publicity campaigns not hiding that fact.

Occasionally, there are *nonremakes.* These movies retain the title of a familiar story and/or the name of its well-known author—for commercial purposes—but, otherwise, give the viewer an entirely new plot, which has a premise somewhat similar to the original one. The 1961 version of *The Thief of Bagdad,* as well as *The Sea Hawk* (1940), illustrate this classification well.

Stanley Rubin, producer of the 1955 edition of *Destry Rides Again,* as well as *The Girl Most Likely* (1958), a musical version of *Tom, Dick, and Harry* (1941), feels that, for a remake to be successful, there must be a *valid* reason for doing it in the first place—aside from the potential financial rewards: "If a studio is going to remake an old film—especially a successful one—they better have something in mind that will make the new picture as good or better than the original.

"For example, maybe the theme is timely again, or, perhaps, there's a 'hot' piece of casting that makes the project an 'exciting' one."

Timeliness has, indeed, been the reason for several remakes during the past few years. *Walk, Don't Run,* a 1966 revamping of *The More the Merrier,* took the 1943 George Stevens comedy about wartime housing conditions in Washington, D.C., and set it against the background of the Tokyo Olympics.

Odd Man Out, a 1947 British film dealing with the IRA and starring James Mason, was used in 1969 as the basis for a Sidney Poitier picture, *The Lost Man,* which had the Academy Award winner playing a black militant. In a similar political switch, John Ford's classic of the 1920s Irish rebellion, *The Informer* (1935), was, in 1968, used by Jules Dassin for *Uptight,* another Black oriented project. Unfortunately, neither remake was well received by audiences or the press.

An even better excuse for remaking is, of course, new casting. Entertainment industry personnel, as well as the public at large, seem to enjoy comparing the performances of current stars to the legendary ones turned in by the Hollywood "greats" of long ago. Finished results aside, Peter Finch seemed like a perfect choice when he was announced for the Ronald Colman role in the 1973 version of *Lost Horizon,* as did Robert Redford doing the Warner Baxter/Alan Ladd part in *The Great Gatsby* (1974), and Richard Burton and Elizabeth Taylor taking over where Mary Pickford and Douglas Fairbanks left off in *The Taming of the Shrew.* On the other hand, many Hollywoodites privately expressed their doubts when Lucille Ball was signed for *Mame* (1974), their feeling being that the popular television comedienne was too much of a "clown" to play the somewhat sophisticated role created by Rosalind Russell.

Possibly the best reason for redoing classic films is to adapt these vintage stories to new screen techniques that have been perfected since the originals were made. The coming of sound, for instance, inspired the studios to film their more popular pictures again, utilizing the new device. A case in point was George Arliss, who was hired by Warner Brothers to star in sound versions of his silent successes: *Disraeli, The Green Goddess,* and *The Man Who Played God.*

Later, when the sound process was perfected to give voices more clarity and allow the camera more fluidity, the studios remade some of their early talkies. At Metro, Joan Crawford played the title role in a 1937 version of *The Last of Mrs. Cheyney,* previously filmed with Norma Shearer in 1929. Over at the Warner lot, Edmund Goulding directed a 1938 version of *The*

---

[1] Today, most contracts for original material provide for additional payments in the event that a remake is later produced and, in some cases, such as the 1974 version of *The Great Gatsby,* rights must be completely renegotiated.

The Informer: **D'Arcy Corrigan and Victor McLaglen.**

Uptight: **Juanita Moore and Julian Mayfield. Liam O'Flaherty's tale of the IRA adapted to deal with a Black revolutionary group. Mayfield did the counterpart to the McLaglen role.**

Gunga Din: **Sam Jaffe, Cary Grant, Victor McLaglen, and Douglas Fairbanks, Jr.**

Sergeants Three: **Frank Sinatra, Henry Silva, Peter Lawford, Dean Martin, and Sammy Davis, Jr.**

Dawn Patrol starring Errol Flynn—almost an exact duplicate of Howard Hawk's original picture with Richard Barthelmess, shot in 1930.

The advent of color and, later, the wide screen, prompted additional remakes of properties that would be enhanced by these new processes—musicals and spectacles being some of the more successful types of films that have benefited from these improvements.

Less obvious were the horror film classics like *Frankenstein* and *Dracula,* which gained a brand new popularity once producers discovered they could be redone in blood-red color.

Often, filmmakers have taken a modern story and, in a remake, given it a western background. John Huston's magnificent 1950 American gangster film, *The Asphalt Jungle,* based on a novel by W. R. Burnett, was later shot as an Alan Ladd western, *The Badlanders* (1958), then reset to modern times in 1963 with a production titled *Cairo.* Along the same lines, Kipling's classic tale of old India, *Gunga Din* (1939) starring Cary Grant, Victor McLaglen, and Douglas Fairbanks, Jr., was spoofed by Frank Sinatra, Dean Martin, and Peter Lawford in the 1962 oater,

Sergeants Three. Two other westerns, *The Magnificent Seven* (1960) and *The Outrage* (1964) were derived directly from Japanese productions— *Seven Samurai* (1956) and *Rashomon* (1951), respectively.

An extremely popular form of remake is a *musical* adaptation of a formerly *straight* comedy or drama. Although attempts like *Lost Horizon* (1973) and *You Can't Run Away from It,* a 1956 version of *It Happened One Night* (1934), met with no success, properties like *Cabaret* (from *I Am a Camera*), *My Fair Lady* (*Pygmalion*), *Carousel* (*Liliom*), and *Oliver!* (*Oliver Twist*), all of which had their musical beginnings on the stage, fared much better.

In doing a *direct* remake, producers hope to draw two types of people into the theaters—those who saw the original film, liked it, and are curious to see how the new stars will handle their roles; and those who have only heard of the original and have decided to see the new version because the old one is not available for viewing.

The great classics of literature have always been popular with moviemakers, and works from such writers as Dumas, Dickens, Stevenson, and Shakes-

The Three Musketeers (1921): **Leon Barry, Douglas Fairbanks, George Siegmann, and Eugene Pallette.**

The Three Musketeers (1939): **The Ritz Brothers.**

The Three Musketeers (1948): **Van Heflin, Gene Kelly, Gig Young, and Robert Coote.**

The Three Musketeers (1974): Richard Chamberlain, Michael York, Oliver Reed, and Frank Finlay.

peare have been filmed on numerous occasions. Not only do these stories have the advantage of a presold title, but virtually all of them are in the public domain, requiring no payment in order to secure the dramatic rights.

A masterpiece like *The Three Musketeers,* first photographed during the earliest days of this century, is dusted off every decade or so in some country and adapted to fit the then-prevelent entertainment tastes. The Dumas swashbuckler became a vehicle for Douglas Fairbanks in 1921, a justification for the comedy antics of the Ritz Brothers in 1939, and an instrument for Gene Kelly's stylish movements in 1948. That successful MGM tongue-in-cheek version of the piece came about when director George Sidney decided that he wanted to make a "musicallike western with swords and feather hats."

Richard Lester's 1974 total burlesque of *Musketeers,* though successful at the box office, missed the boat as far as many swashbuckling aficionados were concerned. Filmed in a realistic style reminiscent of *Tom Jones,* the production totally ignored the romantic elements inherent in earlier pictures of this genre, disappointing those viewers who simply hoped to see a good old-fashioned "swordfight."

Some pictures purporting to be remakes are really no such animal, since the basic source material was never actually filmed in the first place. A good case in point is Hemingway's *To Have and Have Not,* produced in 1944; again in 1950 as *The Breaking Point;* and lastly as *The Gun Runners* in 1958.

Actually, there were only *two* versions of the book, since the 1944 rendition with Humphrey Bogart utilized only the title and leading character—jettisoning the novelist's story line in favor of one more pleasing to its producer-director, Howard Hawks, who recalls how the project came about: "Hemingway and I were talking about *To Have and Have Not* on a fishing trip and I told him I thought it was a lousy novel—probably his worse—but that I could make a picture out of it. He didn't believe me, so I bought the book to prove my point.

"Frankly, I only bought the thing to get the use of Hemingway's name. I hated the story and never really intended to use it. I just wanted the main character."

Michael Curtiz's *The Breaking Point* with John Garfield was much closer to Hemingway's saga and was well received by the press. But *The Gun Runners,* directed by Don Siegel and starring Audie Murphy, was a total "bomb"—a movie that Siegel didn't want to make in the first place: "I did it for the bread. We made an attempt to get as close to the book as possible, which was part of the problem since the story wasn't very good.

"Audie was a lovely person to work with, but to put him in a role that had previously been played by Bogie and Garfield was ridiculous.

"The project never had a chance because, aside from inadequate casting, we didn't have the time or money to make it right."

It's not uncommon for a director to do the remake of one of his own pictures. Among other reasons, it gives the artist an opportunity to correct any mistakes he may have made in the first version. Alfred Hitchcock comments on his two productions of *The Man Who Knew Too Much* (made in 1934 with Leslie Banks and in 1956 with James Stewart): "Let's say that the first version is the work of a talented amateur and the second was made by a professional."

Remakes—especially those based on *successful sound* productions—have seldom been the unqualified hits (either critical or financial) hoped for by their creators. Despite some notable exceptions—*The Dawn Patrol* (1938), *State Fair* (1945), *House of Wax* (1953), and the aforementioned *The Man Who Knew Too Much* (1956), to name a few—most subsequent renditions of the great cinema classics have been complete failures or quickly relegated to programmer

To Have and Have Not: **Walter Sande, Humphrey Bogart, and Lauren Bacall.**

The Breaking Point: **John Garfield, Wallace Ford, William Campbell, and players.**

The Gun Runners: **Eddie Albert and Audie Murphy.**

Beau Geste (1926): **Ralph Forbes and Ronald Colman.**

status. True, many of them might eventually garner a respectable box-office gross and wind up in the black, but they almost never achieve the status of their predecessors.

Why?

Aside from the problems that can plague any film venture—bad script, poor casting, misdirection, inadequate budget—the man doing a remake has some headaches all his own.

He might decide to "improve" the original story when he should have left well enough alone. Such a situation occurred with Universal's 1966 remake of *Beau Geste*. Christopher Wren's famous story about three brothers who join the French Foreign Legion had been successfully produced twice before—a silent edition with Ronald Colman in 1926 and a very popular talkie rendition with Gary Cooper in 1939.

Walter Seltzer, assigned by the studio to produce the newest version starring Guy Stockwell, feels that

the film never should have been done in the first place: "Lew Wasserman [then President of MCA, Universal's parent company] wanted to make *Beau Geste* again. I didn't think we should because it would have been impossible to find a cast to match the memory of Gary Cooper, Ray Milland, Robert Preston, and Brian Donlevy. But, Wasserman thought that the *title* would be the star, so we went ahead and did it."

Seltzer felt the original Wren story should be made more contemporary and that several plot points called for clarity. Among the revisions he and his writers came up with was the elimination of one brother. They also changed the reason that the two remaining siblings joined the Legion in the first place (this alteration eliminated an effective surprise ending that had enhanced the two earlier pictures), and let the leading character of Beau survive at the film's conclusion. In the other versions, he'd been killed. Additionally, the makers of the Technicolor desert epic unsuccessfully

Beau Geste (1939): **J. Carrol Naish, Stanley Andrews, Ray Milland, Gary Cooper, and Brian Donlevy.**

Beau Geste (1966): **Guy Stockwell.**

attempted to delve into the psychological background of the story's sadistic sergeant, portrayed by Telly Savalas. Brian Donlevy, interpreting that role in 1939, had played it straight—simply mean and vicious—and won an Oscar nomination for his efforts.

Few, if any, of the script changes aided the 1966 production and it quickly disappeared from theater screens.

Whereas *Beau Geste* was a project that didn't call for extensive changes, many vintage films do and, in some instances, the updating procedure is next to impossible.

Director Herb Ross comments: "Screenplays, especially those of the thirties and forties, have not dated as well as stage plays written during the same period. Dialogue in a top movie script just doesn't seem to match the often timeless quality in the words of a good play.

"A beautiful example—*Double Indemnity* was a tremendous success when it was filmed in the forties. But, when it was re-done for television some time back, it was a flop and the reason was that they didn't update the dialogue. Instead, they used the original script almost word for word."

Other stories require much more than an updating of the dialogue. In many cases, the moral values or situations in a once-exciting story have become so antiquated that even the best screenwriter cannot make the plot workable for contemporary audiences. Melodramas such as *The Trial of Mary Dugan* and *Back Street*, both of which were remade with disastrous results, are most susceptible to this fate.

The biggest "cross" that the producer of a remake must bear is his audience's memory. "Magnificent" pictures like Bela Lugosi's *Dracula* and John Barrymore's *Svengali* have remained vivid in viewer's minds, but few realize that, seen today as anything except a historical record, these films would be subject to ridicule. Changes in production and acting techniques, as well as the aforementioned maturing social attitudes of the public, have made many early classics anachronisms.

Nevertheless, people cling to their precious memories of a grander cinema in days gone by and, therefore, almost no remake—despite its quality—can shatter the fondness a spectator might hold for the original version he saw in his youth. It's called nostalgia.

Even more unfair, yet just as common, is the movie patron who has never seen the earlier picture, but has heard about it, and knocks the remake because it doesn't live up to his preconceived ideas. That's called stupidity.

Filmmakers have always approached remakes utilizing a certain amount of caution. None seem to be absolutely opposed to the practice, although there are a couple of schools of thought on the subject.

Henry Blanke, who has produced many "second editions" in his time, advises: "Never remake a picture that was previously successful. Remake one that was miscast, miswritten, or misdirected. In other words, a flop."

Producer Hal B. Wallis takes the opposite viewpoint: "If you have a *good* piece of material that has not been filmed for a number of years, there is probably a brand new audience for it. So, *I* wouldn't hesitate to redo a script with a new set of characters. I've done it many times before and I'll probably do it again."

In the motion picture industry, remakes are a fact of life. They have been with us almost from the birth of the art form and, as long as good *fresh* story material is scarce, they will remain.

A remade movie does *not* have to be a bad movie. Produced with a talented cast, a capable director, an intelligent screenplay, an ample budget, and, most important, *good judgment,* these pictures can be thoroughly entertaining and, in some cases, surpass the quality of the original version. To transpose the words of Mr. Wallis: It's happened before and, if audiences and reviewers will accept remakes on their own merits, it will certainly happen again.

Make It Again, Sam

1
An American Tragedy

Theodore Dreiser based his critically acclaimed 1925 novel, *An American Tragedy,* on an actual event—the 1906 killing of Miss Grace Brown by one Chester Gillette at Big Moose Lake in the Adirondacks. Although he followed the true facts of the murder case in his fictionalization, Mr. Dreiser also seized the opportunity to make his 840-page work a powerful social indictment of America's industrial society, which he felt excited indigent youths like his hero, Clyde Griffiths, with dreams of unattainable luxury. Such frustrating goals in weak individuals can, of course, lead to violations of the law, including, as in the case of Griffiths, murder.

The brooding narrative introduces Griffiths as the son of evangelist parents, who run a street mission for derelicts. Ashamed of his squalid surroundings, Clyde longs for a better life and quits school to seek work. A job as a hotel bellhop brings him enough money to attain better clothes and luxuries for himself, but, after he is involved in a hit-and-run auto death, he flees his Kansas City home for Chicago.

Clyde encounters his wealthy uncle, a collar manufacturer from Lycurgus, New York. Impressed with his kin, the elder Griffiths invites the lad to come to work in his factory. Clyde does well at the plant and is soon promoted. To combat his loneliness, he begins an affair with one of the factory girls, Roberta Alden.

He later meets Sondra Finchley, daughter of a wealthy family, and the relationship culminates in a romance between the two. Through marriage to Sondra, Clyde knows that his dreams of a lofty social position can finally be realized. However, these hopes are dashed when Roberta announces that she is pregnant and insists that Clyde set a wedding date.

Panicked that he will lose Sondra, young Griffiths decides to take Roberta out to a desolate lake and drown her. Yet, at the last minute, he can't go through with it. Fate steps in when the rowboat accidentally tips over. Clyde ignores the drowning girl's cries for help and swims away.

Nevertheless, he is soon apprehended and, following a sensational trial, convicted of murder. His claim that he had changed his mind about killing Roberta does not sway the jury. Clyde dies in the electric chair—his last visitor being his mother.

Dreiser's novel concludes with the mother returning to her street mission. Clyde's sister had had an illegitimate child and the reader is left with the impression that this tiny boy will be raised amid the same hopeless poverty and, possibly, come to the same end as his uncle.

The first screen version of *An American Tragedy* was a low-budget affair, released by Paramount in 1931. Sergei Eisenstein had originally been hired to direct the picture but, due to various production problems, eventually withdrew. Josef von Sternberg took over the project, working from a screenplay by Samuel Hoffenstein.

The von Sternberg film touches only briefly on Clyde Griffiths's unhappy background, but includes the fatal auto accident. Once he arrives in Lycurgus, however, the action of the picture follows that of the book quite closely.

Griffiths, as portrayed by Phillips Holmes, is an almost totally unsympathetic character; a selfish, moody, little weakling, caring only about his own gratification—sexual, monetary, and otherwise. He feels nothing for Roberta (Sylvia Sidney) and relatively little for Sondra (Frances Dee), who he pursues only to take advantage of her social position. Mr. Holmes's Clyde is more a villain than a victim of his environment.

The picture concludes with Griffiths's final meeting

An American Tragedy: **Sylvia Sidney and Phillips Holmes.**

An American Tragedy: **Frances Dee and Phillips Holmes.**

An American Tragedy: **Sylvia Sidney and Phillips Holmes.**

with his mother, and avoids Dreiser's sociological implications that were inherent in the scenes dealing with the illegitimate nephew.

Variety said: "As a picture, *An American Tragedy* unreels as an ordinary program effort with an unhappy ending. The other side is that its relations to the book upon which it is based are decidedly strained . . . as Von Sternberg has seen fit to present it, this celluloid structure is slow, heavy and not always interesting drama."

The *New York Times* found fault with the project also: "Granted that the translation of this lengthy work into a motion picture was an enormous undertaking, it seems a pity that the producers did not capture more of the author's analysis of the characters instead of merely using paragraphs from the book and trusting to snatches of dialogue to give effective characterization and motivation. . . . In the trial scene, however, Mr. von Sternberg fires his film with feeling. He really gets down to the author's work. . . ."

An American Tragedy was a total failure at the box office.

A better production of the Dreiser classic was George Stevens's potent *A Place in the Sun* (1951), released by Paramount. The screenplay by Michael

Wilson and Harry Brown updated the action and attitudes from the 1920s to the 1950s.

As Stevens explained in an interview with the *Los Angeles Times*: "It's a story, fundamentally, of the behavior of people in our society as it exists today. The social conditions, the extreme wealth and poverty, don't hold weight anymore. The things that were true to Dreiser's 1925 are not in our picture. Yet the picture is every bit as true to America as America is today."

Abandoning virtually all scenes of George Eastman's (Griffiths's counterpart) impoverished beginnings, and thereby Dreiser's social crusading, Stevens picked up the story with the young man's arrival at his uncle's *swimsuit* factory. Montgomery Clift's interpretation of the character was completely opposite Phillips Holmes's. Eastman was a likable, if weak, chap, who, simply, got into a difficult situation he was unable to cope with. The audience's sympathy was with this young man. He was truly a tragic figure.

Shelley Winters, on the other hand, inherited the Sylvia Sidney assignment (renamed Alice Tripp) and played the part much "bitchier" than her predecessor. Miss Sidney's Roberta was a sweet unfortunate girl, whom audiences felt sorry for, but the "nagging" Shelley Winters did nothing except increase one's empathy for Eastman's plight.

A Place in the Sun: **Montgomery Clift and Elizabeth Taylor.**

A Place in the Sun: **Raymond Burr, Walter Sande, Montgomery Clift, and Fred Clark.**

A Place in the Sun: **Montgomery Clift and Shelly Winters.**

Whereas von Sternberg had shown Griffiths's crime of omission (i.e., his swimming away from a helpless Roberta after the boat had overturned), Stevens dissolved to another scene at that point—leaving the viewer to guess as to the hero's ultimate decision.

Mr. Stevens, in a *New York Times* interview, said: "Clyde Griffiths [is] one of the most fascinating and controversial figures in literature. You can spend weeks debating Clyde's guilt or innocence, his legal immorality over his spiritual immorality."

Stevens played his film as a great tragic love story between Eastman and Angela Vickers (Elizabeth Taylor in the Sondra Finchley role): "The real tragedy occurred when he [Eastman] became 'the luckiest man in the world'—the rich girl accepted him. The rest is mere mechanics."

The 1951 picture maintained the romantic element right to its conclusion, by having Angela visit George on death row to bid him goodbye. As he is led away to be executed, his final thoughts are of this girl that he truly loved.

Variety called the picture: ". . . a film that ranks with Hollywood's finest in the past decade. . . . Helping to make the love story are the flawless performances of its three young stars, Montgomery Clift, Elizabeth Taylor, and Shelley Winters. Each is just right for the character played and each registers an individual triumph."

A Place in the Sun won Academy Awards for Best Director, Screenplay, Black and White Cinematography (William C. Mellor), Dramatic Score (Franz Waxman), Editing (William Hornbeck), and Black and White Costume Design (Edith Head). The film remains Stevens' masterpiece, as well as a glowing monument to a great writer for his eminent contribution to American literature.

An American Tragedy

FILMOGRAPHY

1931: (Par/Josef von Sternberg) Phillips Holmes.
1951: *Place In The Sun, A* (Par/George Stevens) Montgomery Clift.

2
Ben-Hur

According to the reference books, MGM's 1959 production of *Ben-Hur* won eleven Academy Awards—more than any other film in motion picture history. The honors included Best Picture, Best Director (William Wyler), Best Actor (Charlton Heston), Best Supporting Actor (Hugh Griffith), and Best Music Score (Miklos Rozsa). Yet, despite the record number of laurels garnered by that multimillion dollar project, it was the *first* movie version of General Lew Wallace's novel—made in 1907 by the Kalem Company—that achieved the more significant position in motion picture history.

Wallace's tale of the Christ was first published in 1880. It became the basis for a dazzling stage production in 1889 starring Ernest Morgan in the title role and William S. Hart as Messala. The awesome chariot race in that live entertainment was accomplished by having two horses (later increased to five) run on a treadmill while a painted backdrop revolved behind them.

Kalem's abbreviated screen version of the story was directed by Sidney Olcott from an adaptation by Gene Gauntier. Filmed in "sixteen magnificent scenes with illustrated titles," the primitive 1907 production incurred a lawsuit from the book publisher and play producer, who both claimed copyright infringement, since the company had failed to obtain the film rights to the material.

Kalem defended the action by arguing that the picture was good advertising for both the play and the novel, however the courts were not sympathetic to this position and, in 1912, the film company paid damages of twenty-five thousand dollars.

An important legal precedent had been set. The test case established that literary rights existed in all material produced for the screen.

MGM released the second and more polished version of *Ben-Hur* near the end of 1925. That trouble-plagued four-million-dollar production was nearly three years in the making, primarily because of the various difficulties it was subjected to on its Italian location. The project, directed by Fred Niblo, who'd replaced Charles Brabin after the first two years, was finally completed in the Los Angeles area.

Bess Meredyth and Carey Wilson wrote the scenario for the production, which remained relatively faithful to the original material:

Twenty years after the birth of Christ, a wealthy young Jew, Judah Ben-Hur (Ramon Novarro), and his boyhood confidant, Messala (Francis X. Bushman), a Roman centurion, terminate their friendship. The officer had returned to Jerusalem from schooling in Rome to discover that his new-found arrogance made continuing the relationship impossible.

When Judah accidentally knocks a tile off his roof, injuring the Roman Procurator of Judea, the embittered Messala siezes the opportunity to arrest his former friend and have him sentenced to the galleys for life. Ben-Hur's mother (Claire MacDowell) and sister, Tirzah (Kathleen Key), are also imprisoned.

Enroute across the desert to the sea, the thirsty Judah is given water by Jesus, the son of a carpenter.

His hate for Messala keeps Ben-Hur alive in the galleys for over three years. After he saves the life of a Roman tribune during a fierce sea battle, the aristocrat, Quintus Arrius (Frank Currier), adopts Judah and takes him to Rome to teach him the skills of a warrior.

Ben-Hur later returns to Judea, but can find no trace of his mother or sister. Although his family estates have been confiscated, Judah discovers that the actual money of his noble house has been protected and nur-

Ben-Hur (1925): Nigel DeBrulier, Mitchell Lewis, May McAvoy, Ramon Novarro, and players.

Ben-Hur (1925): Francis X. Bushman and Ramon Novarro.

Ben-Hur (1925): **Ramon Novarro.**

tured by Simonides (Nigel DeBrulier), a bond slave of his late father. The young Jew falls in love with Simonides's daughter, Esther (May McAvoy).

Dedicated to the defeat of Messala, Ben-Hur enters a chariot race, driving the horses of the Arabian Sheikh Ilderim (Mitchell Lewis). The contest is a bloody one. Messala attempts to win through foul play, but he himself becomes the victim of his own evil deeds and is crippled for life. The race and glory is won by Judah.

Ben-Hur, who had been hearing about "the son of God" for many years, finally becomes a true believer in the prophet's teachings. He offers to put his entire fortune at Christ's disposal, then, when he learns that the holy man has been arrested, attempts to raise an army to rescue him.

Esther learns that Tirzah and her mother have become lepers. Released from prison, they are taken by Judah's future bride to see the Christ—on his way to be crucified. Before he succumbs, Jesus heals the two women and tells Ben-Hur that he should not attempt to save him, since God willed He should die.

Convinced that Jesus is the Messiah, Ben-Hur embraces Christianity.

Although the picture's performances (especially that of Francis X. Bushman) seem a bit overdrawn today, the 1925 rendition of *Ben-Hur* is still an exciting film to view. At the time of its release, the *New York Times* said: "As a film spectacle, it is a masterpiece of study and patience, a photodrama which is filled with so much artistry that one would like to ponder over some of the scenes to glean all that is in them, instead of seeing just that passing flash. . . . The famous chariot races have been depicted so thrillingly that this chapter evoked no little applause."

Ben-Hur grossed approximately nine million dollars at the box office. A shortened version was released in 1931 with synchronized music and sound effects.

The success of *Quo Vadis* in 1951 gave MGM production head Dore Schary and producer Sam Zimbalist the idea of remaking *Ben-Hur* also, but subsequent problems at the studio—huge financial losses on other films, proxy battles for control of the company, and so forth—forced them to table the project indefinitely.

Joseph R. Vogel, who assumed the presidency of MGM in 1956, decided to take a huge gamble to save the then-faltering Culver City lion and produce a film that was, at that time, the most expensive ever made. The initial budget on *Ben-Hur* was seven million dollars; however at the end of a nine-month shooting schedule at Cinecitta Studios in Rome, that figure had more than doubled.

Shot in Technicolor and Camera 65, the Sam Zimbalist production was directed by William Wyler, an assistant director on the 1925 version. Wyler was intrigued by the story and felt that it could be made with a minimum of changes from the earlier film. He ordered his screenwriters, Karl Tunberg and Christopher Fry (denied screen credit by the Writers Guild), to judiciously eliminate some of the story's subplots, such as the attempted seduction of Ben-Hur by Messala's mistress, and emphasize characterization. Audiences who saw the 1959 release were much more aware of the emotional and spiritual development of the leading character than had been viewers of the 1925 film.

In this new version, the conflict between the Romans and the Jews did not necessarily spring from a general anti-Semitic attitude exhibited by the centurions, as was the case in the Novarro/Bushman picture, but had more of a political basis.

Another modification—Messala was not crippled as a result of the 1959 chariot race, but killed.

The most interesting change that director Wyler made concerned his treatment of Christ: "How we would handle the character of Jesus became our biggest problem. The old film version of *Ben-Hur* was no help to me in this respect because it was too outdated. Also, there is very little research material available on Christ—that is, no *definite* material. Everything else in the era is well researched—but not Christ.

"We finally decided that the audience would never see his face or hear his voice [This was also the case in the 1925 version]. That way, we could treat him either reverently or realistically."

The earlier MGM film had devoted a considerable

Ben-Hur (1959): **Stephen Boyd and Charlton Heston.**

Ben-Hur (1959): **Jack Hawkins and Charlton Heston.**

Ben-Hur (1959): Stephen Boyd and Charlton Heston.

amount of footage to Jesus. In fact, much of that material was completely independent of Ben-Hur's story and could have been extracted from the picture without hurting the story line.

On the other hand, Wyler's project included the nativity scene, and one or two other short sequences dealing with the prophet, but aside from that, the only time audiences saw Jesus was when he came into contact with Ben-Hur, who did not become a believer until late in the movie . . . at the time of the actual crucifixion.

Explains the director: "It was *not* the story of Christ. It was the story of Ben-Hur. So, we only used Jesus in relationship to Ben-Hur."

The leading roles in the production were filled by Charlton Heston (Ben-Hur), Stephen Boyd (Messala), Jack Hawkins (Quintus Arrius), Haya Hara-reet (Esther), Hugh Griffith (Shiekh Ilderim), and Sam Jaffe (Simonides).

As might be expected, the spectacular chariot race, which took second-unit directors Andrew Morton and Yakima Canutt three months to film, garnered the lion's share of the attention and was chiefly responsible for the production's eventual worldwide gross of sixty-five million dollars.

Of the film, the *New York Times* reported: "Without for one moment neglecting the tempting opportunities for thundering scenes of massive movement and mob excitement that are abundantly contained in the famous novel of Gen. Lew Wallace, upon which this picture is based, Mr. Wyler and his money-free producers have smartly and effectively laid stress on the powerful and meaningful personal conflicts that are strong in this heroic tale.

"As a consequence, their mammoth color movie . . . is by far the most stirring and respectable of the Bible-fiction pictures ever made."

Mr. Vogel had rolled a natural.

Ben-Hur

FILMOGRAPHY

1907: (Kalem/Sidney Olcott).
1925: (MGM/Fred Niblo) Ramon Novarro.
1959: (MGM/William Wyler) Charlton Heston.

3

The Blue Angel

Remembered primarily as the motion picture that catapulted Marlene Dietrich to international stardom, *The Blue Angel* (*Der Blaue Engel*) was, in fact, originally conceived to showcase the talents of its star, Emil Jannings. Unfortunately for the German character actor, things did not work out as planned. Once Dietrich sang "Falling in Love Again," the film became hers—and a legend was born.

Jannings, considered at one time to be the screen's greatest actor, departed Hollywood in 1929 to return to Berlin. With the advent of "talkies," his strong gutteral accent had become a liability to him in English-language films.

Joining forces with producer Erich Pommer of Ufa, Jannings requested that Josef von Sternberg, who'd directed him in *The Last Command,* be retained to guide him through a proposed biography of Rasputin. The Austrian director was not enthusiastic about doing a picture about the Russian "mad monk," so, as a compromise, Jannings suggested that they film Heinrich Mann's novel, *Professor Unrat.* The performer was partial to it because, like so many of his American successes, it dealt with the fall from grace of an elderly man.

The story told of Immanuel Rath (Jannings), a respected middle-aged professor of English in a provincial German boy's high school, who pursues several of his wayward pupils to a cheap cabaret called The Blue Angel. There, he becomes infatuated with Lola-Lola (Dietrich), a tawdry singer, and later sacrifices his career to marry her.

The match is doomed from the start. The disgraced professor, unable to teach, works as a stooge in his wife's traveling troupe, selling revealing pictures of her at the various cabarets where she appears.

Returning to the town where he once taught, the professor, now a clown with the company, is humiliated beyond endurance when he is forced to appear before his former associates and crow like a rooster. Rath later finds Lola backstage in the arms of her lover. He tries to strangle her, but the stagehands subdue him and eject the broken man from the club.

That evening, the former instructor wanders back to his old school. Going to his classroom, he sits behind his desk and dies.

Kathe Haach had been set to play the pivotal role of Lola in *The Blue Angel*—that is, until von Sternberg met an unimportant German actress named Marlene Dietrich. The director immediately realized that this girl, whose *artistic* talents were questionable, possessed the exact sexual magnetism that the part required.

Dietrich was signed, coached for weeks to overcome her vocal and English-language deficiencies, and, as they say, the rest is history. Under von Sternberg's attentive direction, the actress gave a sensuous performance, which completely overshadowed Janning's portrayal of the naive professor.

Filmed in both German and English versions, *The Blue Angel* was a heavy melodrama that garnered good notices from critics. Said Mordaunt Hall in a 1930 *New York Times* review: ". . . the final analysis is that it is a decidedly interesting picture with exceptionally fine performances contributed by Mr. Jannings and Miss Dietrich. . . ."

In 1959, Twentieth Century-Fox decided to remake the German film in color and Cinemascope and purchased the rights to the original Ufa script by Karl Zuckmayer, Karl Vollmoeller, and Robert Liebmann. Producer Jack Cummings set Nigel Balchin to write an updated screenplay.

The Blue Angel (1930): **Marlene Dietrich.**

The Blue Angel (1930): **Emil Jannings.**

The Blue Angel (1959): **May Britt.**

Edward Dmytryk, who was assigned to direct, recalls the project: "I, initially, didn't want to do the picture, but agreed to it in order to finish off my Fox contract. Frankly, I enjoyed making it. We shot exteriors in Bavaria and the interiors back in Hollywood.

"I never considered the original to be that much of a classic. That is, I don't think it's in the same league with . . . say . . . a *Stagecoach*. Dietrich was fine, but I think Janning's performance was rather 'hammy.' "

The Fox film starred Curt Jurgens and May Britt as Professor Rath and Lola. With the exception of a revised ending, this version stayed fairly close to the original story line. Instead of having the professor die in the retelling, Balchin's script concluded with Rath being "rescued" by his former principal, who, presumably, helps him reenter the teaching profession. Explains Dmytryk: "We felt there was no valid reason for Jurgens to die. He suffers enough without dying and is, in a sense, an even more tragic figure alive."

Since the first version of *The Blue Angel* was a product of the decadent Germany of the pre-Hitler twenties, Dmytryk felt that a change in tone was also in order: "Ours was not quite as dreary or depraved. We brought it up to date without changing the tack too much; the changes were in shading. Less emphasis on class distinction; and Jurgens, while of middle age, was not as old as Jannings made Professor Rath. Too, there are *attractive* girls in nightclubs these days; it was all on a somewhat higher level."

As he'd expected when he accepted the assignment, Dmytryk's picture got a generally negative response from critics. Miss Britt was no Marlene Dietrich and reviewers took every opportunity to point this out. In all fairness, however, the actress was *competent* in the part, but suffered in comparison to her predecessor.

Dmytryk: "That was our major problem. We didn't have Dietrich. May tried very hard, but was out of her depth. She wasn't a powerful enough personality to carry the film. I'd like to have had somebody else for the role, but there wasn't anyone."

attractiveness under an authentic German academician's mien, impersonating the unworldly schoolmaster with conviction."

The *New York Times* disagreed with the trade paper and said: "He plays the lecherous schoolmaster in such a heavy-paced, pop-eyed, low-voiced way that it is hard to feel any passion or ardor behind this facade."

To a certain extent, audiences and critics were a bit harsh on the Fox release. In itself, the film was rather entertaining and well done. People just *remembered* the original as being better.

According to Dmytryk: "It's 'dangerous' to remake a classic . . . even a second-rate one like *The Blue Angel*."

The Blue Angel (1959): Theodore Bikel, May Britt, and Curt Jurgens.

On the other hand, many critics agreed that Jurgens turned in a much better performance than Jannings. Said *Variety*: "Jurgens proves to be a flexible performer in the Jannings role. He disguises his masculine

The Blue Angel

FILMOGRAPHY

1930: (German/Josef von Sternberg) Marlene Dietrich.
1959: (Fox/Edward Dmytryk) May Britt.

4
The Champ

Sentimental movies dealing with children were good box office during the thirties, and Metro-Goldwyn-Mayer's *The Champ* was one of the best of the genre. Directed by King Vidor, the film's strongest assets were the performances of its two stars, Wallace Beery, receiving a Best Actor Oscar for his portrayal, and moppet Jackie Cooper. Frances Marion's story, which was anything but novel, also garnered an Academy Award.

Simply, the picture tells of The Champ (Beery), an ex-prize-fighter, now addicted to drinking and gambling, and his adoring son, Dink (Cooper), who looks after himself and his father as best he can.

At a racetrack, Dink meets his mother, Linda (Irene Rich), and her kind, wealthy husband, Tony (Hale Hamilton). Linda had divorced Champ when Dink was a baby, giving up her child because she felt that the then-champion fighter could do more for the boy than she could.

After he is arrested for starting a brawl, Champ realizes that Dink would grow up in a better environment if he stayed with his mother. He forces his son to leave by lying that he doesn't "like" him anymore, then striking the boy. But Dink is unhappy living with Linda and runs away—back to his father.

To regain his self-respect and win the money to buy back Dink's racehorse, which he'd lost in a crap game, the determined Champ returns to the ring. Though the fight goes badly at first and Dink urges his father, who is taking a savage beating, to "throw in the towel," Champ finally delivers his opponent a knockout blow and is victorious.

In his dressing room, Champ is felled by a fatal heart attack. Dink, having no other direction in which to turn, runs to Linda, who he now calls "Mother."

Critics were only lukewarm on the picture. The *New York Times* commented: "Mr. Vidor . . . has tackled this venture in a restrained fashion, always permitting the performances of Master Cooper and Mr. Beery to hold up a sequence that might have been banal and trite without them."

Conversely, audiences loved the tearjerker and made it one of the most popular films of 1931. Beery and Cooper were paired again in three later movies, *The Bowery* (1933), *Treasure Island* (1934), and *O'Shaughnessy's Boy* (1935).

It was writer Martin Rackin who conceived the idea of adapting the story of *The Champ* to the talents of comedian Red Skelton—a contract star at Metro during the 1940s and early 50s. Recalls Rackin: "We wanted to do a picture with Red that had a kid in it and utilized the script from Beery's old movie because it seemed to have the same kind of relationship with kids that we wanted to incorporate into our picture. I also thought that a film set against the then-relatively new television industry would be interesting."

Rackin, working with Leonard Praskins, borrowed the basic elements of Frances Marion's story and wrote a screenplay about Dodo Delwyn (Skelton), a former Ziegfeld comedy star, down on his luck, and living with his eight-year-old son, Dink, played by Tim Considine.

Developing along the same plot lines as the earlier film, Dodo hits the bottom of his career when he acts as emcee at a stag party, which is raided by the police. He sends Dink to live with his mother, Paula (Jane Greer), and her husband (Philip Ober), but the boy returns shortly thereafter to find that his father is being offered his own network variety show.

Dodo signs for the live series and, following a grueling rehearsal schedule, is a smash hit on the initial

The Champ: **Wallace Beery and Jackie Cooper.**

The Champ: **Wallace Beery and Jackie Cooper.**

The Clown: **Tim Considine, Red Skelton, Ned Glass, and player.**

Said the *Hollywood Reporter*: "A good combination of mirth and pathos, *The Clown* is a heart-warming, somewhat tragic picture that avoids a soap opera flavor by virtue of two wonderful performances—one by Red Skelton in what stands out as his most brilliant acting stint to date, the other by young Tim Considine, as fine a child actor as the screen has presented. . . . Skelton's performance compels recognition of his genuine acting skill, demonstrating that he is a consummate artist as well as a great comic."

Unfortunately, the moviegoer of the 1950s (when he wasn't in front of his television set) was not attracted by· such maudlin fare and *The Clown* did poorly at the box office.

The Champ

FILMOGRAPHY

1931: (MGM/King Vidor) Wallace Beery.
1953: *Clown, The* (MGM/Robert Z. Leonard) Red Skelton.

telecast. However, the strain has been too much on his body, weakened for years by alcohol and hard living, and he succumbs to a heart attack, leaving Dink to go back to his mother.

The Clown, directed by Robert Z. Leonard, was a fine little picture and, in its own way, was every bit as good as its predecessor. In fact, the general situation in this 1953 release was *more* believable than in the earlier film, since the gulf between Dodo's show business existence and the wealthy society his ex-wife had married into seemed not as great as it had been when Beery dwelled in the sleezy environment of the fight world. At the conclusion of *The Clown,* one feels that young Considine will have an easier time fitting into his new family than did Master Cooper, who was much more a ruffian.

The writers of the new film did well in adapting incidents from the original screenplay to the new format: Instead of having the mother meet Dink at a racetrack, Rackin and Praskins set this scene at a convention dinner where, in the entertainment portion of the program, Dodo is humiliated by working as another comic's "stooge"; the horse that Champ wanted to win back for his son is now an expensive watch—personally inscribed to Dodo by Ziegfeld.

The Clown: **Red Skelton and player.**

5
Destry Rides Again

In the years since she'd starred in *The Blue Angel,* Marlene Dietrich's choices of film roles had not always been the wisest. The German-born love goddess allowed her magnetic personality to be lost in a series of dull vehicles, in which she was required to do little more than be "smothered" by beautiful costumes. By the late 1930s, motion picture exhibitors had labeled her—along with Katharine Hepburn and Joan Crawford—"box-office poison." To say the least, her career was in trouble.

Actually, Paulette Goddard was producer Joe Pasternak's first choice to play the role of Frenchy in Universal's burlesque western, *Destry Rides Again.* When she proved to be unavailable, Dietrich was signed for the part. Marlene's salary was $75,000—considerably less than the $200,000–$450,000 fees that she was used to receiving.

Released in 1939, the picture, co-starring James Stewart, Charles Winninger, Mischa Auer, Brian Donlevy, Irene Hervey, and Allen Jenkins, gave Miss Dietrich, for the first time, a vehicle in which she could exhibit her great flair for comedy. The character of the wild and wonderful dancehall girl was unlike anything she had ever done before. It also gave her the opportunity to sing a couple of rousing ballads, "The Boys in the Backroom" and "Little Joe, the Wrangler," as well as matching her against Una Merkel in one of the most rollicking "cat-fights" in screen history. Audiences loved the film—loved her—and, again, Marlene Dietrich was a *box-office* star.

Universal had originally purchased Max Brand's western novel in 1932 as a project for Tom Mix. That film told the story of an honest cowboy, recently out of prison, who goes after the crooked partner that framed him. The cast included Zasu Pitts, Earle Fox, and Claudia Dell. Ben Stoloff directed from a screenplay by Isidore Bernstein.

Variety was not impressed with the oater: "Mix is the same hard-riding star as of old, but the director does not appear to have realized that the days of old, when range ponies could run miles at about double the speed of a Derby winner, are gone forever. . . . In other ways the story treatment is so old-fashioned as to be creaky in the joints. There is no real conviction to the yarn, and it deprives Mix of the full glory of his comeback after several years with the circus."

Destry Rides Again was forgotten for a number of years—until 1939, when Joe Pasternak resurrected the novel. Recalls the producer: "A friend of mine was kidding me that the only thing I could do was Deanna Durbin musicals. That made me mad and I told him that I produce any kind of picture—even a western.

"I came across this Max Brand property that had been made with Tom Mix. At first glance, it looked alright, so, to show my friend that I meant business, I announced that I was going to film *Destry Rides Again.*

"Then, after I began studying the book closer, I realized that I'd made a mistake. The story wasn't as good as I'd originally thought. Yet, I'd stuck my neck out, so I decided to go ahead with the picture anyway. But, we did some extensive rewriting."

Pasternak jettisoned just about everything from the material except the title, then cast both Dietrich and James Stewart (fresh from his success in *Mr. Smith Goes to Washington*) against type and hired George Marshall—one of the most inventive directors of his day. Marshall: "I brought the light touch to *Destry Rides Again.* Pasternak had been planning a much heavier approach until I convinced him that most westerns being made then were too serious."

The screenplay by Felix Jackson, Henry Meyers, and Gertrude Purcell dealt with the lawless frontier town of Bottle Neck, run by gambler Kent (Donlevy), who cheats ranchers out of their land so he can collect

Destry Rides Again (1932): Claudia Dell and Tom Mix.

a tariff on all cattle driven over the property. Assisting him in fleecing the suckers is Frenchy (Dietrich), a saloon entertainer.

Following the murder of Sheriff Keogh (Joe King), Kent has Mayor Slade (Samuel S. Hinds) appoint Wash Dimsdale (Winninger), former deputy to the legendary lawman Thomas Jefferson Destry, but now the town drunk, as the new peace officer. Wash sends for Destry's son, Tom, Jr. (Stewart), to come to Bottle Neck and serve as *his* deputy.

The easy-going young man arrives in town sans guns (he doesn't believe in wearing them), much to the disappointment of Wash. Kent dismisses Destry's ability to be an effective deputy, until Tom gives a demonstration which proves that, if necessary, he can use a gun quite well.

Not believing the mayor's story that Keogh had gone out of town, Destry begins a search for the sheriff's body. He deputizes Boris Callahan (Auer), then tricks Gyp Watson (Jenkins), one of Kent's henchmen, into revealing the location of the corpse.

Frenchy, who is smitten with Tom, lures him away from the jail so that he will not get hurt when Kent's men break Watson out. Wash is killed in the escape and an angered Destry straps on his father's guns, then enlists the support of the honest townspeople to help him go after Kent.

The gambler and his accomplices barricade themselves inside the saloon. Wanting to avoid as much bloodshed as possible, Frenchy organizes the women of Bottle Neck and gets them to storm the "fortress." In the "battle royal" that ensues, she is mortally wounded by a bullet that has been fired at Destry by Kent. Tom shoots the killer and the fight is over.

With Bottle Neck a peaceful town again, Destry begins to court the attractive Janice Tyndall (Irene Hervey), sister of cattleman Jack Tyndall (Jack Carson).

The *New York Times* commented: "a tightly written, capitally directed show. . . . Good fun every minute of it."

Destry Rides Again (1939): **James Stewart and Marlene Dietrich.**

Destry Rides Again (1939): **Charles Winninger and James Stewart.**

Destry: **Dick Reeves, Audie Murphy, Thomas Mitchell, and George Wallace.**

Destry: **Audie Murphy and Mari Blanchard.**

Frenchie, a dull little western released by Universal in 1950, patterned its two leading characters after Tom Destry and Frenchy. The parts were competently played by Joel McCrea and Shelley Winters. Louis King directed Oscar Brodney's otherwise original script.

Four years later, the studio decided to do a full remake of the Pasternak western and assigned Stanley Rubin to produce. Mr. Rubin reflects on the experience: "Universal wanted to redo the picture as a vehicle for Audie Murphy, who was under contract and was a good box-office property. I wasn't too excited about the project—mainly because I didn't want to do a remake. The fact that George Marshall was agreeable to come back and direct this new version was a major reason why I decided to go ahead with it.

"Marshall is the best comedy/action director in the business. He was marvelous at updating and switching his old gags from the Jimmy Stewart picture. He told me when he started that he didn't want to do the same picture again, but, instead, improve on his earlier material. George seemed to bubble over with comic invention."

The screenplay for the 1954 Technicolor release was written by Edmund H. North and D. D. Beauchamp. Aside from Murphy, the cast included Thomas Mitchell, Lyle Bettger, Edgar Buchanan, and Lori Nelson, taking over the roles played in the 1939 version by Winninger, Donlevy, Hinds, and Miss Hervey respectively.

Brandy, the counterpart to Dietrich's old role, was amateurishly played by Mari Blanchard. Explains Rubin: "The studio *insisted* that I use a contract player in that part. Mari was the only girl on the lot who seemed to have *any* of the Dietrich quality that we wanted to recapture. However, we deliberately gave her a new name and different songs to sing, in order to get away, as much as possible, from an identification with Marlene, that was, of course, inevitable."

Destry was the shortened title of the new film, which, aside from altering a few character names, as well as the name of the town to Restful, stayed pretty close to the basic plot line of its predecessor. One major change, however, was the fact that, in the Murphy project, the women of the town did *not* storm the fortified saloon, as they had in Stewart's picture. Rubin: "We felt that the scene was rather outdated in 1954, so we decided to just have a good old-fashioned shoot-out."

George Marshall had agreed to redo his film because he liked Audie Murphy and thought he might make an interesting Destry. Sadly, the finished 1954 picture played rather straight and lacked the humorous touch that prevailed in the earlier effort. Whereas *Destry Rides Again* had been blessed with some of the best comedic character actors in Hollywood (i.e., Charles Winninger, Mischa Auer, Allen Jenkins, Warren Hymer, Billy Gilbert, and Jack Carson), *Destry* had a cast of basically serious performers. George Marshall: "Thomas Mitchell was one of the best dramatic actors in town, but he didn't possess Winninger's light touch."

The *Hollywood Reporter* remarked: "Under Rubin's supervision, and with George Marshall repeating the directorial chore he handled in the 1939 entry, a good western drama has been fashioned that should have strong appeal to the outdoor fan."

It was never intended that *Destry* should seriously rival the Stewart/Dietrich classic upon which it was based. That would have been an almost impossible dream on the part of its producers. Yet, judged for what it was—an Audie Murphy program western—the picture must be labeled an unqualified success.

Destry Rides Again

FILMOGRAPHY

1932: (U/Ben Stoloff) Tom Mix.
1939: (U/George Marshall) James Stewart.
1954: *Destry* (U/George Marshall) Audie Murphy.

6
Dr. Jekyll and Mr. Hyde

The Strange Case of Dr. Jekyll and Mr. Hyde, Robert Louis Stevenson's classic tale of split personality, supplied the basis for America's first horror movie and has since been filmed more often than any other story of that genre. It is a work that plays down cheap thrills in favor of characterization. Indeed, the 1931 screen version starring Fredric March is the only picture of its kind to have won a *major* Academy Award (i.e., Best Actor).

Written in 1886, the London-based mystery utilizes Mr. Utterson, lawyer for socially prominent Dr. Henry Jekyll, as its "vehicle." Utterson is baffled as to the reasons his client has named Edward Hyde, an ugly fiend, as beneficiary in his will. Jekyll's recent odd behavior also puzzles the attorney. Sometime later, Utterson learns that another of his clients, Sir Danvers Carew, has been murdered by Hyde, who has disappeared from his Soho address.

Jekyll's butler, Poole, informs the lawyer that his master has locked himself in his laboratory and that, when he talks to the doctor through the door, a strange voice replies. Utterson recognizes that voice as Hyde's and, with Poole's aid, breaks down the door. The men find the body of Hyde—a suicide by poison.

The late Dr. Lanyon had left a letter with Utterson, which was only to be opened in the event of the death or disappearance of Jekyll. The message told how Hyde had once appeared before Lanyon at the latter's house to claim some powders left there by Jekyll. The evil man had mixed a green liquid from the salts and, after drinking it, transformed into Jekyll.

It seems that Jekyll had invented a salt that would change his kindly self into a diabolical monster. As he continued to take the solution, the Hyde personality became dominant and Jekyll's only alternative was death.

Beginning in 1887, matinee idol Richard Mansfield made a career out of astounding American audiences by transforming on stage from a handsome Dr. Jekyll into the hideous Hyde. The actor toured in the Thomas Russell Sullivan dramatization for twenty years.

Another popular adaptation of Stevenson's story was written in 1897 by Luella Forepaugh and George F. Fish. This play provided the premise for the first film version of the thriller, shot in Chicago in 1908 by the Selig Polyscope Company. It was also the first horror movie made in the United States. The one-reeler was little more than a record of the abridged stage performance and even incorporated the curtain raising and lowering. Its cast was drawn from the play's road company.

In 1910, there were two other short renditions of the story. Wrench Films, a British company, released *The Duality of Man* and, from Denmark's Nordisk Company came the first filming to name its star—Alwin Neuss. Written and directed by August Blom, the picture concluded with Jekyll waking up and realizing that Hyde had only been a bad dream.

1912 found another American company, Thanhauser, filming *Dr. Jekyll and Mr. Hyde.* Lucius Henderson directed a cast that divided the title role(s) between two actors. James Cruze played Jekyll and, as it was revealed many years later, Henry Benham was Hyde.

Two more versions appeared in 1913. The production from Charles Urban's Kinemacolor Company was the first horror picture released in color. On the other hand, Imp's (later Universal) presentation starring King Baggot had the longest running time (thirty-three minutes) up to that date. Of Baggot, *Moving Picture World* said: "It is a forceful characterization and shows much care and study."

Dr. Jekyll and Mr. Hyde (1920): **John Barrymore and Charles Lane.**

Dr. Jekyll and Mr. Hyde (1920): **Louis Wolheim and John Barrymore.**

The Germans got into the act in 1920 with an adaptation directed by F. W. Murnau, entitled *Der Januskopf*. Conrad Veidt headed a cast that included Bela Lugosi.

That same year, comedian Hank Mann spoofed the tale in a short for Arrow, then Sheldon Lewis played the dual characterization in a production by Louis Mayer for the Pioneer Film Corporation. That film, set in New York, also ended with the hero waking up from a nightmare.

The best 1920 dramatization came from the Famous Players-Lasky Corporation. John S. Robertson directed a scenario by Clara S. Beranger, which was reminiscent, in part, of *The Picture of Dorian Gray,* in that, like the Oscar Wilde character, it gave Jekyll an evil mentor in the person of Sir George Carew.

John Barrymore played the sensitive young doctor, who is introduced to the seedier aspects of life by his future father-in-law, Sir George (Brandon Hurst).

Jekyll is repulsed when sultry Nita Naldi, a cabaret performer, takes a passing interest in him. However, an awareness of his own suppressed desires excites him with the idea of separating the good and evil sides of man's soul. He, therefore, begins his ill-fated experiments.

Miss Beranger's script introduced the characters of Jekyll's prim and proper fiancée, in the person of Martha Mansfield, and Hyde's mistress, portrayed by Miss Naldi. Although counterparts of both these women carried over to future adaptations, the girl from the gutter, virtually a "bit" in the Barrymore picture, became the more dominant of the two roles later on. In fact, Ingrid Bergman's interpretation of the part in the 1941 rendition completely overshadowed Spencer Tracy's performance in the title roles.

All the filmings of *Dr. Jekyll and Mr. Hyde* have been told, at least in part, from Jekyll's viewpoint, rather than through the eyes of a secondary character

Dr. Jekyll and Mr. Hyde (1931): **Holmes Herbert and Fredric March.**

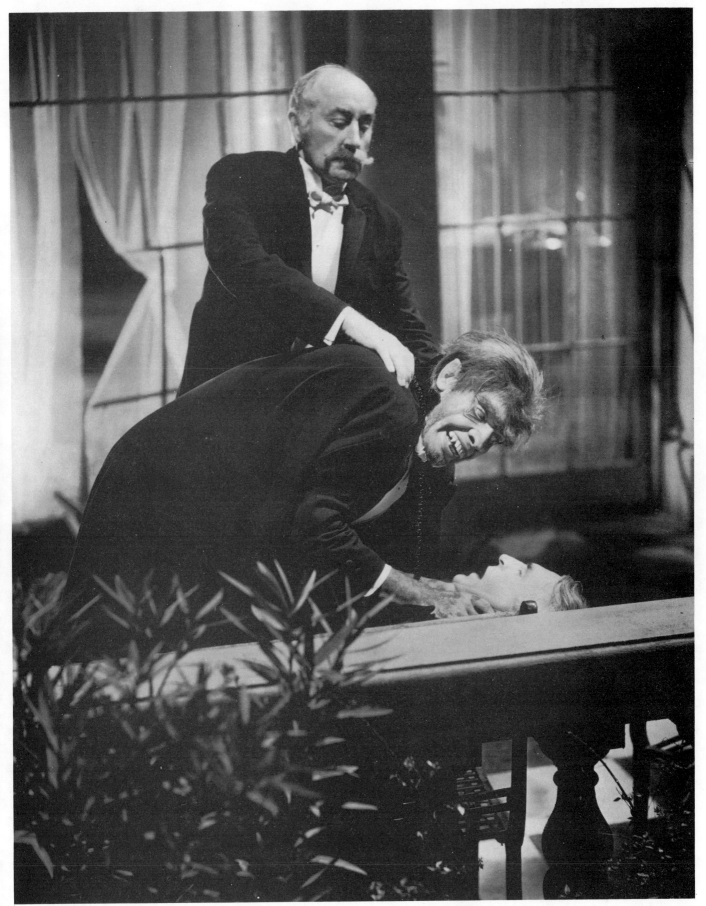

Dr. Jekyll and Mr. Hyde (1931): Fredric March, Halliwell Hobbes, and player.

Dr. Jekyll and Mr. Hyde (1941): Spencer Tracy, Lana Turner, and Donald Crisp.

like Utterson. Such an approach has greater dramatic validity and provides writers, directors, and cameramen the opportunity to create some interesting sequences. For example, in the Barrymore project, we see a gigantic phantom spider melt into the body of a sleeping Jekyll, who then awakes as Hyde.

Many effective scenes graced the Famous Players release. Particularly memorable were the other transformations, in which the handsome Jekyll became a spiderlike Hyde with boney fingers and pointed head.

The *New York Times* said: "Those who expect the photoplay to be good because 'it's just the thing for the movies' will find that it is good because it is just the thing for John Barrymore. It is true that the screen lends itself peculiarly to the story, but it can only be a sufficient medium for Mr. Barrymore's unique ability. It is what Mr. Barrymore himself does that makes the dual character of Jekyll and Hyde tremendous. His performance is one of pure motion picture pantomime

on as high a level as has ever been attained by anyone."

After Stan Laurel burlesqued the story again in a 1925 Standard Cinema Corporation two-reeler entitled *Dr. Pyckle and Mr. Pride,* Fredric March starred in, what many aficionados consider to be, the definitive version of Stevenson's work.

The 1931 Paramount release had an intelligent and well-developed screenplay by Samuel Hoffenstein and Perry Heath, which presented Jekyll as a sincere young physician, who, again, wishes to separate the good and evil elements in man's soul. Following a party given by Muriel Carew (Rose Hobart), his fiancée, and her father (Halliwell Hobbes), Jekyll and his friend, Dr. Lanyon (Holmes Herbert), rescue Ivy Parsons (Miriam Hopkins), a London cabaret singer, from a mugger. Although the attractive woman is unsuccessful in her attempts to seduce Jekyll, the reserved man of medicine is unable to get her out of his thoughts.

March's Hyde is neanderthal in appearance and sensual in nature. The demonic creature induces Ivy to become his mistress, then forces her to submit to his sadistic pleasures. Fearing for her life, she goes to Jekyll for help. He, in turn, assures her that Hyde will not bother her again and, determined to keep his promise, destroys the key that will admit him to his laboratory via a "secret" entrance.

That evening, while enroute to his engagement party, Jekyll reverts to Hyde *without* having taken his chemical mixture. The fiend goes to Ivy's flat and brutally murders her, then, unable to return to the sanctuary of the lab, writes a note—signed by Jekyll—to Lanyon for help.

As per the message, Lanyon obtains several of Jekyll's chemicals from his friend's house. He returns home to find Hyde waiting for him. Suspicious of this monster, Lanyon detains Hyde at gunpoint and forces him to mix and drink the formula in his presence. The subsequent transformation dumbfounds Lanyon.

A weary Jekyll agrees to his colleague's demand that he break off his engagement to Muriel. However, at his fiancée's home, he, once again, turns into his evil self and kills the girl's father.

Lanyon is well aware of the murderer's identity. With the police in tow, he goes to Jekyll's house to find his friend rather agitated. The troubled man claims that Hyde had attacked him, then run from the house. But, as Jekyll speaks, his features transform to their simian state and, in an attempt to escape, he is shot down.

To enhance this atmospheric production, director Rouben Mamoulian, working with cinematographer Karl Struss, decided that the face of his Dr. Jekyll would transform into Mr. Hyde before the eyes of the

Dr. Jekyll and Mr. Hyde (1941): **Spencer Tracy and Ingrid Bergman.**

movie audience. They accomplished this task brilliantly, through the use of successive camera exposures of March's gradually changing makeup.

Reviews on the picture were mixed. *Variety* said: "General effect is of misjudged values; the picture doesn't build to an effective climax, and it seems that the reason is the too labored approach in the climaxes. . . . March does an outstanding bit of theatrical acting. His Hyde make-up is a triumph of realized nightmare."

As previously noted, March tied with Wallace Beery (*The Champ*) for the 1932 Best Actor Oscar.

A decade later, Spencer Tracy assumed the Jekyll/Hyde characterization in a slick Metro-Goldwyn-Mayer production, which utilized the Hoffenstein/Heath screenplay as its basis. Although John Lee Mahin's script was virtually a scene-by-scene recreation of the earlier film, the writer *did* tone down the sexual aspects of the story, update the dialogue, and tighten the action.

Mahin: "The film was written especially for Tracy, who had to be coaxed into doing it. I'm sure I was influenced by the March version, however I added the opening sequences dealing with Barton MacLane as the madman who disrupts the church services. That character set the tone for the rest of the picture."

Tracy's transformations to Hyde were accomplished sans grotesque makeup—relying, for the most part, on subtler changes that simply hardened the actor's facial features. It was an interesting approach, but most observers felt Tracy was "wrong" for the part. The

Dr. Jekyll and Mr. Hyde (1941): **Spencer Tracy.**

New York Times: "Mr. Tracy's portrait of Hyde is not so much evil incarnate as it is the ham rampant. When his eyes roll in a fine frenzy like loose marbles in his head he is more ludicrous than dreadful. When he blows grapeskins upon the fair cheek of Miss Bergman, the enchantress of his evil dreams, it is an affront to good taste rather than a serious, and thereby acceptable, study in sadism."

Ingrid Bergman's portrait of Ivy, on the other hand, was highly praised by the press. The supporting cast included Lana Turner as Jekyll's fiancée, Donald Crisp as her father, and Ian Hunter as Lanyon. Victor Fleming directed the 1941 release, which audiences found to be a generally entertaining thriller. Since it subsequently proved to be a box-office success, one finds it difficult to fully agree with the aforementioned *Times* review when it concludes: "Out of ham and hokum the adaptors have tried to create a study of a man caught at bay by the devil he has released within himself. And it doesn't come off either as hokum, significant drama, or entertainment."

Louis Hayward was the *Son of Dr. Jekyll* for Columbia in 1951; Abbott and Costello "met" the horror duo, courtesy of Boris Karloff, at Universal in 1953; and, for Allied Artists in 1957, Gloria Talbott turned up as the *Daughter of Dr. Jekyll*. Stevenson's story was kidded again in *Dr. Jekyll's Hyde*, a 1958 Sylvester the Cat cartoon from Warners,[1] then, a year later, Britain's Hammer Films produced *The Ugly Duckling*, a silly comedy adaptation starring Bernard Bresslaw.

House of Fright (aka *The Two Faces of Dr. Jekyll*), also produced by Hammer, was released in the United States by American-International in 1961. Filmed in color, the screenplay by Wolf Mankowitz presented Jekyll, played by Paul Massie, as a mild-mannered, bearded Victorian doctor, who, as Hyde, becomes suave, cleanshaven, and, naturally, evil.

Jekyll, a recluse, is married to an unfaithful wife (Dawn Addams). Under the influence of Hyde, he arranges the demise of her lover (Christopher Lee)— from the bite of a serpent—then drives his mate to suicide. Several murders later, to avoid capture by the police, Hyde frames the doctor's death. Nevertheless, in the end, good Jekyll is able to destroy the now-dominant fiend by temporarily seizing control of his body—long enough for the police to recognize the ruse and arrest him.

[1] Tom and Jerry had already been seen in *Dr. Jekyll and Mr. Mouse,* a 1947 animated short from MGM.

Terence Fisher directed the production, which, unlike its predecessors, had Jekyll taking his "magic fluid" by injection, rather than orally.

Said *Variety*: "Mankowitz has palpably distorted and, in fact, jettisoned Stevenson's original story and the affair becomes mostly a straightforward horror meller, but with the benefit of some good opportunities for characterization and a useful climax."

Another spoof of *Dr. Jekyll and Mr. Hyde* came along in 1963—thanks to the efforts of writer (with Bill Richmond)/director/performer Jerry Lewis. Paramount's *The Nutty Professor* cast the comic as nebbish Professor Julius Kelp, preformula, and swinger Buddy Love, postformula. Of Lewis' characterization(s), the *New York Times* reported: "The surprising, rather disturbing result is less of a showcase for a clown than the revelation (and not for the first time) of a superb actor."

Christopher Lee played the Jekyll/Hyde roles in *I, Monster,* a 1971 film from Amicus Productions, with a release through British Lion. In the March 1974 issue of *Famous Monsters of Filmland,* the actor discussed the project: "We reproduced Stevenson's Jekyll and Hyde exactly as he wrote it—with one or two minor exceptions, insofar as I was Dr. Marlowe and Mr. Blake! Don't ask me why! Everybody else had the right names! But, I couldn't be Jekyll and Hyde—that's been done before!"

Directed by Stephen Weeks, with a screenplay by Milton Subotsky, the film utilized the characters of Utterson (Peter Cushing) and Lanyon (Richard Hurdall) much as they had been employed in the

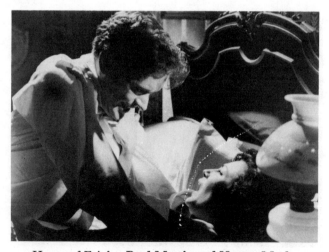

House of Fright: **Paul Massie and Norma Marla.**

Dr. Jekyll and Sister Hyde: **Ralph Bates and Martine Breswick.**

Stevenson original. The climax has Hyde (or Blake) going to Utterson's house in order to kill him. In the ensuing struggle, the villain catches fire and falls to his death.

The *Monthly Film Bulletin* commented: "Certainly, in terms of horror, *I, Monster* must be one of the most reticent Jekyll and Hyde films ever made, for it contains only one murder, and even that is after extreme provocation. In fact, Marlowe's so-called 'evil' alter ego becomes increasingly pathetic in the course of the action; and when he is finally humiliated by his ugliness, Christopher Lee convincingly conveys the feeling of a frightened, hunted animal. Unfortunately, despite its stylized direction and evocative trappings, *I, Monster* is dogged by an extremely repetitive script, and some of the performances . . . are highly stilted."

The most interesting off-shoot of *Dr. Jekyll and Mr. Hyde* emerged from Hammer in 1972, with a United States release through American-International. *Dr. Jekyll and Sister Hyde* was exactly what the title implied. Jekyll (Ralph Bates), experimenting with ways to prolong life, reluctantly murders so he can obtain the human organs needed for his formula, which, ultimately, turns him into the exotically beautiful, if homicidal, Sister Hyde (Martine Breswick). The remainder of the picture has all the bloody elements of a typical horror exploitation film, with the leading man/woman meeting his/her end in a fall from a building.

Roy Ward Baker directed the Technicolor feature from a Brian Clemens screenplay. *Variety*: "As with the Hammer horror pix, production values and performances are of a high standard. Director Roy Ward Baker has set a good pace, built tension nicely and played it straight, so all seems credible. . . . Ralph Bates and Martine Breswick, strong, attractive, personalities, bear a strange resemblance to each other, making the transitions entirely believable."

The possibilities for variations on the Jekyll/Hyde theme are seemingly endless. It should, therefore, be interesting to observe the fate of the next Dr. Jekyll when he drinks his elixir. Will he emerge as a man? Woman? Monster?

Who knows?

Dr. Jekyll and Mr. Hyde

FILMOGRAPHY

1908: (Selig).
1910: *Duality of Man, The* (British).
1910: (Danish/August Blom) Alwin Neuss.
1912: (Thanhauser/Lucius Henderson) James Cruze.
1913: (Kinemacolor).
1913: (Imp) King Baggot.
1920: *Januskopf, Der* (German/F. W. Murnau) Conrad Veidt.

1920: (Pioneer) Sheldon Lewis.
1920: (Famous Players/John S. Robertson) John Barrymore.
1931: (Par/Rouben Mamoulian) Fredric March.
1941: (MGM/Victor Fleming) Spencer Tracy.
1961: *House of Fright* (British/Terence Fisher) Paul Massie.
1971: *I, Monster* (British/Stephen Weeks) Christopher Lee.
1972: *Dr. Jekyll and Sister Hyde* (AIP/Roy Ward Baker) Ralph Bates.

7

Four Daughters

Among the more popular movie soap operas of the 1930s was Warner Brothers' *Four Daughters*. Based on Fannie Hurst's novel, *Sister Act,* the picture, directed by Michael Curtiz, starred the Lane sisters (Priscilla, Rosemary, and Lola), Gale Page, Claude Rains, Jeffrey Lynn, and, making his first *important* film appearance. John Garfield.

The screenplay by Julius J. Epstein and Lenore Coffee told of the idyllically happy and saccharine Lemp family. Papa (Rains), a professor of music, has utilized the talents of his attractive daughters (the Lane girls and Page) to form a household quintet with himself as leader.

Into this "paradise" full of music and youthful femininity comes an exciting young composer, Felix Deitz (Lynn), and he soon wins the heart of one of the girls, Ann (Priscilla Lane). A short time later, orchestrator Mickey Borden (Garfield) arrives to work on Felix's new Broadway show. Ann is fascinated by this rude and fatalistic young man—an eternal outsider.

Eventually, Felix proposes to Ann, but when she learns that one of her sisters is also in love with the handsome composer, she sacrifices her own happiness by eloping with Borden. Their life together is not easy and, on a Christmas visit back home, the "born loser" commits suicide by crashing his car into a tree.

With the coming of Spring, Felix returns to be reunited with Ann.

The *New York Times* called *Four Daughters*: "a charming, at times heartbreakingly, human little comedy. . . . It may be sentimental, but it's grand cinema." In fact, so successful was the film with both critics and audiences alike, that the studio produced two inferior sequels, *Four Wives* (1939) and *Four Mothers* (1941).

Taking top acting honors in the original film was John Garfield as the doomed Mickey Borden. Said the *New York Times*: "Garfield bites off his lines with a delivery so eloquent that we still aren't sure whether it is the dialogue or Mr. Garfield who is so bitterly brilliant." As would be expected, Garfield became a top Hollywood star and the screen's first "angry young man."

Following the 1953 release of Columbia's *From Here to Eternity,* Frank Sinatra was one of the most sought-after actors in the motion picture industry. Jack Warner, anxious to secure the performer's services for a film, asked the recent Oscar winner if there was a property that interested him. Sinatra had always been intrigued with Garfield's role in *Four Daughters* and indicated to the studio head that he'd be willing to remake that story—as a semimusical.

Henry Blanke, associate producer of the original 1938 picture, was assigned to the color project, which was made under the banner of Arwin Productions, a company owned by Doris Day and her husband, Marty Melcher. Gordon Douglas directed.

Titled *Young at Heart,* Liam O'Brien's adaptation of the Epstein/Coffee screenplay closely followed the original story. However, in order to accommodate the placing of several tunes into the picture, one of the daughters was eliminated.

Joining Sinatra in the cast were Miss Day, essaying the Priscilla Lane role; Robert Keith, playing the father with less eccentricities than Rains's interpretation; Gig Young as the composer; and Dorothy Malone and Elisabeth Fraser as the other two sisters. The new script also changed the names of the characters.

Gordon Douglas recalls why Sinatra insisted that the ending of the story be changed in this remake:

Four Daughters: **John Garfield and Jeffrey Lynn.**

Four Daughters: **Lola Lane, Priscilla Lane, Gale Page, Claude Rains, and Rosemary Lane.**

Four Daughters: **John Garfield and Priscilla Lane.**

Young at Heart: **Gig Young, Doris Day, Frank Ferguson, Frank Sinatra, and Elisabeth Fraser.**

Young at Heart: **Doris Day and Elisabeth Fraser.**

Young at Heart: **Frank Sinatra and Doris Day.**

"Frank had been 'killed' in his last two pictures and he didn't want to get a reputation in movies as a leading man who always died. So, we had him recover from the auto accident and he and Doris went on to a happy finish."

Many critics felt that the altered finale was unconvincing and weakened the drama. According to the *Hollywood Reporter*: "The present script does little to bridge this gulf between the basic characters and backgrounds of a super-normal girl and a morose, abnormal man. A great love is about the only thing that an audience would believe could span such a chasm. But the script has Doris (who is engaged to Gig) give him up to marry Frank—not because she loves Frank but because she thinks her sister loves Gig. This is a fool's motive, since it promises permanent unhappiness for three people. Later we are told that she really loves her piano player, but the fineness of the actors never quite makes up for the weakness of the story."

Reviews for the picture were mixed—with some critics claiming that Sinatra was better than Garfield, while others felt that he lacked the bite and sharpness of his predecessor.

But, in spite of what the papers might have said, the public was satisfied and *Young at Heart,* like *Four Daughters,* was a huge box-office success.

Four Daughters

FILMOGRAPHY

1938: (WB/Michael Curtiz) John Garfield.
1954: *Young at Heart* (WB/Gordon Douglas) Frank Sinatra.

8
Goodbye, Mr. Chips

Some literary masterpieces are endowed with a simplicity so fragile that, in a dramatization, should the basic elements of the piece be exaggerated or mishandled even slightly, the author's entire conception can be lost. One such work is James Hilton's 1934 novelette, *Goodbye, Mr. Chips.*

Metro-Goldwyn-Mayer has produced two film versions of Hilton's story. The first, made in 1939 with Robert Donat, was a relatively low-budget affair, which, among its other virtues, managed to capture the nostalgic and unpretentious values of the original story. Ultimately, it became a cinema classic.

A 1969 musical remake did not fare as well. Although the 151 minute roadshow picture was a good piece of family entertainment, it discarded the unaffected quality of its predecessor in favor of a disastrous change of focus in the story, a dozen forgettable songs by Leslie Bricusse, and an overblown production design.

Mr. Hilton's *Goodbye, Mr. Chips* tells, via flashbacks, the story of Arthur Chipping, a twenty-three-year-old Latin teacher, who, in 1870, accepts a position at the Brookfield School for Boys. Following some problems in disciplining his students, Chipping adjusts his methods and gains a reputation as a competent, if unremarkable, instructor.

Twenty-five years pass before shy Mr. Chipping meets the young and beautiful Katharine Bridges while on a European walking tour. The couple marry after a short courtship and Katharine dubs her husband with the nickname that will stick with him for the rest of his life—"Mr. Chips."

Katharine immediately captivates Brookfield's students and faculty with her charm. She is a good influence on Chips and helps him to broaden his views and

opinions, as well as teaching him compassion. It isn't long before he becomes a very popular teacher at the school.

After only three years of marriage, Chips' world falls apart when both Kathy and their infant son die in childbirth.

Years later, a retired Chips is called back by Brookfield at the outbreak of World War I to become headmaster—a position that he'd aspired to attain during his forty-two-year tenure at the school, but was denied then by the Board of Governors. Since all younger men are going off to do battle, Chips is the logical one to assume leadership of the institution throughout this difficult period.

The war ends and Chips goes back into retirement. Still keeping active ties with Brookfield, he prepares the school directory, meets with visiting dignitaries, and regularly invites the students to his rented rooms for tea.

A veritable institution at the school, the beloved, if eccentric, Mr. Chips dies in 1933. As the old man's life slips away, the doctor remarks to an instructor from Brookfield that it was too bad his patient never had children. With his last breath, Chip's replies: "But I had hundreds of children . . . all boys."

Metro's 1939 film version of *Goodbye, Mr. Chips* was shot in England under the direction of Sam Wood, from a screenplay by R. C. Sherriff, Claudine West, and Eric Maschwitz. Victor Saville produced. Aside from Robert Donat, who won an Academy Award for his portrayal, the excellent cast included Greer Garson, making her motion picture debut in the role of Katharine, young Terry Kilburn, playing four generations of the Colley family, all of whom were Brookfield students, John Mills, Milton Rosmer, and Paul von Hen-

Goodbye, Mr. Chips (1939): **Robert Donat.**

Goodbye, Mr. Chips (1939): **Greer Garson and Robert Donat.**

Goodbye, Mr. Chips (1939): **Terry Kilburn and Robert Donat.**

reid (he later dropped the "von" from his name).

It was an impeccable production—warm and senti-mental—that has endeared itself to the millions who have seen it through the years. The *New York Times* commented: "Mr. Hilton's adapters obviously have stenciled each page of their script with a 'handle with care' and there is evidence that director Sam Wood, Robert Donat, Greer Garson, and the rest heeded their injunction. They have played out the drama at their own leisurely pace, which was the appropriate tempo. . . . The picture has no difficulty in using two hours to retell a story that was scarcely above short story length. Mr. Chips is worth its time."

And, of Mr. Donat's brilliant performance, the same paper said: "It is an incredibly fine characteriza-tion, not merely for its ability to make its convincing transition from young schoolmaster to octogenarian institution, but for its subtle underlining—if underlin-ing can be subtle—of the dramatic moments in an essentially undramatic life. . . . Mr. Donat has wisely understated him [Chips], played him softly, doubled his poignance."

The 1969 musical remake of *Goodbye, Mr. Chips* encountered so many problems in preproduction that it's almost a miracle it even went before the cameras in the first place. Conceived in 1963 by composers André and Dory Previn, who brought the idea for the project to producer Arthur P. Jacobs, *Chips* lost two leading men, two leading ladies, a director, and the composers from its ranks prior to the start of actual production.

Jacobs liked the idea of doing *Chips* as a musical and immediately proceeded to make a deal with Metro for the rights to the property. Once this was accomplished, Terence Rattigan's services were secured to do the screenplay, while Gower Champion was signed to direct. The Previns, of course, were set to supply the score with André also assigned to serve as musical director.

Initially cast in the two starring roles were Richard Burton and Samantha Eggar, but they were replaced a few months later by Rex Harrison and Lee Remick (the plan, at that time, was to make Katharine an American). Finally, when contract negotiations with Harrison broke down, which was the same cause for Burton's withdrawal, Peter O'Toole was set as Chips and, since she seemed to be more compatible casting opposite the former *Lawrence of Arabia*, Petula Clark replaced Lee Remick. Miss Remick, incidentally, sued the production for breach of contract, but the matter was settled out of court.

Goodbye, Mr. Chips (1969): **Michael Redgrave and Peter O'Toole.**

Commitments on other projects forced André Pre-vin to withdraw as musical director in November of 1967, followed a week later by the resignation of Gower Champion, who'd decided that he didn't want to move his family to England for a year. The original intention had been to film the picture in Hollywood on the MGM backlot, but producer Jacobs later concluded that a British location would work better.

Then, in January of 1968, the Previns abandoned the production completely. André explained to the press: "It was impossible to create a score the way Jacobs wanted us to do it. The artistic differences were completely irreconcilable. Therefore, we would prefer not to do the picture at all, rather than com-promise."

Jacobs signed choreographer Herbert Ross to make his directorial debut with *Chips*, as well as Leslie Bri-cusse to supply a fresh score. John Williams became the new musical director.

Mort Abrahams, an associate producer on the proj-ect, remembers how Hilton's sensitive little story was adapted to a Metrocolor roadshow production: "The addition of music and the required length of the pic-ture forced us to make certain changes in the story.

Goodbye, Mr. Chips (1969): **Petula Clark and Peter O'Toole.**

Goodbye, Mr. Chips (1969): **Peter O'Toole.**

The most logical place to add material was in the relationship between Chips and his wife. Otherwise, the musical sections of the film would have had too many male voices.

"Almost none of us liked the idea of utilizing flashbacks, as we all felt it was a clumsy device. We also updated the story to involve the Second, instead of the First, World War.

"In retrospect, I don't feel that the story lent itself to a roadshow production. We were forced to create new material that, simply, didn't work. And, of course, we were unfavorably compared to the original film. I think we'd have been much better off if the picture had been only two hours long."

Indeed, it was the enlarging of Katharine's role that caused the major problems in the remake. The part, in the earlier version, was limited to approximately one-third of the film, but, in the 1969 picture, Katharine was present almost from the beginning to end. That production commenced just before Chips left on a visit to London, where he met his future wife, and· she was killed (by a German bomb) shortly before the picture's conclusion. Whereas the 1939 *Goodbye, Mr. Chips* told the story of a man's love for his profession, Jacobs' film gave us a tale about a man's love for a woman.

The roadshow picture presented Katharine as a London musical-comedy star with a "scandalous" past, who gave up her career to marry the schoolmaster. Other plot changes were merely incidental and were only made to accommodate the new story focus.

Herbert Ross: "I entered the project late and had very little to do with the script or the score, which I felt was weak, though better than the one that the Previns had written.

"I think that the major mistake was made by *not* using flashbacks. Had we gone with this device, we would have gotten a much better feeling of the passage of so many years and the many generations of students.

Flashbacks would have allowed us to jump around in the story by utilizing subjective recall, rather than straight narrative."

Goodbye, Mr. Chips (1969) was, in fact, an enjoyable motion picture for those members of the audience who didn't know the book or the 1939 version. The score was pleasant, though nothing to get excited about, and Ross's direction was quite inventive. The highlight of the film, however, was O'Toole's portrayal of Chips, which was easily as good, as if not better than, Donat's.

Said *Variety*: "O'Toole creates a man of strength and dignity, whose tendency to appear ridiculous at times is an enduring human fallibility rather than a weakness. From the too-prim young man to the doddering, senility of the 85 year-old man who can no longer separate past and present, O'Toole always is totally convincing. As a singer, however, he is no Rex Harrison."

Of the picture itself, the trade paper added: "Euphemists may talk about production values, but the sum total is considerably less than the parts, many of which have great charm but don't mesh effectively to sustain drama or emotional appeal."

Color and wide screen added much to the visual beauty of the story, but, at the same time, the producers had diluted the sentimentality and ungarnished quality of the piece—the primary characteristics that had made the 1939 production so popular.

Goodbye, Mr. Chips

FILMOGRAPHY

1939: (MGM/Sam Wood) Robert Donat.
1969: (MGM/Herbert Ross) Peter O'Toole.

9
High Sierra

By the early 1940s, Hollywood's gangster film cycle had pretty much run its course. Stars like Edward G. Robinson and James Cagney were tired of being on the wrong side of the law and turned to less violent roles, such as in *Dr. Ehrlich's Magic Bullet* and *Yankee Doodle Dandy.* Audiences, too, were looking for a new kind of screen fare.

As a finale to the genre, Warner Brothers produced *High Sierra,* the story of "Mad Dog" Roy Earle, a Dillinger-like gunman, who had become an anachronism in his own time. Based on a novel by W. R. Burnett (of *Little Caesar* fame), the Raoul Walsh-directed film presented its central character as a tragic figure and endowed him with a sensitivity that was completely atypical of other movie gangsters.

The screenplay by Burnett and John Huston began with Earle's release from an Illinois prison—his pardon having been secured by Big Mac, an old gangland associate. Mac wants the legendary gunman to come to California so he can engineer a holdup at an exclusive resort hotel. He is to be aided by Babe Kozak and Red Hattery, two "punks," who have brought dancehall girl Marie Garson to their mountain hideout.

Starved for affection during his years in the penetentiary, Roy makes a pet of a stray dog and becomes acquainted with Velma Goodhue. He falls in love with this crippled girl from the Middle West, paying for the surgery to have her club foot corrected. She, in turn, jilts him for a younger man.

The robbery itself goes well, but Babe and Red panic and are killed in the getaway. Roy and Marie, along with the dog, escape with the loot. Upon reporting to Big Mac, Earle finds the elderly leader dead of a heart attack.

Earle, on the rebound from Velma, takes up with Marie. The couple plan to dispose of the stolen jewels, but the desperado is recognized and hunted to the cold and lonely heights of the Sierras. Trapped on a mountain peak, he is killed by the police after leaving a note that exonerates Marie.

Humphrey Bogart, a contract player at Warner Brothers since 1936, inherited the role of the doomed gangster after it had been refused by both Paul Muni and George Raft. It was the first important assignment for the actor who, up until that time had only done leads in "B" pictures and secondary parts in the major ones. Of his memorable portrayal, the *New York Times* commented: "Mr. Bogart plays the leading role with a perfection of hard-boiled vitality. . . ."

The remainder of the cast was also fine: Ida Lupino as Marie; Joan Leslie as Velma; Alan Curtis and Arthur Kennedy as the "punks"; and, in one of his early assignments, Cornel Wilde doing Mendoza, the "inside" man for the robbery—all were effective in their individual roles.

Summing up the 1941 release, the *New York Times* said: "As gangster pictures go, this one has everything —speed, excitement, suspense, and that enobling suggestion of futility which makes for irony and pity . . . it's a perfect epilogue."

Raoul Walsh recalls that he was the one who originally conceived the idea of doing Burnett's story as a western: "Warners needed a picture to fill out their release schedule. I didn't have a project I was interested in at the time and there were no scripts 'on the shelf' that I liked. So, I suggested that we change *High Sierra* to a western format. It was a relatively easy task and we found we could shoot the picture very quickly."

Colorado Territory, directed by Walsh, was released in 1949. Joel McCrea and Virginia Mayo headlined

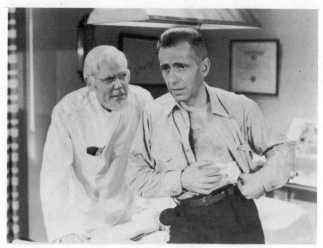

High Sierra: **Henry Hull and Humphrey Bogart.**

High Sierra: **Arthur Kennedy, Ida Lupino, Alan Curtis, and Humphrey Bogart.**

High Sierra: **Ida Lupino and Humphrey Bogart.**

the cast as Wes McQueen and Colorado Carson—the counterparts to Roy Earle and Marie.

Beginning along the same lines as its predecessor, the screenplay by John Twist and Edmund H. North has train and bank robber McQueen escaping from a Missouri jail. Dave Rickard (Basil Ruysdael), an aging desperado, had sprung Wes, so that the latter could rob a train of a $100,000 payroll.

On a stagecoach to Colorado, the outlaw meets Julie Ann (Dorothy Malone) and her father (Henry Hull).[1] McQueen becomes smitten with Julie, as she reminds him of a now-dead girl he'd once loved.

Wes meets his young accomplices, Reno and Duke (John Archer and James Mitchell), in a ruined Spanish village, which is to be the gang's hideout. Also present is frontier waif, Colorado Carson.

In spite of the treachery of the two confederates, as well as a double-cross by the train conductor, who was the "inside" man, McQueen successfully pulls off the robbery and leaves Reno and Duke tied up for the posse. Escaping with Colorado, he takes refuge at Julie Ann's ranch. The two-faced girl attempts to turn the bandit over to the law so she can claim the reward money, but Colorado thwarts her effort.

McQueen then realizes that he loves Colorado and the pair make a vain attempt to get married at the Spanish village. After he gives the stolen money to the Church, Wes rides for the Mexican border. Cornered by the posse in an old indian cliff dwelling, Colorado tries to help him escape—but the couple are shot down.

In many respects, the romantic assumptions and

---

[1] Hull, incidentally, had been in *High Sierra,* playing a shady, but wise old doctor, who philosophizes to Earle: "Remember what Johnny Dillinger said about guys like you and him; he said you're just rushing toward death—that's it, you're rushing toward death."

Colorado Territory: **Henry Hull, Virginia Mayo, and Joel McCrea.**

Colorado Territory: **Joel McCrea.**

sentimental qualities of *High Sierra* worked better in a western than they had in a modern-day setting. The *New York Times* said: "... its obviously fictionalized hero looks much nobler robbing a train with his six-shooter cocked than pulling a stick-up at the point of a nasty tommy-gun."

The *Hollywood Reporter* called the picture "a colorful and well-acted western period drama. . . . Raoul Walsh's masterly direction makes the action sequences outstanding and he builds up the suspense and drama in the yarn most effectively."

Filmed in 1955, the most recent version of *High Sierra* had originally been intended as a vehicle for Frank Sinatra, but when the actor/singer demanded fifty percent of the box-office net, Warner Brothers broke off negotiations and hired Jack Palance on a straight salary.

The remake, entitled *I Died a Thousand Times*, was shot in Warnercolor and Cinemascope, under the direction of Stuart Heisler. W. R. Burnett, who again did the screenplay, recalls that he made few changes from his original: "I toned down some of the sentimental aspects in the script, as I felt that Mark Hellinger, who'd produced the first version, had gone a

I Died a Thousand Times: **Jack Palance and Earl Holliman.**

bit overboard in this area. But, otherwise, the only thing I really did was to tighten up what I'd previously written."

The only noticeable script changes in the 1955 picture were ones of omission. Whereas the Bogart film began with Earle's release from prison and his initial readjustment to the outside world, the new production picked up the story with the gunman enroute across the desert on his way to his rendezvous with Big Mac's front man. By making such cuts, Burnett certainly telescoped his story, but, at the same time, he eliminated several scenes, which had helped audiences to more fully understand the character of Roy Earle in the 1941 version.

Supporting Palance in Heisler's picture were Shelley Winters as Marie, Lee Marvin and Earl Holliman as the two accomplices, Lori Nelson as Velma, and Lon Chaney, Jr., as Big Mac.

Of Palance's interpretation of Earle, the *Hollywood Reporter* said: "... he does not seem as doomed from the outset as Bogart did and he does not seem to symbolize the universal yearning of an aging man for his woman and his dog as his predecessor did. Palance stresses tension and has his own technique. According to the Warners publicity department, he runs up and down the back of the sound stage and does pushups so that he begins every scene with every corpuscle tingling."

With the exception of Ted McCord's color photography that took full advantage of the magnificent snow-capped Sierras, audiences were rather unimpressed with the picture. Writer Burnett thinks the production failed because the casting was wrong: "Palance was too much of a villain to be as sympathetic as Bogie was."

I Died a Thousand Times: **Shelley Winters and Jack Palance.**

On the other hand, the *New York Times* argued: "But the reason this film is not so touching is because it is antique and absurd. . . . It is an insult to social institutions and to public intelligence to pull this old mythological hero out of the archives and set him on a mountain top again. The pretense is so blunt and sentimental that it makes the whole thing a total cliché."

Valid as the *Times* comments may be with regard to *I Died a Thousand Times,* it does not alter the fact that, done well, this same "clichéd" material becomes a potent drama, which continues to retain its vitality as a nostalgic piece of fictional Americana. That's a basic reason why, after more than thirty years, *High* *Sierra* remains an engrossing film—one of the finest of its kind.

High Sierra

FILMOGRAPHY

1941: (WB/Raoul Walsh) Humphrey Bogart.
1949: *Colorado Territory* (WB/Raoul Walsh) Joel McCrea.
1955: *I Died a Thousand Times* (WB/Stuart Heisler) Jack Palance.

10
House of Strangers

Although it was a powerful motion picture drama, director Joseph L. Mankiewicz's 1949 production of *House of Strangers* had only moderate success at the box office and could never, in any sense of the word, be considered a "classic." Yet, its basic story of family conflict (reminiscent of Shakespeare's *King Lear*) was strong enough to inspire two remakes within a twelve-year period.

Philip Yordan's screenplay (from a novel by Jerome Weidman) utilized a flashback technique: Following a seven-year prison term, Max Monetti (Richard Conte) returns to New York's Little Italy to settle an old score with brothers Joe (Luther Adler), Tony (Efrem Zimbalist, Jr.), and Pietro (Paul Valentine), who now head the Monetti Trust Company. The brothers attempt to placate Max with a money offer, which he refuses—leaving the trio to worry that their younger brother plans to avenge their father's betrayal.

Max goes to see his former girl friend, Irene Bennett (Susan Hayward), then visits the old Monetti mansion, where he remembers the events that led up to his imprisonment and his father's death.

In the early thirties, Gino Monetti (Edward G. Robinson), the tyrannical patriarch of the clan, was a powerful money lender, generously giving out loans at high interest rates. With the exception of Max, his favorite, Gino treated his sons with contempt and used them to suit his own purposes. They, in turn, felt nothing but hate for their father—continuing to work for him only because he controlled the purse strings. Max's attempts to bring the family together proved unsuccessful.

The elder Monetti's banking methods eventually led to his being indicted. Joe, Tony, and Pietro deserted Gino, but Max, an attorney, defended him and,

when the trial took a turn for the worse, attempted to bribe a juror. On a tip from Joe, the police arrested Max, who was sent to prison. Gino went free on a mistrial, but his three disloyal sons took over the loan business.

While in Sing Sing, Max was visited by his father, who demanded that he make his brothers pay for stealing the company from him. Shortly thereafter, Gino died—a broken man.

As he stands before his father's portrait in the deserted mansion, Max realizes that Gino was a vicious man and that, if he carries out his vendetta, he (Max) would be destroying his own life.

Led by Joe, the brothers arrive at the house to kill Max. But, they are soon fighting among themselves, leaving Max to depart with Irene.

The Twentieth Century-Fox release was well received by the nation's critics. The *New York Times* said: "Edward G. Robinson, as usual, does a brisk and colorful job of making 'Papa' Monetti a brassy despot with a Sicilian dialect, and Paul Valentine, Luther Adler, and Efrem Zimbalist, Jr. are good as his weak sons. Likewise Richard Conte plays Max with a fine, superior air. And, say what one will, Mr. Mankiewicz knows how to make points when he directs."

Producer Sol C. Siegel felt that the plot of *House of Strangers* had a sound enough formula to utilize a second time. So, in 1954, he convinced 20th to let him remake it as a western—starring Spencer Tracy in the role of the father. Robert Wagner co-starred as the loyal son, with Richard Widmark, Hugh O'Brian, and Earl Holliman as his brothers. The romantic interest was supplied by Jean Peters.

Edward Dmytryk directed *Broken Lance,* which was written by Richard Murphy and filmed in color and

House of Strangers: **Richard Conte, Thomas Browne Henry, and Edward G. Robinson.**

House of Strangers: **Richard Conte and Susan Hayward.**

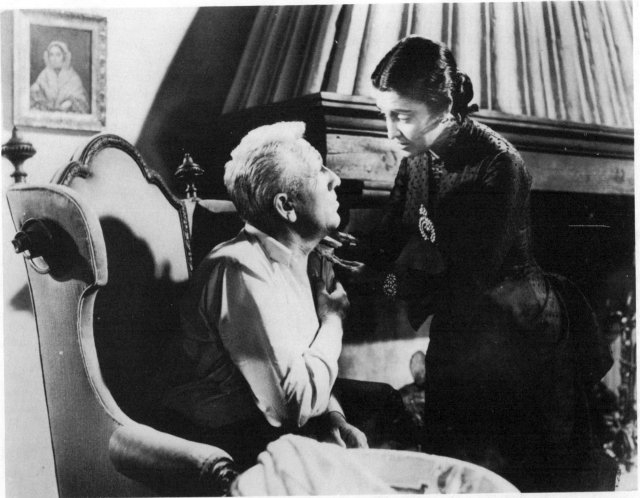

Broken Lance: **Spencer Tracy and Katy Jurado.**

Broken Lance: **Robert Wagner, Hugh O'Brian, Earl Holliman, Spencer Tracy, Richard Widmark, and Robert Burton.**

Cinemascope. Aside from the fact that the story was now set in the old West, this new version was a literal transference of the original plot construction—virtually point by point. The only new story angle of any consequence was a racially oriented subplot dealing with Tracy and his Indian wife.

Again told via a flashback, the film presented Tracy as Matt Devereaux, ruthless head of a cattle empire. Wagner was his son by a marriage to Comanche "princess" Katy Jurado and only a *half*-brother to the other offspring.

In the remake, Devereaux is brought to trial after he raids a copper works that is polluting his water. Unable to use his wealth or political power to save himself, the pioneer rancher avoids responsibility by dividing his property among his sons. Joe (Wagner), the only one that doesn't despise his father, accepts the blame for the raid and is sentenced to three years in prison. While the young man is incarcerated, Matt dies of a stroke, brought on by the rebellion of his other sons.

The final confrontation between the brothers involves only two of them this time—Joe and Ben (Widmark)—with the younger one being saved from death by Two Moons (Eduard Franz), the indian ranch foreman.

Unlike *House of Strangers*, in which one feels that Gino is "reaching out from the grave" to get Max to avenge him, there is no mystic bond between father and son in the 1954 film. According to Edward Dmytryk: "When Tracy dies, he's gone . . . and that's all there is to it."

Other changes were minimal. Sol C. Siegel: "We stayed pretty close to the original on this one. It was a good story, so there was no real need to deviate from it."

Broken Lance fared well with both critics and the public. It won the Silver Spur Award for the Best Western of the Year and Philip Yordan garnered an Oscar for Best Motion Picture Story. The *New York Times* said: "Although the saga of the self-made, autocratic cattle baron who helped shape the West is familiar fare, *Broken Lance* . . . makes a refreshingly serious and fairly successful attempt to understand these towering men. The standard clichés of the Western are plentifully evident in this drama, but they do not debase it to any great degree. And the rugged, vast and beautiful terrain of the Southwest is impressive and pleasing in the colors and Cinemascope in which it was filmed."

Tracy turned in a splendid portrayal, bringing forth many more values in his characterization than Rob-

inson had discovered earlier as the Italian banker. It may have been the more subtle of the two performances, but it was just as powerful in its final result.

Seven years later, executive producer Robert L. Lippert was looking for a story that would play well against a European circus background. James B. Clark had been with 20th for some time and suggested that the plot of *House of Strangers/Broken Lance* was adaptable for this purpose. Lippert liked the idea and the project proceeded under the title of *The Big Show*. Ted Sherdeman wrote the screenplay, which did *not* credit its origins, and also co-produced with Clark, the director of the picture.

Nehemiah Persoff was cast as the harsh father of a German circus family; Cliff Robertson was the good son; and Robert Vaughn, Franco Andrei, and Kurt Fecher, the brothers. Top-billed Esther Williams played Robertson's love interest. This version also gave the family a younger sister (Carol Christensen), who becomes romantically involved with an American soldier (David Nelson).

Instead of a bank or cattle ranch, the family "battled" for control of a circus. As did its predecessors, the film opens with Josef (Robertson) returning home, after completing a prison term. He announces to his brothers, led by Klaus (Vaughn), that he plans to take the circus away from them.

The flashback method is, again, utilized to tell the bulk of the story: Bruno Everard (Persoff), a domineering ex-trapeze flier, built and ran the European circus, which bore his name. Legal turmoils developed when a faulty turnbuckle gave way during a performance, causing the deaths and injuries of several highwire performers. To prevent financial ruin, Bruno transferred ownership of the circus into his children's names. At the trial, Josef took full responsibility for the accident and was sent to prison.

Angered at the way Bruno had treated him through the years, Klaus seized control of the business and turned his father out. Bruno vowed to start all over again and staged a trapeze act in a deserted park— planning to pass a hat for coins. When he tried to do his old act as a flier, the patriarch died of a heart attack.

Back in the present, Josef and Klaus fight it out in the deserted circus arena—with the latter being killed when he gets too close to a polar bear cage.

Josef and his other two brothers get back together again and the famous trapeze act of the flying Everards once more becomes the star attraction of the circus.

The Big Show: **Nehemiah Persoff and Cliff Robertson.**

The Big Show: **Cliff Robertson and Esther Williams.**

Sherdeman added one rather interesting plot twist to this Fox release: Early in the story, Bruno is anxious to merge his circus with a successful animal show. To accomplish this, he orders a reluctant Josef to marry the frustrated daughter of the show's owner. However, instead of Josef, Klaus courts and weds the girl, who, when she learns that her husband doesn't love her, commits suicide by allowing herself to be mauled by a trained polar bear.

The 1961 movie was the weakest rendition of the potent story. In most instances, the acting was very good, but the basic conflict seemed to have lost its once powerful bite. The fault lay in a change of focus from the original plot line.

Whereas the first two pictures had the father as the story's central figure, in *The Big Show,* the role is relegated to supporting status. The audience is told by the other characters that Bruno is a cruel and dominating force in the family, but they never witness this for themselves. Instead, they are presented with a portrait of a rather nasty man, who lacks any color whatsoever—a factor so important to the characterizations created by Robinson and Tracy.

Director James B. Clark gives an explanation: "I was caught in a 'mouse-trap.' The studio insisted that we use Esther Williams in what was a secondary role. After we paid her, we could no longer afford to hire a major star to play the father. Nehemiah Persoff was a nice man and a fine actor . . . but he wasn't a powerful personality, which is what the part called for.

"With all our money going for Williams, the focus of the story had to be shifted to Robertson and her, which was a big mistake."

On the plus side, the movie, filmed, in part, in Munich, offered handsome color photography, Cinemascope, and a genuinely diverting atmosphere. As the *Hollywood Reporter* said: "But what is unusual and interesting is the general feeling of a European circus that Sherdeman's screenplay and Clark's direction have achieved. This is something special and colors the film with exceptional lustre and variation of hue."

Conversely, the *New York Times* commented: "There is little lightness or imagination in either the script or the directing."

The original story concept of *House of Strangers/ Broken Lance/The Big Show* is still a vital one and it would not be surprising if, at some point in the future, Fox decides to film it a fourth time.

House of Strangers

FILMOGRAPHY

1949: (Fox/Joseph L. Mankiewicz) Edward G. Robinson.

1954: *Broken Lance* (Fox/Edward Dmytryk) Spencer Tracy.

1961: *Big Show, The* (Fox/James B. Clark) Nehemiah Persoff.

11
The Hunchback of Notre Dame

French novelist Victor Hugo never intended *The Hunchback of Notre Dame* to be a "horror" story and, frankly, neither did the various producers who have filmed the literary masterpiece over the years. Yet, because the central character of Hugo's graphic word portrait of medieval Paris is a grotesque freak and was most notably played on the screen by silent horror star Lon Chaney, movie historians and buffs often rank the great work with the "monster" classics —*Frankenstein, Dracula,* and *Phantom of the Opera.* To pigeonhole the book in this superficial manner is grossly unfair and incorrect, since it is no more a tale of horror than Steinbeck's *Of Mice and Men,* which also has as its "hero" one of society's outcasts.

Set in Paris of the late fifteenth century during Louis XI's reign, *The Hunchback of Notre Dame* tells of Quasimodo, the deformed bell ringer of the famed cathedral, and his love for Esmeralda, a wild young gypsy dancer. Claude Frollo, the Archdeacon of Paris and Quasimodo's benefactor, is also taken with the girl. He orders the hunchback to seize Esmeralda, but the gypsy is rescued by Captain Phoebus de Chateaupers of the King's Archers.

Quasimodo is sentenced to the pillory for his crime. To the surprise of the cruel mob that stones him, it is Esmeralda who comes to his aid when the unfortunate cries for water.

Angered that the beautiful dancer has fallen in love with Captain Phoebus, Frollo stabs the officer. Esmeralda is arrested and the Archdeacon charges her with sorcery. A visit to the torture chamber elicits a quick confession. The fact that Phoebus has recovered makes no difference to the court and Esmeralda is condemned to death by hanging on the city gibbet.

Quasimodo rescues the girl. Shouting "Sanctuary!" —he carries her inside Notre Dame and up to his bell tower.

In an attempt to rescue her, Esmeralda's friends— the vagabonds and thieves of the city—are led to the cathedral by poet Gringoire, her husband in name only, and Clopin, king of the beggars. The hunchback fears that the mob wishes to harm the girl and throws wooden beams and stones down upon them. The battle ends with the arrival of the King's Archers.

In the meantime, Frollo has persuaded the girl to leave the tower and accompany him to safety, but when she refuses his advances, the Archdeacon orders her execution carried out.

Quasimodo discovers that Frollo has murdered Esmeralda. Infuriated, he throws the man he once "worshipped" off the tower.

The bell ringer disappears from Notre Dame. Two years later, the deformed skeleton of a man is found in close embrace with that of a woman in a burial vault. To quote Hugo: "When those who found this skeleton attempted to disengage it from that which it held in its grip, it crumbled into dust."

Hunchback, written in 1831, has served as the basis for six *faithful* film adaptations, as well as numerous imitations. The first two versions were made by the French. In 1906, Alice Guy directed a one-reeler entitled *Esmeralda* starring Denise Becker in the title role of the gypsy dancing girl and Henri Vorins as Quasimodo. Five years later, in 1911, Henri Krauss and Stacia Napierkous appeared in a three-reel rendition, released by Pathé under the book's French title, *Notre Dame de Paris.* Unlike many of the later filmings, this production retained the tragic conclusion of the original material. The *Moving Picture World* said: ". . . the photoplay *Notre Dame de Paris* has exceptional merits. It has extracted a connected narrative from a rambling work of fiction; it is a marvel of setting, interior and exterior; the types are admirably

The Darling of Paris: **Theda Bara.**

chosen and the acting little short of superb."

The first U.S. production was shot in 1917 by the Fox Film Corporation, under the title of *The Darling of Paris*. Vamp Theda Bara starred as Esmeralda, Glen White played Quasimodo, and Walter Law was Frollo. J. Gordon Edwards directed Adrian Johnson's adaptation. Of the six-reel silent, *Photoplay* said: ". . . the screening is characteristically vigorous and opulent, and the surface manifestations of time and people are gone into in much motional detail. Miss Bara throws herself into her delineation with the wholeheartedness for which she is noted, and is an Esmeralda passably true to novel and period."

Today, the general public's familiarity with Hugo's work is due, primarily, to the next three movie versions of the piece—appearing in 1923, 1939, and 1957 respectively—all of which stayed relatively close to the original story line, with the exception of the ending.

The best-known filming of *The Hunchback of Notre Dame* was released in 1923 by Universal Pictures, starring Lon Chaney in the title role and Patsy Ruth Miller as Esmeralda. Wallace Worsley directed the scenario by Edward T. Lowe, Jr., which was from Perley Poore Sheehan's adaptation.

Although the film maintained Hugo's basic plot, there were some alterations:

To avoid offending the Church, the character of Frollo became Jehan—*brother* of the Archdeacon.

Esmeralda was not a gypsy by birth, but had been kidnapped by a band of these vagabonds when she was a baby. Her real mother discovers her true identity while the dancer is being led to the gibbet.

Phoebus (Norman Kerry) and Esmeralda are happily reunited at the film's conclusion, but Quasimodo is fatally stabbed by Jehan (Brandon Hurst) just prior to tossing the villain off the tower.

The story changes worked well in the silent produc-

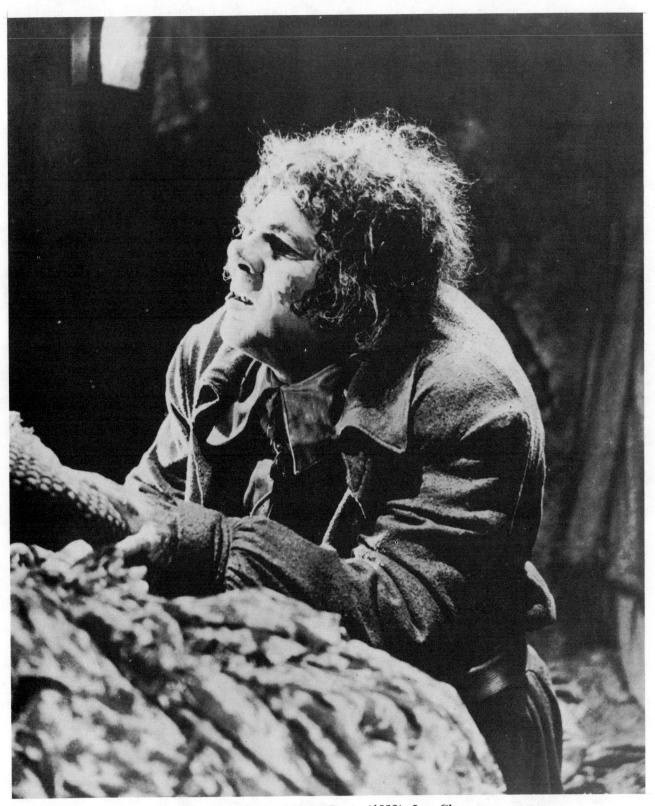

The Hunchback of Notre Dame (1923): Lon Chaney.

tion, which was to establish Lon Chaney as a major Hollywood star. Commenting on his performance, the *New York Times* said: "Chaney throws his whole soul into making Quasimodo as repugnant as anything human could very well be, even to decorating his breast and back with hair."

The paper called the film itself "a strong production, on which no pains or money have been spared to depict the seamy side of old Paris. . . . It is a drama which will appeal to all those who are interested in fine screen acting, artistic settings and a remarkable handling of crowds who don't mind a grotesque figure and a grim atmosphere."

British character star Charles Laughton was the first actor to play Quasimodo in talkies. The 1939 RKO-Radio production was written by Sonya Levien from an adaptation by Bruno Frank. William Dieterle directed a cast that included Maureen O'Hara as

Esmeralda, Alan Marshal as Phoebus, Thomas Mitchell as Clopin, and Edmond O'Brien as Gringoire.

Whereas in this atmospheric version, Frollo, superbly played by Sir Cedric Hardwicke, remains the Archdeacon's brother, he is also the Lord High Justice of Paris. Near the end of the film, he confesses that *he* and *not* Esmeralda is guilty of Phoebus's murder.

Frollo then goes to the tower where Quasimodo is fighting off the rabble and tries to execute the gypsy girl. The bell ringer saves Esmeralda by killing his former friend. Immediately thereafter, word arrives that Esmeralda has been pardoned and she goes off with Gringoire. Quasimodo, alone in the tower, looks at one of the gargoyles and sadly asks: "Why was I not made of stone like thee?"

Despite this contrived "happy" ending, the overall production played quite well. Laughton's makeup, in its own way, was just as hideous as Chaney's had been—if not more so. Director Dieterle, working for

The Hunchback of Notre Dame (1923): **Lon Chaney and Patsy Ruth Miller.**

In interviews given at the time of the film's production, Quinn dismissed the idea that he was attempting to recreate Chaney's characterization: "Chaney was too much of a master for me to try to imitate him. My makeup is not as grotesque and we are making my Quasimodo less a monster and more a human being."

Still not wishing to slight the Church, the screenwriters of this rendition again denied Claude Frollo his holy garb and made him an alchemist, who claims to Louis XI that he can manufacture gold. The role was ineptly portrayed by Alain Cuny.

Said *Variety:* "This foreign version of the Victor Hugo classic, although beautifully photographed and extravagantly produced, is ponderous, often dull and

The Hunchback of Notre Dame (**1939**):
Charles Laughton.

The Hunchback of Notre Dame (**1939**):
Maureen O'Hara.

a considerable amount of shock value in his scenes, still allowed the actors to deliver extremely sensitive portrayals and finally brought in an intriguing film that presented a meticulous picture of Paris during the fifteenth century.

According to the *Motion Picture Herald*: "Produced by Pandro S. Berman on a scale undreamed of in the period when the earlier *Hunchback* was made, this version exceeds in sheer magnitude any similar film in history. Sets are vast and rich in detail, crowds are immense, and camera uses of these are versatile, varied, and veracious. . . .

"Charles Laughton's portrayal of the hunchback is among the half dozen best acting achievements on record."

The most recent version of *The Hunchback of Notre Dame* was filmed in Technicolor and Cinemascope by producers Robert and Raymond Hakim. A 1957 Allied Artists release, the project was shot in Paris under the direction of Jean Delannoy, from a screenplay by Jean Aurenche and Jacques Prevert. It starred Anthony Quinn as the bell ringer and Gina Lollobrigida as the sexiest Esmeralda of all.

far overlength [103 minutes]. Subject as presented is old-fashioned for today's American audiences. . . ."

The trade paper's "decision" on the major performances was a "draw": "Miss Lollobrigida appears to be somewhat miscast as a naive gypsy girl of 15th century Paris, but occasionally displays flashes of spirit. Quinn, as the hunchbacked bell-ringer of Notre Dame . . . gives a well-etched impression of the difficult role."

Oddly, this, the weakest filming of Hugo's work, offered an ending more true to the original book than either of its two immediate predecessors: In attempting to escape the tower during the hunchback's battle with the mob, Esmeralda is felled by an arrow from one of the King's Archers. Quasimodo sees her body being dragged away, thus inciting him to kill Frollo. Afterwards, he joins his beloved in death at the burial vault.

The Hunchback of Notre Dame (1957): **Anthony Quinn.**

The Hunchback of Notre Dame (1957): **Anthony Quinn and Gina Lollobrigida.**

The failure of the Allied Artists release cannot be blamed *entirely* on its producers. Perhaps time had finally caught up with Hugo's once magnificent melodrama—making it nearly impossible to inject any freshness into the tired story. The astute *New York Times* had, interestingly, expressed doubts as to the tale's continued viability when they'd reviewed the Laughton version eighteen years earlier: "The *Hunchback* belongs between the covers of his book or back in the simpler days of the movies; he's a bit too coarse for our tastes now."

The Hunchback of Notre Dame

FILMOGRAPHY

1906: *Esmeralda* (French/Alice Guy) Henri Vorins.

1911: *Notre Dame de Paris* (French) Henri Krauss.

1917: *Darling of Paris, The* (Fox/J. Gordon Edwards) Theda Bara.

1923: *Hunchback of Notre Dame, The* (U/Wallace Worsley) Lon Chaney.

1939: *Hunchback of Notre Dame, The* (RKO/William Dieterle) Charles Laughton.

1957: *Hunchback of Notre Dame, The* (AA/Jean Delannoy) Anthony Quinn.

12
Jesse James

Contrary to American folklore, Jesse James was *not* a Robin Hood of the old West, stealing from banks and railroads, then turning the spoils over to weeping widows. History tells us that he was simply a cold-blooded thief and killer, who carried out his evil deeds for his own self-gratification and gain.

According to the facts, at sixteen, Jesse was riding with Charles Quantrill, the leader of Missouri's bloodiest guerilla band during the War Between the States. Then, following that conflict, he and his brother Frank, along with the notorious Younger Brothers, staged at least seventeen bank and train robberies, which netted them about two hundred thousand dollars. In September of 1876, the gang was shot apart in an ill-fated attempt to rob the First National Bank at Northfield, Minnesota. Jesse went into hiding. He died in St. Joseph, Missouri, on April 3, 1882, shot in the back by "that dirty little coward," Bob Ford.

Hollywood's tendency in dealing with real heroes and badmen of the West has been to romanticize them. Jesse James is no exception. In films of varying quality, the Missouri outlaw has been played by such performers as Fred Thompson, Audie Murphy, Robert Duvall, Willard Parker, Wendell Corey, and Roy Rogers. But the most popular interpreter of the role was handsome and dashing Tyrone Power in the 1939 Twentieth Century-Fox production, *Jesse James*.

This highly fictionalized account of the desperado's life had him moving to the wrong side of the law so that he could carry out a vendetta against the St. Louis Midland Railroad. Jesse's mother (Jane Darwell) was killed by a bomb thrown into her home by a railroad representative (Brian Donlevy) after she refused to sell her land to that company at an unreasonably low price.

The Missouri populace are sympathetic toward Frank (Henry Fonda) and Jesse James's crusade against the railroad, since many of them had also been victims of that company's land-grabbing tactics. Among their supporters are Zee (Nancy Kelly), Jesse's future wife, Will Wright (Randolph Scott), a local peace officer, and Major Rufus Cobb (Henry Hull), the cantankerous newspaper publisher, who continually editorializes that "If there is ever to be law and order in the West, the first thing we've got to do is take all lawyers out and shoot them down like dogs."[1]

Jesse James: **Charles Tannen, Tyrone Power, and John Carradine.**

[1] He has a similar attitude toward railroad presidents, dentists, governors, and anybody else who upsets the order of uncivilized existence.

88

Jesse James: **Tyrone Power and Randolph Scott.**

The outlaws pull off a series of successful train and bank robberies—all directed against the St. Louis Midland, headed by Mr. McCoy (Donald Meek). But years spent as a fugitive causes Jesse to lose sight of his original "enemy" and he decides to rob the bank in Northfield, Minnesota. To collect the reward on the James Brothers, which had been offered to him by Pinkerton-like detective Runyan (J. Edward Bromberg), Robert Ford (John Carradine), a member of the gang, informs the law of the planned raid. The posse is waiting for the outlaws in Northfield and the only ones to escape the ensuing massacre are Frank and Jesse.

Wounded, Jesse makes his way home to St. Joseph, Missouri, where Zee and their child are waiting. She nurses him back to health and he promises to go straight. However, Ford cancels Jesse's plans when he puts the fatal bullet in his back.

At the funeral, the eulogy delivered by Major Cobb is one that glorifies the outlaw.

Nunnally Johnson's screenplay, based on historical data assembled by Rosalind Shaffer and Jo Frances James (Jesse's granddaughter), completely ignored the existence of the Younger Brothers. Conversely, for story purposes, it fabricated the characters of Will Wright, Major Cobb, and Mr. McCoy, as well as the incidents involving them. The betrayal at Northfield by Bob Ford was also fiction. That raid had actually been thwarted when an alert citizen recognized the gang on its way into town and sounded the alarm.

Yet, the Technicolor release was a popular one—with both audiences and critics alike. The *New York Times* said: "Handsomely produced by the Messrs. Darryl Zanuck and Nunnally Johnson, stirringly directed by Henry King, beautifully acted by its cast—

Jesse James: **Nancy Kelly, Tyrone Power, and Henry Fonda.**

notably Henry Hull, Henry Fonda, and even its star, Tyrone Power—and buoyed by a brilliantly and slyly humorous screenplay by the versatile Mr. Johnson, it becomes an authentic American panorama, enriched by dialogue, characterization, and incidents imported from the Missouri hills."

As entertaining and well done as it was, *Jesse James* was a whitewash that left viewers with a false impression that the government and law enforcement officials were, indeed, the villains, while the outlaw was akin to a saint.

So successful was the picture that the following year the studio starred Henry Fonda in an equally good sequel, *The Return of Frank James.*

1957 found Twentieth Century-Fox digging Nunnally Johnson's old script out of the vaults and re-

making it—at least in part. The new screenplay by Walter Newman retained most of the key sequences from the original, but, on the other hand, it eliminated all of the fictional elements Johnson had created.

Titled *The True Story of Jesse James,* this new project attempted, as much as possible, to tell the outlaw's story as it actually happened—allowing, of course, for a certain amount of dramatic license.

In an interview given to the *Los Angeles Times* during the film's production, director Nicholas Ray explained that he, writer Newman, and producer Herbert B. Swope, Jr., had sifted millions of words written about the bandit and his times and taken events that all agreed happened. Said Ray: "In the first place, ours isn't the 'true' story of Jesse. But it's as true as anyone living these days, and possessed of our insight, can make it.

"In effect, we put Jesse James on trial—something the forces of law and order were unable to do in his lifetime. Our witnesses are not completely free of prejudice, we suspect; but we are being careful to film the events exactly as they saw them. To this extent, we are presenting 'the true story.'

"Our technique was suggested by *Citizen Kane*—but we have no particular feeling of guilt about this. Art is long and life is short, and dramatic techniques are all derivative by this time."

In this serious telling of the story, the major roles were filled by three Fox contractees. Robert Wagner played Jesse, Jeffrey Hunter was Frank, and Hope Lange essayed the part of Zee. Additionally, Agnes Moorehead did Jesse's mother, Alan Hale, Jr., was Cole Younger, and John Carradine, who'd played Bob Ford in the original, was back, cast, this time, as a preacher.

The Newman/Ray treatment brought a modern psychological approach to the saga. Beginning with the Northfield raid, the film told (via flashbacks) how Frank and Jesse were forced outside the law by the antagonism of their neighbors in Missouri. The James family had been Confederates during the Civil War, which caused their Northern-sympathizing neighbors to persecute them after the conflict ended.

Initially, Jesse planned only a single robbery—one that would give him and his "rebel" friends enough money to save their farms. But soon thereafter, he forgot his purpose for the thefts and began to enjoy what he was doing, since it satisfied a twisted urge within him.

The principal antagonist in this film is not the railroad, but Yankee law and order. Following the bombing of the James household, in which the outlaws' mother loses an arm and their little brother is killed, the public's sympathy leans heavily in Jesse's favor and amnesty is proposed. But the bandit shatters any hope of freedom when he cannot control his hatred and shoots down the neighbor responsible for the bombing.

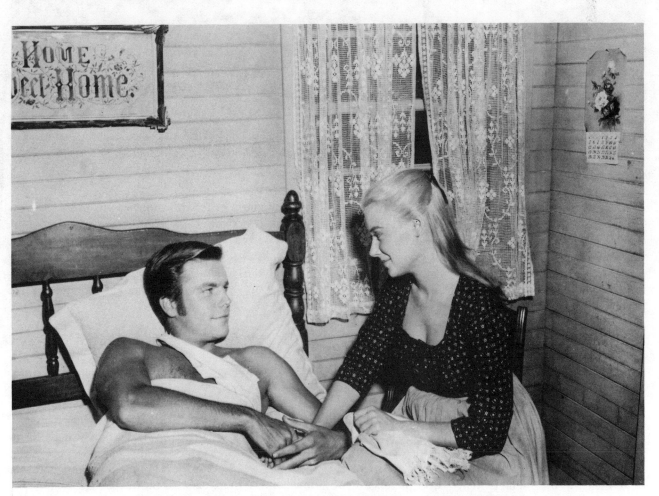

The True Story of Jesse James: **Robert Wagner and Hope Lange.**

The True Story of Jesse James: **Robert Wagner, Jeffrey Hunter, and players.**

As in the Tyrone Power picture, Jesse is shot in the back by Bob Ford (played by a very youthful Carl Thayler), after he has decided to go straight and move his family farther West. Ford's primary motive in this version is not the reward money, but the glory he will achieve by killing the notorious desperado.

The film concludes with Ford rushing from the house proclaiming his deed, while an elderly black minstrel walks down the street singing Billy Gashade's famous folk ballad about Jesse. The glorifying eulogy at the funeral is, thankfully, absent.

Newman's inclusion in the script of several real-life characters greatly enhanced the authentic quality of the film. It would have been easy for the writer to streamline his story by omitting roles like the James Brothers' stepfather, Dr. Samuel, or, for that matter, Zee's kinfolk. Whereas they added little to the forward movement of the main plotline, their presence cer-

tainly made it easier for audiences to grasp the psychological motivations of the leading characters.

Critics liked the Cinemascope/Deluxe color feature. The *Hollywood Reporter* said: "*The True Story of Jesse James* is a first-rate adventure story. . . . The picture has an excellent cast . . . and Nicholas Ray's direction is analytical and well-paced, probing and exciting."

Yet, some reviewers felt that Robert Wagner and Jeffrey Hunter were poor substitutes for their predecessors. Commented the *New York Times*: "These two earnest lads, as Jesse and brother Frank, while adorned with sideburns and mustaches, never approach the easy leatheriness of Mr. Power and Henry Fonda."

Nevertheless, their rather straightforward performances were as well suited to this factual approach to the story of Missouri's most infamous bandit, as Power and Fonda's more colorful portrayals had been to the

The True Story of Jesse James: **Carl Thayler, Robert Wagner, and Frank Gorshin.**

romantic treatment of Johnson and Henry King.

Folk heroes never die—nor do they fade away. As long as movies about Billy the Kid, Wyatt Earp, and Jesse James remain good box office, producers will continue to find new approaches for filming these legends over and over again.

Jesse James

FILMOGRAPHY

1939: (Fox/Henry King) Tyrone Power.
1957: *True Story of Jesse James, The* (Fox/Nicholas Ray) Robert Wagner.

13
Les Miserables

Les Miserables, Victor Hugo's long, scathing indictment of French injustice, has served as the basis for eleven motion pictures, yet only one of them—the 1935 version with Fredric March and Charles Laughton—made any lasting impression with either critics or the public.

Briefly, the literary masterpiece, which was written in 1862, tells of Jean Valjean, a French peasant who, to feed his sister and her seven starving children, steals a loaf of bread. He is caught and sentenced to serve five years in the galleys. Subsequent escape attempts increase his term to nineteen years. Valjean finally emerges from confinement in 1815, a bitter and insensitive derelict.

Unable to secure food or shelter because of his ex-convict status, Valjean is taken in by Bishop Myriel. The churchman treats him as an equal, but unable to accept his kindness, Jean departs during the night—taking the Bishop's silver along with him.

When Valjean is captured the next day by gendarmes, Myriel tells the officers to release him, and that the valuables had been a gift to the convict. The Bishop's compassion results in Valjean reversing his negative attitude toward life.

Settling in a Northern French town, the ex-convict adopts the name of M. Madeleine. He utilizes the silver to begin a manufacturing business and soon becomes a wealthy and popular industrialist. Five years later, he is elected mayor.

The inspector of police in Madeleine's town is Javert —a merciless official whose strict devotion to the law stems from the fact that his father, of whom he is ashamed, was a convict. Since he was stationed in the galleys during the early part of his career, Javert recognizes something familiar about the mayor and begins to investigate his background.

Madeleine befriends a former employee of his fac-tory, Fantine. The dying woman entrusts her daughter, Cosette, to the mayor's care.

Javert suspects that his superior is, in truth, Jean Valjean, who is currently wanted for committing a minor theft. Knowing that Madeleine could never let an innocent man go to prison in his place, the inspector informs the mayor that Valjean is on trial in a neighboring town. Madeleine proceeds to the courtroom and reveals his true identity. He is later arrested, then returned to the galleys, but, shortly thereafter, is reported to have drowned.

In actuality, Valjean has escaped and, after rejoining Cosette, who now thinks of her fifty-five-year-old benefactor as a father, attempts to establish a new life for both himself and the girl. However, Javert appears on the scene again and the pair must flee. They eventually find themselves in a convent, with Cosette becoming a student and Valjean working as a gardener.

Years go by. Cosette has grown into a beautiful young woman and, with Valjean (now calling himself Fauchelevent), has moved to Paris. The girl falls in love with Marius, a young revolutionary.

During a battle with French authorities, the revolutionaries capture Javert and offer Valjean the opportunity of executing his old nemesis. The ex-convict finds that he cannot kill the inspector. Upon being released, a disturbed Javert admits to Valjean: "I would rather you killed me."

Marius is wounded in the fighting and is carried by Valjean through the sewers of Paris to safety. When he emerges from the city's depths, the fugitive finds Javert waiting to arrest him.

The inspector allows Valjean to take the youth home, but, as he waits for his prisoner, finds himself torn between his lifelong belief in following the letter of the law and the realization that he cannot arrest the man who saved his life. Unable to cope with his

Les Miserables (1917): **William Farnum and player.**

dilemma, Javert ends his life in the Seine.

Marius and Cosette are married. Sometime later, Valjean dies—a free and happy man.

The numerous film versions of Hugo's massive novel have varied in story line only slightly and, for the most part, these differences did not involve any actual plot alterations, but rather the amount of material that was utilized from the original source.

Initial silent versions of the work were relatively insignificant efforts. Vitagraph released a primitive four-reel rendition in 1909, followed in 1913 by a French version from the Electric Film Company, directed by Albert Capellani and starring Henri Krauss as Valjean. This picture was imported into the United States by George Kleine of the Motion Picture Patents Group.

The Fox Film Corporation adapted Hugo's story in 1917 and, under the direction of Frank Lloyd, who, along with Marc Robbins was responsible for the scenario, came up with a production that the *New York Times* called "intelligently directed and highly interesting . . . quite the best picture that has been seen hereabout for a considerable period." William Farnum starred as Valjean.

In 1922, Lynn Harding played the fugitive in a British picture from Masters Films, *Tense Moments With Great Authors,* which presented scenes from several classic works of literature.

The French remade the story again in 1925. Directed by Louis Manpas, the Cinéromans Cie production starred Gabriel Gabrio as Valjean and Jean Toulout as Javert.

Whereas Manpas's original film ran thirty-two reels, the United States distributor, Universal, edited their 1927 domestic release prints down to eleven. It was a mistake, since the major surgery took much depth out of the picture, as well as eliminating the important character of Fantine. Said *Variety*: "This version in its boiled down form has all the breathless haste and fierce economy of a 'synopsis of chapters already published' in a magazine serial. Not for a single moment

Les Miserables (1935): Charles Laughton and Fredric March.

Les Miserables (1935): Fredric March, Charles
Laughton, and John Carradine.

does it live and breathe with any touch of human interest. Instead it is a long and tiresome parade of stiff and stilted melodrama."

A two-reel short entitled *The Bishop's Candlesticks,* based on an incident in *Les Miserables,* was produced by Paramount Famous Lasky Corporation in 1929. Walter Huston starred.

The most highly regarded version of *Les Miserables* to date was produced by Twentieth Century (prior to its merger with Fox) and released through United Artists in 1935. Fredric March was cast as Valjean in this production, with Charles Laughton essaying the role of Javert. Richard Boleslawski directed a fine screenplay by W. P. Lipscomb, but unlike many of the earlier, as well as subsequent, versions, it did *not* attempt to dramatize Hugo's *entire* novel. Instead, the writer selected the incidents in the book that best illustrated the novelist's basic points and thereby captured the intrinsic quality of the piece in an effectively compressed 109-minute film.

Darryl F. Zanuck's classic production, which concluded with Javert's suicide, rather than Valjean's death, garnered excellent reviews from the nation's critics. The *New York Evening Post* said: "A superlative effort, a thrilling, powerful poignant picture, produced on a tremendous scale, yet retaining all the color, passion and intimacy of Hugo's fiercely dramatic tale of nineteenth-century France."

Performances were also well praised. According to *Variety*: "March makes the screen Jean Valjean a living version of the panegyrical character. . . . There is studied acting in the March performance, but none of it tends to sacrifice Valjean for flashy histrionics. Side by side with March, throughout the picture, is Laughton as Javert, the cop. His performance is much more on the quiet side, but equally powerful and always believable."

The supporting cast included Cedric Hardwicke as the Bishop, Rochelle Hudson as Cosette, John Beal as Marius, and Florence Eldredge as Fantine.

Another French version of *Les Miserables,* running over six hours in length, had been filmed in 1934 by Pathé-Nathan Productions, under the direction of Raymond Bernard, who also wrote the screenplay with André Lang. Harry Baur and Charles Vanel played fugitive and pursuer respectively in that project—cut to 162 minutes for its domestic English-titled release by Franco-American in 1936.

Shown in the United States with a five-minute intermission, the picture was warmly received by the critics. Comparing it to the preceeding versions of Hugo's novel, *Variety* said: ". . . this Pathe-Nathan production is by all odds the most faithful, longest, and meritorious. . . . In acting, direction, and over-all conception it generally deserves its self-coronation as a French film classic."

The excellent film was hurt at the U.S. box office by the fact that, less than a year earlier, the March/Laughton version of *Les Miserables* had saturated audiences with the Hugo story and the public was not interested in paying to see another retelling of the same material—no matter how well it was executed. The picture passed quickly into obscurity.

Italian producer Carlo Ponti tackled the property in 1946, hiring Gino Cervi as Valjean, John Hinrich as Javert, and Valentina Cortesa in the dual role of Fantine/Cosette. Ricardo Freda directed the screenplay he'd written with Mario Monicelli, Stefano Vanzina, and Nino Novarese.

Lux Films released a 140-minute English-dubbed rendition of Ponti's epic in 1952, which was the recipient of good notices, yet failed to draw audiences. In its review, *Variety* called the import: ". . . a neat version, with the dubbing into English highly successful for the most part."

Later that year, Twentieth Century-Fox remade their relatively short 1935 version of Hugo's novel. Richard Murphy, who penned the screenplay, recalls the project: "It was [producer] Fred Kohlmar's idea to redo *Les Miserables*. Things were rather slack at Fox then, so I agreed to take on the assignment.

"I screened the March film, then decided that I'd rather start pretty much from scratch, as there were certain elements in the earlier version that I had difficulty accepting. For example, I objected to Fredric March looking like an 'animal' in the first part of the movie, then, after virtually one quick dissolve, he turns into the handsomest son-of-a-bitch who ever lived."

The 1935 picture had indeed jumped several years via a title card and a dissolve, from the ex-convict's confrontations with Bishop Myrial to Valjean living under the guise of the successful M. Madeleine. Murphy decided to *show* how his hero achieved such a lofty position and, therefore, added scenes dealing with Jean's becoming involved in a pottery business, which he subsequently purchased with the funds he obtained from the sale of the Bishop's silver.

The writer also added the character of Robert (played by James Robertson Justice), who both managed Madeleine's business and served as his confidant.

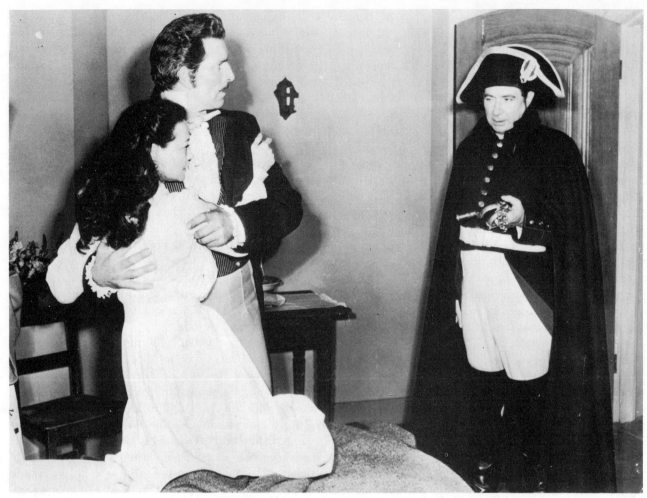

Les Miserables (1952): **Sylvia Sidney, Michael Rennie, and Robert Newton.**

Les Miserables (1952): **Cameron Mitchell and Michael Rennie.**

The 1952 release ran 105 minutes and, like the March/Laughton film, ended with Javert's suicide, which, in Murphy's script, Valjean tried to prevent. Explains the writer: "I felt that Valjean was too 'big' a man to let Javert kill himself."

Unable to secure the services of Burt Lancaster, his first choice for Valjean, Kohlmar cast contract player Michael Rennie as the fugitive and veteran character actor Robert Newton as Javert. Debra Paget made an attractive Cosette, while Sylvia Sidney did well in the role of her mother. Edmund Gwenn as the Bishop and Cameron Mitchell as Marius were also featured.

Lewis Milestone directed the rather glossey production, about which the *New York Times* commented: ". . . Richard Murphy's script and Lewis Milestone's direction are combined effectively in extracting the action, if not the genuine emotion of the book."

Regarding the actors, the *Hollywood Reporter* said: "Michael Rennie's brilliant performance as Jean Valjean should soon make his name a magnetic one. . . .

"Robert Newton turns in a wonderful deadly performance as Javert, playing the policeman with such dedicated sincerity that he commands at least understanding if not sympathy. The only flaw in the portrayal of Javert lies in omission of scenes which would furnish more logical motivation for his suicide."

The most recent motion picture version of Hugo's work was a sweeping French-made Technicolor epic, filmed primarily in East Germany by Pathé-PAC. The four-hour production featured Jean Gabin as Valjean and Bernard Biler as Javert. Jean-Paul Le Chanois directed the screenplay he'd written with Rene Barjavel.

Although the 1958 domestic release offered a fine performance by Gabin, it did not cause much excitement in the United States. Perhaps Hugo's book had been done one too many times on the screen. *Variety* said: "But, in all, the pic is an overdrawn, plodding odyssey with pruning in order."

It is an accepted rule of screenwriting that in adapting great novels to film, the more important task is to capture the true spirit of the piece, rather than to recreate and dramatize each and every scene of the work. The fact that Zanuck's successful 1935 production of *Les Miserables* is a sterling example of this thesis makes it easy to understand why *that* version of Hugo's work, over all other editions, has become a cinema classic.

Les Miserables

FILMOGRAPHY

1909: (Vit).
1913: (French/Albert Capellani) Henri Krauss.
1917: (Fox/Frank Lloyd) William Farnum.
1922: *Tense Moments with Great Authors* (British) Lynn Harding.
1925: (French/Louis Manpas) Gabriel Gabrio.
1929: *Bishop's Candlesticks, The* (Par) Walter Huston.
1934: (French/Raymond Bernard) Harry Baur.
1935: (20th/Richard Boleslawski) Fredric March.
1946: (Italian/Ricardo Freda) Gino Cervi.
1952: (Fox/Lewis Milestone) Michael Rennie.
1958: (French/Jean-Paul Le Chanois) Jean Gabin.
1976: Remake announced.

14
Macbeth

Shakespeare wrote *Macbeth,* his shortest play, in 1606. He based much of its plot on Holinshed's *Chronicles* (1577), a work that recorded the career of a real Macbeth who killed a Scottish king in 1040, then seized the throne—only to be overthrown by the son of the murdered monarch seventeen years later.

Scholars have described the tragedy as a study in fear: Two of King Duncan's generals, Macbeth and Banquo, meet three witches on a deserted heath. The "wierd sisters" prophesize that Macbeth will be Thane of Cawdor, then King of Scotland; and that Banquo will be the *father* of kings. After the witches disappear, two noblemen arrive to inform Macbeth that he has, in fact, been named Thane of Cawdor, since the former holder of that title was discovered to be a traitor and condemned to death.

An ambitious Lady Macbeth urges her reluctant husband to murder Duncan, so that he can gain the crown. Macbeth carries out the evil deed and is proclaimed King. Fearing the remainder of the witches' prophecy, the new ruler has Banquo murdered and is, subsequently, haunted by the dead man's ghost.

Duncan's son, Malcolm, and Macduff, a thane loyal to the late king, raise an army in England to recapture the crown from Macbeth, who, in retaliation, slays Macduff's family.

Plagued with a guilty conscience, Lady Macbeth goes mad. Ultimately, she commits suicide. Malcolm and his forces, utilizing Birnam Wood as cover, attack Macbeth's castle—with Macduff slaying the villainous sovereign to avenge the murders of his wife and children. Malcolm becomes the new King.

Of all Shakespeare's works, *Macbeth* has provided filmmakers with the most interesting possibilities for innovation—including adaptation to another time and place. Not only have experimental directors like Welles and Polanski tackled the material—with varying results—but the plot has also supplied the basis for a Japanese samurailike movie from Kurosawa, as well as a modern Chicago-based gangster epic.

In 1905, the American Mutoscope and Bioscope Company filmed the *Duel Scene From "Macbeth."* This was followed by several other short versions of the work—1908 from Vitagraph; 1909 from Italy's Cines Company; and in 1910 from Pathé of France.

A somewhat longer rendition was staged for the camera by the Frank R. Benson Company in the Shakespearian Memorial Theatre at Stratford-on-Avon in 1911. Benson and his wife, Constance, starred. Released by Britain's Co-Operative Cinematograph Company, the production was described by *The Bioscope* as being "wonderfully and vividly portrayed with the plot clearly told and full of action."

Arthur Bouchier and Violet Van Brugh played the Macbeths in a 1913 German-made picture from the Big A Film Corporation, released in the United States three years later (1916). *Moving Picture World* condemned the project as "so ridiculously inadequate in every respect that one may seek in vain for a redeeming quality."

Another, more important, production of *Macbeth* was also released during 1916. Presented by D. W. Griffith through Triangle/Fine Arts, the film starred well-known stage performers Sir Herbert Beerbohm Tree and Constance Collier, with direction by John Emerson. The *New York Times:* ". . . the star of the screen *Macbeth* is the director. . . . The imagination revealed, the impressive panoramas, the fine sense of composition, the cunning uses of impressionism, the prevailing good taste bespeak the presence of a man who is something of an artist. Mr. Emerson prepared

Macbeth (1916): **Sir Herbert Beerbohm Tree and Constance Collier.**

the scenario and consulted with Sir Herbert in the direction. The product is among the best things in motion pictures. All the detail of costuming and background is excellent, the vision of the wierd sisters a triumph. Indeed, the supernatural element in *Macbeth* gives the director chances after his own heart, so that the cave scenes are peopled with fine phantoms and the ghost of Banquo is more truly spectral than the stage can ever make him."

The last silent version of *Macbeth* was British in origin, appearing in 1922 under the direction of H. B. Parkinson. Russell and Sybil Thorndike were the leading players.

Theatrecraft did the next adaptation. The English company dramatized both the murder of Duncan and Lady Macbeth's sleepwalking scene in a sixteen minute short starring Wilfred Lawson and Cathleen Nesbitt. The film, released in 1945, was produced by Sidney Box and directed by Henry Cass.

1946 found producer/writer/cinematographer/editor/actor David Bradley turning out an ambitious amateur rendition of Shakespeare's play—at a total cost of five thousand dollars. A 16mm project, it was shot, for the most part, in and around Illinois' Northwestern University over a three-month period. Thomas A. Blair, who also played Banquo, staged the picture, which featured Bradley and Jain Wilimovsky in the central roles. Costumes were designed by an aspiring young actor named Charlton Heston.

Taking into consideration the film's primitive production techniques, as well as its unpolished per-

formances by a group of nonprofessional actors, most critics were quite complimentary to Bradley's seventy-three-minute work—citing him, in particular, for his inventive visual design.

Orson Welles, Hollywood's revolutionary young filmmaker of the 1940s, had long been interested in doing a motion picture version of *Macbeth,* but, unfortunately, no major studio was particularly keen about financing such a project, since Shakespeare had never been very popular at the box office. At last, the director was able to talk Herbert Yates of Republic into bankrolling the venture on a limited budget ($700,000) and shooting schedule (twenty-one days).

Welles agreed to do the film on the modest budget because he knew he had an ace in the hole. Recently, he'd staged the play at the Utah Centennial Festival in Salt Lake City and it was his plan to utilize much of that same cast, who, of course, were well rehearsed in their roles. The one major change in the company was radio actress Jeanette Nolan—signed for the role of Lady Macbeth after both Agnes Moorehead and Tallulah Bankhead were found to be unavailable.

Unlike Laurence Olivier's Shakespearean films, which remained faithful to the original text, Welles simply used the Bard's words as a vehicle for his own imaginative directorial technique. He altered the play, cutting it down to eighty-six minutes running time, simplified the characters, and staged the whole thing in low-key lighting against some wild scenic backgrounds. Few critics could deny that, if nothing else, Welles's innovations certainly made it an interesting production.

The *Hollywood Reporter* dissented: *"Macbeth* is slow, dull and monotonous. It is made so as much by

Macbeth (1948): **Peggy Webber, Christopher Welles, Orson Welles, and players.**

Macbeth (1948): **Orson Welles, Jeanette Nolan, and players.**

the direction of Welles as his gloomy, shabby production. It is photographed against a background of smoky haze. The characters appear from nowhere, speak their lines, and then depart into the mist. One is barely distinguishable from the other, thanks to their hideous make-ups and the aborted text. Welles even implements Shakespeare by forming a composite of several characters and calling him a holy Father. The fellow, incidentally, played by Alan Napier, gives the nearest thing to a legitimate performance in the entire film."

Of the writer/producer/director's portrayal of the title role, the *New York Times* said: "Especially does Mr. Welles favor the pointing of the camera at himself from all sorts of distorting angles and in close-ups that make his face bulk large. Also he uses heavy make-up to darken and crease his countenance so that his Macbeth, much given to pondering, has a monstrous quality. Except that he offers the suggestion

that this fatally ambitious man took rather heavily to drinking in the later phases of his bloody career, he accomplishes no illumination of the classical character."

The 1948 release featured Dan O'Herlihy as Macduff and Roddy McDowall as Malcolm. Its continued popularity, especially with film societies, is due, almost entirely, to the cult of fans who worship Mr. Welles' work.

A rather good seventy-eight-minute color rendition of the tragedy was filmed in 1951 by South Carolina's Bob Jones University and released through Unusual Films. Directed by Katharine Stenholm, the film starred Jones, Barbara Hudson Sowers, and the students and faculty from that educational institution.

The World's a Stage (1953), a British film, produced and directed by Charles Deane, featured scenes from several of Shakespeare's plays, including a thirteen-minute sequence from *Macbeth*. Ronald Howard served as narrator.

Writer Philip Yordan conceived the idea of adapting the *Macbeth* story to an American gangster movie format and, in 1954, received support for his plan from M. J. Frankovich at Columbia Pictures. *Joe Macbeth* was released two years later with Paul Douglas and Ruth Roman playing the counterparts to the Thane of Cawdor and his spouse. The film, shot in England, had Ken Hughes as its director.

Yordan's screenplay made some obvious adjustments on Shakespeare's original text: Macbeth, instead of being a general, became the triggerman for a gang boss; the three witches were changed to a sole fortuneteller; and most of the killings were accomplished via a tommy-gun.

Reviews were less than enthusiastic. The *New York Times*: "They have paraphrased the plot of the Scottish intrigue with sophomoric precocity, and Mr. Frankovich has assembled a good cast to play their consequent charade. . . . They have merely overlooked one little matter: the sweep and mightiness of Shakespeare's play reside in the high position of the characters and in the eloquence of the words. A plot of rather routine proportions is simply routine when the characters are thugs and the words are such things as, 'All you have to do is put the finger on Banky [Banquo]' or 'I don't want that hag around here.' "

The most straightforward filming of *Macbeth* to date was produced in England and Scotland by George Schaefer for a 1960 airing on NBC-TV's "Hallmark Hall of Fame." The Technicolor feature, starring Maurice Evans and Judith Anderson, later received a limited theatrical release through Prominent Films.

Mr. Schaefer, who also directed, recalls the project: "We made the film on a $500,000 budget. It was, actually, the first *major* picture shot for television and

Joe Macbeth: **Paul Douglas and Ruth Roman.**

Macbeth (1960): **Judith Anderson and Maurice Evans.**

became the prototype for the movies that you see on the 'tube' today.

"Regarding the text, we decided to make the film as true to Shakespeare as possible—so that school kids could view it with 'scripts in hand.' I think we were successful in that respect.

"There were no major problems working in England, although I did feel a bit of coolness from a few individuals there. It had something to do with the fact that, a couple of years previous, Laurence Olivier and Vivien Leigh were unsuccessful in raising the financing for *their* proposed movie of *Macbeth* and were forced to abandon it. I guess there were those who resented the idea of an American company producing this play by England's greatest playwright when that country's finest performer had been unsuccessful in getting *his* version off the ground."

Variety called the picture: "the equal, to be sure, of present day top screen thrillers."

Surely no free adaptation of *Macbeth* has garnered as much praise as Arira Kurosawa's *Throne of Blood,* produced through Japan's Toho Productions and released in the United States by Brandon Films in 1961. Mr. Kurosawa directed a screenplay by himself, Shinobu Hashimoto, Ryuzo Kikushima, and Hideo Oguni, which transported Shakespeare's character to sixteenth-century Japan, making him a warrior named Washizu (Toshiro Mifune), who is told by an old soothsayer that he will become the chief war lord. He, of course, assassinates the elderly lord and, from that juncture, the film follows the dramatic high points of the original quite closely, concluding with Washizu being felled by a shower of arrows. The

Throne of Blood: **Toshiro Mifune.**

Macbeth (1971): **Francesca Annis and Patricia Mason.**

Lady Macbeth role was played by Isuzu Yamada.

Time magazine: "It is a nerve-shattering spectacle of physical and metaphysical violence, quite the most brilliant and original attempt ever made to put Shakespeare in pictures. . . . The structure of the film is stark but never static; Kurosawa impels his drama with demonic drive."

"I see Macbeth as a young, open-faced warrior who is gradually sucked into a whirlpool of events because of his ambition. When he meets the wierd sisters and hears their prophecy, he's like the man who hopes to win a million—a gambler for high stakes." So said director Roman Polanski in a 1972 interview with *Playboy* magazine, following the release of his surrealistic version of *Macbeth,* which he'd scripted with Kenneth Tynan. That 1971 production from Columbia also marked *Playboy* publisher Hugh Hefner's debut as a film producer.

In the same article, Mr. Tynan elaborated on Polanski's position: "When actors in their 20s take on the leading roles [the parts had always been played middle age], they take on a stronger, more human pathos. Their lack of experience allows a greater chance of error. Here is a superb young general in the prime of his condition who has thrown away his own life in the space of a few seconds, by one murderous action. But all the time, the Macbeths see themselves as participants in a success story, not a tragedy."

As might be expected with such a highly publicized film from *Playboy,* the expensive Technicolor epic had its fair share of nudity, with not only the witches romping around in the buff, but also Lady Macbeth doing her famous sleepwalking scene sans a nightgown.

According to the *Hollywood Reporter:* "This *Macbeth* is definitely a movie. Polanski and his co-scenarist, Kenneth Tynan, have casually—almost blithely—sliced and trimmed and rearranged Shakespeare's text, and they have, indeed, made a screenplay out of it.

"But as beautifully made as it is, Polanski's *Macbeth* is also rather dull to sit through. The reason it seems to me, is that Polanski really doesn't have much to bring to *Macbeth,* apart from his characteristic fascination with bloodshed. . . . Polanski has simply not

Throne of Blood: **Isuzu Yamada and Toshiro Mifune.**

Macbeth (1971): **Jon Finch.**

supplied enough details of characterization or behavior to make it very interesting."

Most critics felt that newcomers Jon Finch and
Francesca Annis played the leading roles in a pedes-
trian manner.

Like the earlier film versions of *Macbeth,* this one
was also a financial failure. In fact, movie audiences
just don't seem to buy Shakespeare at all.[1]

[1] According to *Variety,* the most successful Shakespearean
film from the standpoint of box office was Franco Zeffirelli's
Romeo and Juliet (1968). Its domestic gross alone was nearly
17.5 million dollars.

Macbeth

FILMOGRAPHY

1908: (Vit).
1909: (Italian).
1910: (French).
1911: (British/Frank R. Benson) Frank R. Benson.
1913: (German) Arthur Bouchier.
1916: (Triangle/John Emerson) Sir Herbert Beerbohm Tree.
1922: (British/H. B. Parkinson) Russell Thorndike.
1946: (Amateur/Thomas A. Blair) David Bradley.
1948: (Republic/Orson Welles) Orson Welles.
1951: (Unusual/Katharine Stenholm) Bob Jones.
1956: *Joe Macbeth* (Col/Ken Hughes) Paul Douglas.
1960: (Prominent/George Schaefer) Maurice Evans.
1961: *Throne of Blood* (Japanese/Arira Kurosawa) Toshiro Mifune.
1971: (Col/Roman Polanski) Jon Finch.

15
Madame X

Presented before a contemporary audience in its original form, Alexandre Brisson's *Madame X* would be laughed off the stage. Laws and moral values have changed so radically since the classic tearjerker of mother love was first performed on Broadway in 1910 that the once-powerful melodrama has become archaic.

Brisson's relatively simple story is set in Paris. Jacqueline Floriot deserts Bernard, her wealthy politician husband, and their young son, Raymond, to run off with another man. Years later, having realized her mistake, she attempts to return to her family, but is thwarted by a bitter Bernard, who has informed Raymond that his mother is dead. Jacqueline departs without seeing her child and, filled with feelings of guilt, begins to drink—eventually becoming addicted to absinthe.

More years pass. Jacqueline takes up with a rather shady character, Laroque. When he learns that his mistress's former husband is now the Attorney-General of France, Laroque plans blackmail. Jacqueline, to prevent her now-grown son from being hurt by the revelation of his mother's past, kills the villain.

As fate would have it, fledgling attorney Raymond Floriot is appointed to defend the mysterious woman named Madame X, who refuses to admit the reasons for her crime. Initially, neither lawyer or client are aware that they are mother and son. However, after she sees Bernard in the courtroom, Jacqueline knows Raymond's true identity and, out of sympathy for him, takes the witness stand to confess, without using names, that she shot Laroque to protect her son. During a court recess, the gravely ill Jacqueline dies—her son never learning her real name.

The first of six filmings of *Madame X* was by Pathé in 1915. Henry W. Savage both produced and directed the six-reeler, which had a scenario by William E. Burlock. The cast included Dorothy Donnelly, star of the Broadway production, as Jacqueline and John Bowers as Raymond, her son.

It was a relatively accurate adaptation of the Brisson play, as were the following four movie versions. *The Bioscope* said: "... a more emotional and heart-throbbing portrayal than of Miss Dorothy Donnelly ... it would be difficult to conceive. If we paused to consider the probabilities of the story we might be tempted to say that her downfall, from the time that her husband thrust her from his door to the time when, a generation later, she is defended on a murder charge by her own son, is perhaps unnecessarily thorough and heart vending. But in this case the probabilities do not really matter, as all the elements of the plot are deftly blended until they culminate in the tremendous trial scene in which the outcast woman is tried for her life."

Frank Lloyd directed the second rendition of the French melodrama from a scenario he'd written with J. E. Nash. Filmed through Goldwyn Pictures, the 1920 production starred Pauline Frederick and Casson Ferguson as mother and son.

Although many reviewers felt that the story was somewhat artificial, they also had high praise for the production's performances, direction, and other creative aspects. Regarding Miss Frederick, the *New York Times* said: "Whatever the story has of life, however persuasive it is, is due as much to her performance as to everything else combined. In makeup and acting, she gives Madame X definiteness, and, by her restraint,

Madame X (1920): **Sidney Ainsworth and Pauline Frederick.**

Madame X (1920): **Lionel Belmore, Pauline Frederick, and Casson Ferguson.**

avoids the ever present danger of letting her become simply a burlesque queen."

Since the play is essentially a drama of words, it was only natural that *Madame X* would become one of the first "all-talking" pictures. Such a production was released by Metro-Goldwyn-Mayer in 1929, with Lionel Barrymore assuming the directorial reins. Ruth Chatterton essayed Jacqueline, Raymond Hackett was the son, and Lewis Stone played Floriot. Dialogue was credited to Willard Mack.

Excellent reviews greeted the movie upon its release—most of them noting that it was one of the better sound films to date. According to *Variety*: "Pictures of this calibre and their makers are entitled to untold commendation, whether too early or no, in lending to the screen a quality that the screen needs. Pictures like *Madame X* confound the reformers, elevate the name of pictures and tell the world that there is an art in film making."

The *New York Times* was also enthusiastic about the project, especially the acting: "There are a number of competent performances, several of which elicited genuine applause, but without a doubt the acting of Ruth Chatterton in the title role is the outstanding achievement of the picture. She portrays the emotional spells of the saddened woman with intelligence and artistry. She abandons all idea of good looks in the latter stages of this chronicle, and sometimes as the absinthe victim and on other occasions as the remorseful mother, Miss Chatterton lends to her part acting rarely beheld on the screen."

Unfortunately, when Metro remade the picture in 1937, sound was no longer a novelty and the Brisson

Madame X (1929): **Sidney Toler, Richard Carle, and Ruth Chatterton.**

play was forced to stand on its own two aged feet. Some critics tried, in vain, to be kind in writing about this competently played version of a once-viable play. *Variety*'s comments were typical: "Time has dulled the poignancy of Jacqueline Fleuriot's sin, suffering, grief and sacrifice. Numerous pleas for mercy in film criminal courts by brothers, sisters, cousins, and aunts have taken the edge from Raymond's impassioned argument that his mother be spared the ignominy of a murderess' fate. The years have passed, and entertainment tastes have quickened. *Madame X* is a fine old play, dated and outmoded. Audiences will leave the theaters expecting to find the coachman with horse and buggy."

John Meehan wrote the faithful adaptation, which was directed by Sam Wood. The talented cast was headed by Gladys George (Jacqueline), John Beal (Raymond), Warren William (Bernard), and Henry Daniell (Laroque).

New York audiences had a brief opportunity to view a Greek version of Bisson's work in 1960. Directed by Orestis Laskos, the film starred Mme. Kyveli in the title role. Reviews were not good.

Much of Hollywood must have chuckled when Ross Hunter announced in 1965 that he would star Lana Turner in a Technicolor remake of *Madame X*. True, the producer had been quite successful in updating such soap operas as *Magnificent Obsession, Imitation of Life,* and *Back Street,* but Alexandre Bisson's play was well over fifty years old and it seemed like an impossible task to adapt it to modern tastes.

Madame X (1929): **Ruth Chatterton and Eugenie Bresserer.**

Madame X (1937): **Gladys George and Warren William.**

Madame X (1937): **Gladys George and John Beal.**

Madame X (1965): **Ricardo Montalban and Lana Turner.**

Madame X (1965): **Lana Turner and Burgess Meredith.**

Writer Jean Holloway, who accepted the assignment because it gave her an opportunity to pen something other than the musicals she'd been use to, experienced innumerable difficulties in coming up with a workable script: "In studying the original play, I discovered that all I could really use from it was the basic premise—the woman loving her husband and child, making a mistake, and sacrificing herself to protect them. Very few *specific* incidents from Brisson's material worked in my updating."

At one point, the frustrated writer went to Hunter and complained that the play was too hopelessly old-fashioned and out of date. The producer smiled and said: "Everybody has problems—that's yours."

After she'd reset the story to take place in the United States, Miss Holloway decided that it would be better if Clay Anderson, the husband (played by John Forsythe), were a sympathetic character ("In order to make the audience care about the people, the villainy could not be the husband's"). She, therefore, gave him a strong-willed mother, Estelle (Constance Bennett in her final screen appearance), who learns of the wife's infidelity to her son. When Holly (Miss Turner) accidentally kills her lover (Ricardo Montalban), her wealthy mother-in-law forces her to abandon her family and travel around the world—living on a generous annual allowance. Estelle informs her politically active son that his wife has died by drowning.

Miss Holloway: "Many elements that were essential if we were to keep some identity with the original play, just didn't work by today's standards. For example, in America, the police always book a person without identification as 'John' or 'Jane Doe.' Well, we couldn't change the title of the movie to *Jane Doe,* so, in the scene where Holly signs a confession to the murder of the blackmailer [as played by Burgess Meredith], I had her, in a drunken stupor, scrawl an 'X'."

There were other adjustments also: "I found out that, because it produces a degenerative effect on the brain, absinthe has not been allowed in *any* country since 1928. Anybody familiar with *Madame X* knew she was famous for drinking that liqueur. Therefore, I gave Burgess a *secret* contact for obtaining the drink.

"But, my biggest problem was the trial sequence. Considering Madame X's mental state at the time of her arrest, it's highly unlikely that she would stand trial. More believable is that she'd be sent to a mental institution. Ergo, during the questioning by police, I gave her a line . . . something like, 'I knew *exactly* what I was doing.'

"Incidentally, unlike the trial scenes in the previous versions, I had the son [Keir Dullea] incorporate an argument about the law vs the spirit of the law into his final summation."

To the surprise of many observers, the 1966 Universal release worked well in its updating, benefiting not only from the carefully revised screenplay, but also from fine performances and the rich production values that had become Mr. Hunter's trademark. Director David Lowell Rich wisely decided to play the story "straight," so the basic emotion of the piece would come through: "Lana Turner is a fine actress and her talent helped bridge the precarious gap between soap opera and classic theatre."

The *Hollywood Reporter*: "David Lowell Rich's direction, Jean Holloway's screenplay, and a superb cast of players take this rather shabby old piece and give it immediacy, vigor, and credibility. It plays and plays beautifully. . . . In the end, thanks to director, writer, and actors, we have allowed that willing suspension of disbelief, and the emotions we feel are as genuine as the people."

Madame X made money at the box office, but was not as financially successful as some of Hunter's earlier efforts in the same genre. The public had tired of these lavish remakes of famous soap operas and were, frankly, interested in seeing pictures with more topical themes.

Madame X

FILMOGRAPHY

1915: (Pathé/Henry W. Savage) Dorothy Donnelly.
1920: (Goldwyn/Frank Lloyd) Pauline Frederick.
1929: (MGM/Lionel Barrymore) Ruth Chatterton.
1937: (MGM/Sam Wood) Gladys George.
1960: (Greek/Orestis Laskos) Mme. Kyveli.
1966: (U/David Lowell Rich) Lana Turner.

16
The Maltese Falcon

Prior to the release of *The Maltese Falcon* in 1941, the major emphasis in detective films seemed to be fast action, blended with a goodly share of light comedy. More often than not, these melodramas were of a programmer quality (an exception being *The Thin Man* series at Metro) and left little lasting impression on audiences.

John Huston's underplayed version of Dashiell Hammett's novel accented psychology and characterization, rather than superficial thrills. It made the formula detective movie obsolete and became the model for a new kind of private-eye film.

The plot line of this Warner Brothers classic is quite familiar to most devotees of the cinema:

Private detectives Sam Spade and Miles Archer are hired by a Miss Ruth Wonderly to follow Floyd Thursby. Archer is murdered while on the assignment. Then, later the same night, Thursby is killed. In a second meeting with his client, Spade gets Miss Wonderly to admit that her real name is Brigid O'Shaughnessy and that she is in danger. Attracted by the woman's beauty, as well as an additional fee, the sleuth agrees to help her.

Shortly thereafter, two unusual characters contact Spade—Joel Cairo, an effeminate type, and Casper Gutman, the "fat man," who has the detective brought to him by his "gunsel," Wilmer Cook. Both men express an interest in gaining possession of a black, jewel-encrusted statue of a falcon, which is, presumably, worth a fortune.

Spade pretends to know the whereabouts of the "black bird" and, on a second visit to Gutman, the portly gentleman slips him a "mickey." Recovering, the detective is visited by a mortally wounded Captain Jacobi of the S. S. LaPaloma, who gives him the falcon. Spade leaves the prize in a checkroom—returning

to his apartment to find Brigid waiting outside and Gutman, Cairo, and Wilmer inside.

Following Spade's suggestion, Gutman agrees to let Wilmer become the "fall guy" for the murders of Archer, Thursby, and Jacobi. The fat man also promises to pay Spade ten thousand dollars for the statue and the latter has his secretary reclaim, then deliver it to the apartment. The Maltese Falcon proves to be a fake and, during the ensuing confusion, Wilmer escapes. Gutman and Cairo decide to continue to look for the real thing, while Brigid indicates she will remain with Spade.

The detective, who had himself been under suspicion for the murders, tells the police to pick up the three men, after which, he gets Brigid to confess that she was the one who killed Archer. Her pleas that she loves him fall on deaf ears and Spade turns the treacherous woman over to the authorities.

John Huston, already a respected Hollywood screenwriter, made his debut as a director with *The Maltese Falcon*. Gathering together a brilliant cast, which included Humphrey Bogart as the sardonic Sam Spade, Mary Astor as Brigid, Sydney Greenstreet as Gutman, Peter Lorre as Cairo, Elisha Cook, Jr., as Wilmer, and his own father, Walter, playing a cameo role as the ill-fated Captain Jacobi, the thirty-five-year-old Huston created a picture, filled with tension, that the *New York Times* called: "The best mystery thriller of the year."

Actually, Huston's film was the *third* screen version of Hammett's novel. Warners' original was made in 1931 with Ricardo Cortez as Spade, Bebe Daniels as Brigid, Dudley Digges as Gutman, Otto Matieson as Cairo, and Dwight Frye as Wilmer. The screenplay by Maude Fulton, Lucien Hubbard, and Brown

The Maltese Falcon (1931): **Ricardo Cortez and Bebe Daniels.**

Holmes was directed by Roy Del Ruth.

The story differences in the two pictures are minimal, but worth noting:

Both versions contain a subplot dealing with the fact that Spade is having an affair with Archer's wife. The husband remains unaware of the relationship in Huston's film, but in the earlier telling, he overhears an "incriminating" phone conversation between his partner and spouse.

Whereas, in the 1941 picture, we *see* Archer being shot, this murder is committed offscreen in the original. Also in Del Ruth's film, the crime has a witness—a Chinaman.

Digges's Gutman, who is *not* fat, slips Spade the drug on his first visit—not the second.

The 1931 movie retained a scene from the novel, which Huston omitted because censorship regulations were stricter in 1941. When, at Spade's apartment, Gutman suggests that Brigid stole a thousand dollar bill from an envelope containing ten times that amount, the detective takes the girl into the kitchen and forces her to strip, so that he can search her.

Later in the same film, we learn from the police that when, on Spade's tip, they'd attempted to arrest Gutman and Cairo, Wilmer appeared and shot the two men down. In the 1941 version, the criminals are, simply, arrested.

Finally, Del Ruth's film concludes with Spade, now working as an investigator for the district attorney's office, visiting Brigid in jail and expressing his affection for her. The later edition ends in the apartment—while she is being led away by the police.

Taking into consideration the acting styles and production techniques that were employed during the early thirties, Del Ruth's *The Maltese Falcon* was probably a pretty good little film and suffers only in comparison to the 1941 remake. Unfortunately, it's difficult for one who has become familiar with Huston's masterpiece to view this earlier effort with any degree of objectivity.

However, critics at the time were quite impressed. Said the *New York Times*: "The adventures of Sam Spade, private detective of the firm of Spade and Archer . . . are here reported smoothly, fluidly, with cultivated humor and a keen intelligence, these qualities being manifest all the way along. Played with disarming ease and warmth by Ricardo Cortez, the character of Sam Spade is enormously unique and attractive."

In comparison to Bogart's interpretation of the antihero private eye, Cortez played Spade as a ladies' man with much more charm and less ruggedness than his successor. Dudley Digges, on the other hand, created a Gutman who was almost a comical character—bearing little resemblance to Greenstreet's pompous, yet quite dangerous, fat man.

By today's standards, several of the scenes in the 1931 film seem to be terribly overacted. For example, Captain Jacobi's staggering into Spade's office is played so broadly that one can hardly avoid laughing at this "serious" moment in the melodrama.

The overall "look" of both pictures is also totally different. Del Ruth places *his* Spade in a very swanky environment, as opposed to the rather seedy atmosphere Huston created for his detective to operate in. This latter approach goes far in helping to create a proper mood for the intriguing story.

The second filming of Hammett's tale took place in 1936. Warners needed a property for Bette Davis and, lacking anything better, decided to adapt the mystery story to her talents. Associate producer Henry Blanke reflects on the project, titled *Satan Met a Lady*: "It was the worst picture I ever made. Jack Warner ribbed me about it for years afterward.

"We decided that we could redo the story so soon

Satan Met a Lady: **Warren William and Bette Davis.**

after the original by switching certain elements around and turning the whole thing into a comedy. But, as I later found out, the director had no flair for that kind of film and it failed."

Brown Holmes's screenplay, directed by William Dieterle, made only two major changes in Hammett's story. Instead of a black falcon, the characters were looking for a horn filled with priceless gems. In addition, the Gutman character was rewritten for a woman —Alison Skipworth. Other variations of time and place did little to affect the basic plot.

All of the characters' names were changed. Warren William overplayed the detective, while Miss Davis was wasted in the role of his mysterious client. Most amusing was British character actor Arthur Treacher doing the counterpart to Joel Cairo. His initial scene with William, where he returns to the sleuth's apartment after having ripped it apart in search of the horn, is the film's highlight.

The *New York Times* summed up the picture best: "A cynical farce of elaborate and sustained cheapness, it causes still other intelligent actors and actresses— including Warren William, Arthur Treacher, and Alison Skipworth—to behave like numskulls, and deserves to be quoted as a classic of dullness, in future press notices, as often as *The Thin Man*—also based on a Dashiell Hammett theme—has been quoted as a classic of scintillating wit."

By 1941, John Huston was becoming tired of writing screenplays (such as *Jezebel, High Sierra,* and *Sergeant York*) for other directors, so, with the help of producer Blanke, he got a commitment from the studio to let him *direct* a film—subject, of course, to the property.

Recalls Blanke: "John wanted to do *The Maltese Falcon* and the fact that it had been done twice before didn't bother him.

The Maltese Falcon (1941): **Humphrey Bogart, Mary Astor, and Jerome Cowan.**

The Maltese Falcon (1941): **Sydney Greenstreet and Humphrey Bogart.**

The Maltese Falcon (1941): **Mary Astor, Humphrey Bogart, and Peter Lorre.**

"He followed the book exactly. He took two copies of it . . . cut them up to give him something to work from, then based his entire screenplay on what Hammett had already written. Much of the dialogue in the film came directly from the novel.

"Four weeks after he began, Huston came to me with the thing all finished. I told him to stick the manuscript in a drawer and go fishing for eight weeks, since no studio head would have much faith in a screenplay that was written in such a short period of time."

George Raft had been the first choice for Sam Spade, but when the actor refused the assignment be-cause he didn't want to work with an inexperienced director, Bogart inherited the role. His chilling, but captivating, interpretation of the detective subsequently made Bogie a major star.

Blanke continues: "When we showed Jack Warner our finished picture, he didn't like it. He thought it was confusing . . . and *he was right,* so we came up with the idea of adding the written forward that told the history of the falcon. It made all the difference in the world. Without Jack Warner's suggestion, the picture might have been a big flop."

Of the film's creator, the *New York Times* said: ". . . Mr. Huston gives promise of becoming one of the smartest directors in the field. . . . He has worked out his own style, which is brisk and extremely hard-boiled. . . ."

Few, if any, mystery films have ever surpassed the artistry of Huston's *The Maltese Falcon*. More than three decades after it was made, it remains the definitive achievement of its genre.

The Maltese Falcon

FILMOGRAPHY

1931: (WB/Roy Del Ruth) Ricardo Cortez.
1936: *Satan Met a Lady* (WB/William Dieterle) Bette Davis.
1941: (WB/John Huston) Humphrey Bogart.

17
Moby Dick

Hollywood producers have seldom been hesitant to bring the great works of world literature to the screen. During the 1930s and 40s, the studios turned out excellent renditions of such classics as *A Tale of Two Cities, Les Miserables, Mutiny on the Bounty,* and *Jane Eyre.* Therefore it is rather odd that, not until 1956 was a *definitive* film adaptation of Herman Melville's masterpiece, *Moby Dick,* even attempted.

True, Warner Brothers had previously utilized the tome as the basis for two John Barrymore vehicles, yet these productions bore only a fleeting resemblance to Melville's lengthy allegorical novel.

Written in 1851, *Moby Dick* tells the story of the last voyage of the *Pequod,* as seen through the eyes of Ishmael, a young sailor, who, along with the exotic harpooner, Queequeg, signs aboard the doomed vessel.

Captain of the whaling ship is Ahab, intent on killing Moby Dick, the great white whale that took his leg from him. Gaining the crew's support for his mad quest for revenge, Ahab begins a chase that takes the *Pequod* halfway around the globe.

The final confrontation with Moby Dick is a costly one. Ahab, his ship, and the entire crew, save Ishmael, are destroyed by the sea monster. After two days of grasping onto a floating coffin, the youth is rescued by a passing ship.

Warner Brothers first used Melville's tale in 1926 as the inspiration for a silent John Barrymore feature, *The Sea Beast.* Fearing that the lack of a love interest in the film would severely hamper box-office potential, the studio assigned writer Bess Meredyth to devise a scenario that would include a leading lady.

Miss Meredyth's substantially original story told of half-brothers Ahab (Barrymore) and Derek (George O'Hara) Ceeley, rivals for the attentions of Esther

Harper (Dolores Costello), the daughter of a missionary. Jealous because Esther favors Ahab, Derek pushes his harpooner brother overboard during a whaling expedition. Ahab loses his leg in the jaws of Moby Dick, the white whale, and returns to Esther an embittered man.

After Derek falsely tells him that Esther no longer loves him, the driven Ahab becomes captain of a whaler, setting out to destroy Moby Dick. Ultimately, he learns of Derek's treachery and, following the slaughter of the white whale, kills his brother in a

The Sea Beast: **John Barrymore.**

The Sea Beast: **Dolores Costello and John Barrymore.**

fight. Ahab returns to New Bedford to find Esther waiting for him.

Reviews for the Warner release were mixed. The *New York Times* said: "Millard Webb, who directed this production, often spars for suspense and misses it, and frequently loses his dramatic value by long close-ups, first of one person and then another. For this reason the production drags quite a good deal. . . . This is a good production and one which contains much interest, but it is not a great photoplay."

The Sea Beast was, as the trade called it, a "money picture" and for that reason the studio decided to remake it with sound in 1930. This time, however, they chose to retain Melville's original title—*Moby Dick*.

Barrymore again played the fun-loving harpooner who loses his leg to the white whale. Sadly, four short years of hard living had taken their toll on the actor's once-magnificent features and, instead of the dashing young sailor that he portrayed in the earlier film,

audiences saw a tired, dissipated Barrymore—a shadow of his former self.

J. Grubb Alexander wrote the screenplay for the film, which was directed by Lloyd Bacon. Joan Bennett co-starred as Faith, the counterpart to Esther in the 1926 version, and Lloyd Hughes was Derek. Whereas *The Sea Beast* had had a bit player doing the role of Queequeg, this new picture expanded that part slightly and also included the Melville characters of Starbuck, Ahab's first mate on the *Pequod,* and Elijah, the "prophet" who predicts the destruction of the ship.

Moby Dick followed the basic storyline of *The Sea Beast.* Yet, there were a few differences:

First, Faith was definitely Derek's girl at the start of the film, but she becomes infatuated with Ahab after he stumbles into the local church—slightly inebriated.

Second, Ahab loses his leg to the whale when he *accidentally* falls out of the boat. Derek's only sin against his half-brother is the lie about Faith's true feelings toward him.

Moby Dick (1930): **John Barrymore.**

Moby Dick (1930): **Walter Long, John Barrymore, and Nobel Johnson.**

Finally, it is Queequeg who kills Derek—not Ahab. The harpooner from the South Seas commits the act in order to stop the treacherous brother from killing his captain.

Incidentally, Ahab's ship in this version is the *Shanghai Lil*—not the *Pequod*.

Considering the limitations that sound techniques had placed on moviemaking during this period, *Moby Dick* was a superior adventure film. In the areas of story construction, acting, direction, and especially special effects, it was a vast improvement over *The Sea Beast*. The scenes of battle with the whale are still exciting to behold and have seldom been equaled.

Surprisingly, critics were not bothered by the fact that the film was quite unlike Melville's work. *Variety* said: "*Moby Dick* is stirring, even if you don't believe in whales."

Of the star's performance, the *New York Times* commented: "John Barrymore, who fills the role of the indomitable, half-crazed Ahab Ceeley, gives a performance that puts his work, even the latter part of the mute offering, in the shade. . . . Mr. Barrymore is Mr. Barrymore of the stage in this film, and not the great silent lover who is made to turn his profile to the camera on the slightest provocation. Words bring out his true talent, whether he is affording humor or

Moby Dick (1956): **Leo Genn and Gregory Peck.**

delivering a grim impression of a man who wants to even up matters with a white whale."

John Huston had been intrigued with the idea of filming an *honest* adaptation of Melville's novel for many years. Initially, he'd wanted to make it with his father, Walter Huston, in the pivotal role of Ahab, but after the death of the veteran character actor, the director temporarily lost interest in the whole idea.

He later got Warner Brothers enthusiastic about the project. However, once again, that studio expressed their doubts in the advisability of not having a romantic subplot in the story. As a compromise, Huston agreed to cast a *top* male star as the fanatical Captain Ahab—eventually choosing Gregory Peck for the role. He also attempted to secure the services of Montgomery Clift to play the part of Ishmael, but, unsuccessful, settled on Richard Basehart. Other cast members included Leo Genn as Starbuck, Friedrich Ledebur as Queequeg, Royal Dano as Elijah, and Orson Welles in a brief appearance as Reverend Maple, the New Bedford preacher who delivers a God-fearing sermon on Jonah and the whale.

In a 1955 interview with the *Los Angeles Times*, Huston discussed his film: "I tried to make the picture itself very faithful to the spirit of Melville's novel. It's a very philosophical work, one of the deepest ever written; at the same time there's wild action. The combination of the two gives the picture its peculiar flavor."

Moby Dick, released by Warner Brothers in 1956, was shot over a two-year period: on location in Ireland; then off the coast of Madeira, Cardiff, Wales; followed by studio filming in London; and, finally, in

Moby Dick (1956): **Gregory Peck.**

the Canary Islands. Poor weather conditions, accidents, and other problems raised the total negative cost of the picture to nearly five million dollars.

Adding to the increased expense was a successful effort on the part of the producer/director to create, in collaboration with camerman Oswald Morris and Technicolor, new color shadings for his film, so that the scenes would look like steel engravings of sailing ships. Explained Huston: "We wanted to express visually what the novel stands for in our own—the reader's—thoughts.

"We finally came up with this process, not a hard effect to achieve—at least till you go to print it. A black-and-white negative is drawn from the color negative and then the two are superimposed—'married.' That way you get more of a sense of form, as in black and white; 'looms powerfully' is a phrase that describes it."

Ray Bradbury's thoughtful screenplay, though telescoping many scenes, was true to Melville's original work. Technical aspects of the picture—costumes, settings, color, and, of course, special effects were without fault in recreating nineteenth-century New Bedford, the sailing ships, and whale hunts.

The film contained many memorable scenes: the dockside prophecy of doom by Elijah; the initial appearance of Ahab with his artificial leg of whale bone; the "duel" between the *Pequod* and Moby Dick; and the chilling final shot of the drowned captain, lashed to the white whale by harpoon lines, as his dead hand seems to beckon his crew onward. Each moment stayed with audiences long after they'd left the theater.

Unfortunately, the reviews were not what Huston had hoped for. According to *Variety*: "*Moby Dick* in its final 116 minute form is interesting more often than exciting, faithful to the time and text more than great theatrical entertainment."

Garnering the severest criticism was star Gregory Peck. Of his contribution, the trade paper reported: ". . . Peck often seems understated and too gentlemanly for a man supposedly consumed by insane fury. When Ahab is intent on working his will upon the crew, asking them to pass up commercial kills for the sake of his grand revenge, the dramatic effects are inherent in the faces of the crew members rather than in Peck's own inwardness."

Huston had made a valiant attempt, but, despite the film's merits, his *Moby Dick* was destined to become a box-office failure. And yet, a better production of Melville's classic is not likely to come along for quite some time.

Moby Dick

FILMOGRAPHY

1926: *Sea Beast, The* (WB/Millard Webb) John Barrymore.
1930: *Moby Dick* (WB/Lloyd Bacon) John Barrymore.
1956: *Moby Dick* (WB/John Huston) Gregory Peck.

18
The Mummy

The "curse" of King Tut's tomb, which had been discovered by British archaeologists in 1922, was the inspiration for Universal's minor horror masterpiece of a decade later, *The Mummy. Dracula* and *Frankenstein* had been box-office hits and the studio was anxious to find a "new" monster to scare movie audiences. Bringing an ancient Egyptian mummy back to life seemed like the perfect idea.

John L. Balderston's screenplay, based on a story by Nina Wilcox Putnam and Richard Schayer, concerns Im-Ho-Tep, High Priest of the Temple of the Sun at Karnak, who, 3,700 years ago, stole the sacred Scroll of Thoth, so he could return to life the woman he loved—Princess Anck-es-en-Amon. Caught, the priest was buried alive in a casket containing the scroll.

The remains of Im-Ho-Tep are unearthed in 1921 by a British archaeological expedition. A young member of the party, Ralph Norton, discovers the scroll and reads the chant aloud. The mummy comes alive, takes the scroll, and disappears into the desert—leaving Norton stark raving mad.

Ten years later, the elderly Ardath Bey (actually Im-Ho-Tep in more human form) leads scientist Frank Whemple to the tomb of Princess Anck-es-en-Amon. Bey's efforts to revive her mummy at the Cairo Museum fail because her soul has been reincarnated in Helen Grosvenor, an attractive Anglo-Egyptian girl.

Ardath Bey attempts to embalm Helen so their souls can be joined eternally, but he is thwarted when a statue of the god Iris comes to life and, through its mystic powers, crumbles the long-dead High Priest into dust.

Boris Karloff, the screen's Frankenstein monster, was set by Universal to play Im-Ho-Tep/Ardath Bey.

Billed simply as "Karloff," his effective low-keyed performance assured his succession to Lon Chaney, Sr., as Hollywood's top interpreter of the macabre.

The supporting cast included Zita Johann as Helen, David Manners as Frank Whemple, and Bramwell Fletcher as Norton.

Director Karl Freund's production was a rather slow-moving affair, which concentrated on establishing an eerie mood. The *New York Times* reported: "For purposes of terror there are two scenes in *The Mummy* that are weird enough in all conscience. In the first, the mummy comes alive and a young archaeologist, going quite mad, laughs in a way that raises the hair on the scalp. In the second, Im-Ho-Tep is embalmed alive, and that moment when the tape is drawn across the man's mouth and nose, leaving only his wild eyes staring out of the coffin, is one of decided horror. But most of *The Mummy* is costume melodrama for the children."

Universal produced four other *Mummy* movies during the first half of the 1940s. Whereas in the 1932 film Karloff had only appeared as the bandage-wrapped High Priest in a single scene, then switched over to a wizened-faced Ardath Bey, Tom Tyler and Lon Chaney, Jr., who essayed the role in the subsequent productions,[1] stayed mute and in their mummified makeup throughout the entire pictures.

These cheaply made spinoffs gave the mummy a new name, Kharis, and changed his status from High Priest to a prince in love with the Princess Ananka. The Princess died and Kharis stole not the Scroll of Thoth, but forbidden Tana leaves, the juice of which

---

[1] Tyler played the part in *The Mummy's Hand* (1940), while Chaney did it in *The Mummy's Tomb* (1942), *The Mummy's Ghost* (1944), and *The Mummy's Curse* (1945).

The Mummy (1932): **Boris Karloff.**

The Mummy (1932): **Boris Karloff and Bramwell Fletcher.**

will revive the dead. After the prince was caught, his tongue was cut out, *then* he was buried alive.

Additionally, each of these new pictures had a High Priest, whose job it was to keep Kharis alive, so he could kill those who desecrated Ananka's tomb. Of course, in most instances, his potential victims were the epic's hero, heroine, or their friends.

Hammer Film Productions, a British company, had revitalized the horror film in the late 1950s with such well-made efforts as *The Curse of Frankenstein* (1957) and *Horror of Dracula* (1958). Filmed in blood-soaked color, the productions were a refreshing change from the low-budget monster movies that had dominated theater screens for the several years previous. Audiences enjoyed these exciting new productions, as did the critics.

By the end of the decade, Hammer was the acknowledged new leader in producing horror fare. Therefore, it was not unexpected when they negotiated a deal with Universal to remake several of that studio's copyrighted horror classics. The first of these to go into production was *The Mummy*.

Directed by Terence Fisher from a screenplay by Jimmy Sangster, the 1959 Universal-International Technicolor release was actually closer in concept to the Tom Tyler/Lon Chaney, Jr. films than the old Karloff classic, in both the story line and the fact that Kharis never doffed his bandages.

Set near the end of the nineteenth century, the plot tells of how three English archaeologists, led by John Banning (Peter Cushing), discover the tomb of Prin-

The Mummy (1959): **Christopher Lee and players.**

cess Ananka and her buried-alive priest/lover, Kharis (Christopher Lee). Following their return home to place the mummies in the British museum, Banning's two associates are murdered by Kharis, who has been brought back to life through the use of a mystic scroll by a worshiper of the old Nile gods.

Only the likeness of Banning's wife (Yvonne Furneaux) to Ananka distracts Kharis from killing the scientist. The thing from a time long past carries the woman off, but is shot down in a swamp by her husband and a group of rescuers.

The "lavishly-produced" programer was one of the weaker entries to come from Hammer. As stated by the *Hollywood Reporter*: ". . . the pace is slow and it is becoming apparent that this British company needs to ferret out better stories for its horror programs."

Despite the poor critical reception, Hammer went on to produce several other *Mummy* pictures, which would indicate that their original did rather well at the box office.

The Mummy (1959): **Christopher Lee and Peter Cushing.**

The Mummy

FILMOGRAPHY

1932: (U/Karl Freund) Boris Karloff.
1959: (U/Terence Fisher) Christopher Lee.

19
Mutiny on the Bounty

Whereas Metro-Goldwyn-Mayer's 1935 version of *Mutiny on the Bounty* was the first filming of Charles Nordhoff and James Norman Hall's much-acclaimed novel, it was *not* the first motion picture to deal with that dramatic incident from British naval history. A poorly executed semidocumentary by Expeditionary Films of Australia had been produced in 1933. Entitled *In the Wake of the Bounty,* the seventy-minute "epic" starred a then-unknown actor named Errol Flynn as Fletcher Christian.

Mutiny on the Bounty, published in 1932, was the first part of a trilogy that included *Men Against the Sea* (dealing with Captain Bligh's journey across the ocean in an open boat) and *Pitcairn's Island* (about the flight of the mutineers), both of which appeared in 1934. MGM purchased the film rights almost immediately and assigned Talbot Jennings, Jules Furthman, and Carey Wilson to adapt the material into screenplay form. Frank Lloyd was set to direct.

The 1935 release details the final voyage of H.M.S. *Bounty,* a British war vessel, which, in 1787, sets sail for Tahiti on a scientific mission to bring back breadfruit plants.

Midshipman Roger Byam (Franchot Tone) is shocked at the sadistic methods the ship's master, Captain Bligh (Charles Laughton), uses to discipline his crew. Fletcher Christian (Clark Gable), the first mate, shares the young man's views and is continually at odds with the captain. The crew is subjected to further hardship during the long voyage when Bligh cuts their food rations so that he can fatten his own pocketbook.

As punishment for denouncing him as a cheat, Bligh, upon arrival in Tahiti, confines Christian to the ship, while the rest of the crew is allowed to go ashore. The native chieftain, at Byam's urging, ar-

ranges for Fletcher to leave the *Bounty* and, on shore, the first officer meets and falls in love with Miamiti (Mamo). Byam, meanwhile, has taken up with another island girl, Tehani (Movita).

When the time comes for the *Bounty* to depart, five crew members attempt to desert, but are captured and ordered flogged. The unnecessary death of the elderly Dr. Bacchus (Dudley Digges), as well as continued mistreatment of the men, leads Christian to the conclusion that he must take action against Bligh.

In the Wake of the Bounty: **Errol Flynn.**

Mutiny on the Bounty (1935): **Clark Gable, Charles Laughton, Donald Crisp, and players.**

Mutiny on the Bounty (1935): **DeWitt Jennings, Ian Wolfe, Charles Laughton, Clark Gable, and Dudley Digges.**

He seizes control of the ship and sets the captain adrift with several still-loyal members of the crew.

The mutineers return to Tahiti where Christian and Byam marry their native girls. Eventually, the first mate and his crew depart the island in search of a safer place to settle. They leave Byam and five other men who had not taken part in the mutiny behind. The *Bounty* reaches the incorrectly charted island of Pitcairn and the mutineers, deciding to stay there, burn the vessel.

Determined to have his revenge, Bligh reaches safety, then leads a search to capture the renegades. He picks up Byam and his party, taking them back to England to stand trial.

The men are convicted and sentenced to hang. Byam denounces Bligh in court for his cruelties and is, subsequently, pardoned. The film concludes with the midshipman returning to duty.

Albert Lewin's film garnered nothing but rave notices from critics. *Variety* said: "As a production of the type that used to be known as a 'spectacle,' as an example of superb screen authorship and as an exhibition of compelling histrionics, this one is Hollywood at its very best. The story certainly could not be presented as powerfully through any other medium. . . .

"Laughton, Gable and Tone are all that Producer Al Lewin and Director Frank Lloyd could have wished for in the three key roles. Laughton is magnificent. Gable, as brave Fletcher Christian, fills the doc's prescription to the letter. Tone, likeable throughout, gets his big moment with a morality speech at the finish and makes the most of it."

The MGM presentation won the Academy Award as the Best Picture of 1935 and, today, ranks as one of the screen's all-time great adventure classics.

Metro's lavish 1962 remake of *Mutiny* was the victim of poor planning, artistic temperament, and plain bad luck. Although the box-office gross for the hard-ticket Technicolor/Ultra Panavision attraction was a large one (nearly ten million dollars—domestic), the total return was not enough to offset the picture's final cost of $19.2 million.

The idea of redoing the Laughton/Gable picture, taking advantage of modern film techniques, was quite valid and there was no question that the story contained all the right elements to merit a reserved seat treatment. A budget of $8.5 million was allotted for the production, with initial expenditures going for a new and *expanded* screenplay, and the construction of a $750,000 replica of the *Bounty* by a Nova Scotia shipbuilding firm.

Coming up with a workable script that would satisfy the studio, producer, and star Marlon Brando was not an easy task. In fact, four writers (Eric Ambler, Borden Chase, William Driskill, and Ben Hecht) worked on the project before Charles Lederer, who received sole screen credit, was called in—ten days before filming was to commence in Tahiti.

As Brando recalled in a 1961 interview with Vernon Scott of *UPI*: "They started shooting without a completed script and eventually had seven scripts on the picture. The studio sent the entire cast and crew on location to Tahiti where it cost them $32,000 a day and we were out there for six months."

Sir Carol Reed, the original director, resigned after several months of mounting difficulties and was replaced by Lewis Milestone. Speaking to Murray Schumack of the *New York Times* early in 1962, the new director, whose credits included such films as *All Quiet on the Western Front* and *Of Mice and Men*, attempted to shed light on the reasons for Reed's departure, as well as the other rumors that were circulating about the seemingly "cursed" project: "Reed was use to making his own pictures. He was not use to producer, studio, and star interference. But those of us who have been around Hollywood, we are like alley cats. We know this style. We know how to survive.

"The big trouble was the lack of guts by management at Metro. Lack of vision. When they realized that there was so much trouble with the script, they should have stopped the whole damn production."

Milestone also commented on the problems he'd had with Brando: "Marlon did not have approval of the story, but he did have approval of himself. If Brando did not like something, he would just stand in front of the camera and not act. He thought only of himself. At the same time, he was right in many things he wanted.

"If they [the studio] did not like Marlon's behavior, they should have told him that he must do what they wished or else they should have taken him out of the picture. But they just did not have the guts."

Three months later, MGM president Joseph R. Vogel issued a statement in an effort to put aside the numerous stories that had been published concerning the inflated production cost of *Mutiny on the Bounty*: "A combination of circumstances, including delay in completion and delivery of our specially built ship which forced rearrangement of a shooting schedule, a break-out of fire on the ship on its way to Tahiti, tropical storms and otherwise unfavorable weather; clashes of temperament among director, producer, writer and principal players, illness and death among the cast,

Mutiny on the Bounty (1962): **Trevor Howard and Marlon Brando.**

particularly the illness and resignation of the original director, and other problems which not infrequently arise on a location far distant from the full facilities of a Hollywood studio, all contributed to a final cost beyond the amount budgeted for the picture. While one or more of these problems may be expected to arise in the course of producing a picture of such unprecedented size and scope, *Mutiny on the Bounty* was plagued by them all."

Producer Aaron Rosenberg's sweeping entertainment ran nearly an hour longer than its predecessor (185 minutes plus intermission) and, naturally, differed from the 1935 film in a number of ways:

First, unlike the earlier rendition, which drew its plot from only the first two books of *The Bounty Trilogy,* this underplayed production utilized material from all three works—concluding with the renegades on Pitcairn's Island. When Christian, as played by Brando, suggests that they should return to England to present their case at a court-martial, the men set fire to the ship. The first officer is killed while trying to save the sextant from the blazing inferno.

Secondly, the remake eliminated the Roger Byam character, telling the story of the mutiny, via flashback, through the words of William Brown (Richard Haydn), the *Bounty's* gardener, whose job it was to care for the breadfruit plants. Brown, the last surviving crew member on Pitcairn, relates the saga to the captain of a passing British ship several years after the mutiny. An epilogue, in which the captain tells Brown that the crew has been exonerated, was also shot, but was only added to the film for its television airing. The theatrical version concludes immediately after the death of Christian—an unwise decision, since it put the entire story out of focus and left audiences wondering about the fate of the *Bounty* crew.

Third, Bligh, effectively played by Trevor Howard, does not confine Christian to the ship during the stay in Tahiti, but instead, in a highly amusing sequence, orders his first mate to make love to the native chief's daughter (Tarita), lest the girl be offended.

Christian's decision to mutiny is more spontaneous in the remake, than in Frank Lloyd's film. In that earlier effort, the ship's officer, angered because of the

Mutiny on the Bounty (1962): **Tarita and Marlon Brando.**

doctor's death, waits until *the next day* to decide that he's had enough of Bligh. He then incites the more militant members of the crew to join him in taking control of the vessel.

Conversely, in the 1962 picture, Christian's emotions reach their limit when Bligh kicks from his hand a ladle of water intended for a gravely ill seaman. Incensed, and almost without thinking, the officer hits the captain across the face. Christian realizes that, since he has committed a hanging offense, there is no turning back and he orders the revolt.

Without doubt, *this* interpretation of the story's climactic scene played considerably better than the Laughton/Gable confrontation.

Despite a somewhat uneven script by Mr. Lederer, *Mutiny on the Bounty* (1962) had its share of exciting moments and, as far as its visual aspects were concerned, received considerable praise from the press. Said the *Hollywood Reporter*: "Whether this *Mutiny* matches or surpasses the original of nearly 30 years ago is an academic question. It is a different kind of picture, made in a different time. Performances admired 30 years ago would not go today. Certainly in its scope and sweep, the present production eclipses anything possible when the *Bounty* first sailed. Some of the visual images alone, in limpid Technicolor and the almost dimensional Ultra Panavision 70 are unforgettable. Seascapes of the *Bounty* placid on an orange, sunwashed sea; the *Bounty* fighting for its life on the gray, boiling seas off Cape Horn. The pulsating dance sequences where the men of the *Bounty* face in Tahiti, for the first time, the friendly guileless natives of the friendly islands. The charm of a fishing scene, with a seemingly endless chain of Tahitian beauties forming an undulating human net. . . .

"Milestone's direction is magnificent, balancing the spectacle with the intimate."

Coming under the greatest criticism was Brando's unorthodox portrayal of Fletcher Christian. Reported the *New York Times*: "Where Trevor Howard puts wire and scrap-iron into the bulky, brutal character of Captain Bligh, making him really quite a fearful and unassailable martinet, Mr. Brando puts tinsel and cold-cream into Christian's oddly foppish frame, setting him up as more a dandy than a formidable ship's officer . . . he maintains the airs, to the point where one feels the performance is intended either as a travesty or a lark."

This extreme departure from Gable's quite masculine interpretation of Christian disappointed a great many viewers and, according to some "insiders," was probably the principal reason that the project failed to garner the huge box-office receipts it needed to break even, let alone wind up in the black.

Mutiny on the Bounty

FILMOGRAPHY

1935: (MGM/Frank Lloyd) Clark Gable.
1962: (MGM/Lewis Milestone) Marlon Brando.

20
One Sunday Afternoon

It's no secret that improper casting has been the ruin of many motion pictures. A studio or an individual producer will acquire the rights to a successful novel or play, then, in order to put a commercial package together, cast a well-known star in the lead—failing to take into account whether that performer is actually the best choice for the role. Such was the case with the 1933 version of *One Sunday Afternoon*.

The Paramount release was based on a fairly successful stage play of the same name, which had starred Lloyd Nolan as its quick-tempered hero. The actor, well-suited for the part, later made a name for himself as a movie tough guy.

Had the studio been wise, they would have set Nolan to repeat his performance on film, but, unfortunately, they decided that a better-known player would be more desirable in the role and proceeded to miscast Gary Cooper.

The screenplay by William Slavens McNutt and Grover Jones followed James Hagan's Gay 90s play rather closely:

Biff Grimes (Cooper), an ex-convict, is having little success in building his dental practice. Married to Amy (Frances Fuller), Biff holds a grudge against Hugo Barnstead (Neil Hamilton), who the dentist feels, years ago, stole his girl, Virginia Brush (Fay Wray), from him and was also responsible for his prison term. When Biff gets an emergency call on a Sunday afternoon to extract one of Hugo's molars, he contemplates giving his old enemy an overdose of sleeping gas.

Via a flashback, we learn that both Biff and Hugo had once courted Virginia, but the shallow-minded girl had ultimately decided to elope with the fast-talking Barnstead, since she disapproved of the aspiring dentist's rowdy manner. On the rebound, Biff married Virginia's best friend, Amy Lind.

One Sunday Afternoon (1933): **Fay Wray and Gary Cooper.**

A few years later, Biff, who was at that time employed in a box factory owned by Hugo's uncle, received an offer from his old boyhood chum to act as a paid informant and report on his fellow wage earners' reliability. When he refused the job, Hugo made things rough for Biff at the plant, which resulted in the worker losing his temper and quitting.

One Sunday Afternoon (1933): **Frances Fuller, Gary Cooper, and players.**

Hugo refused to pay Biff for the time he'd put in, so Grimes attempted to collect his wages at gunpoint. He was arrested and spent two years in prison. Upon his release, Amy was waiting for him.

Back in the present, Biff decides not to kill Hugo after he sees what an ill and unhappy man he has become. Virginia, the girl he'd once worshiped, is now a nagging nuisance. Biff realizes that, by marrying Amy, he did, in fact, get the better of the two girls.

Directed by Stephen Roberts, *One Sunday Afternoon* was poorly received by both critics and audiences. Said *Variety*: "... it is still pitched in stage tempo for the screen and unfolds haltingly. Its substance is delicate character humor and elusive sentimental appeal and these are qualities that are difficult to translate from footlight to celluloid."

Mr. Cooper's out-of-place interpretation of the leading part naturally had a negative effect on the overall production. As reported by the *New York Times*: "The role of the redoubtable Biff Grimes . . . is played in the film by Gary Cooper, whose performance, like the picture as a whole, is praiseworthy in many respects but fails to impress one with the character's aggressive personality. The author's Biff Grimes went around with a chip on his shoulder, but Mr. Cooper portrays him in a milder fashion, which does not help the story."

Hagan's play lay dormant until 1940 when producer William Cagney came across the work and suggested it to Warner Brothers as a possible vehicle for his brother James, who was then under contract to that studio. All parties involved liked the idea and Warners proceeded to purchase the rights from Paramount.

Cocky Jimmy Cagney was the perfect choice to play the pugnacious Biff Grimes, and screenwriters Julius J. and Philip G. Epstein gave a fresh insight into the character's quarrelsome personality by creating a drunken father for him to contend with. The colorful new role was amusingly portrayed by Alan Hale.

Julius Epstein recalls that "the most important change we made from the original was to switch the locale of the story from a small town to New York City. That new environment made a considerable difference in the believability of the characters and situation."

The writers also came up with a more workable way for Grimes to get into trouble with the law. This new version has Hugo making Biff a vice-president in his construction business. In truth, however, Barnstead is using the naive Biff as a "stooge" to put over his crooked dealings.

Due to the use of inferior building materials, one of the company's projects collapses and Biff is held responsible. He is sentenced to five years in prison.

Cagney was surrounded by a fine ensemble of players. Jack Carson was Hugo, while the distaff half of the cast featured Olivia DeHavilland as Amy and Rita Hayworth (replacing Ann Sheridan) playing Virginia. Raoul Walsh directed the production, which had a new title—*The Strawberry Blonde*.

Whereas the earlier filming of Hagan's play was a rather sluggish affair, the 1941 Warner Brothers release had exactly the opposite result. Not only did Walsh turn the simple sentimental story into a well-paced, engrossing motion picture, but he also managed to capture the charm of the Gay 90s—probably better than any other director has before or since. It was a thoroughly enjoyable piece of nostalgic entertainment.

The *New York Sun* called *The Strawberry Blonde* "an unusual picture, a film with a definite individuality. It not only tells a very human story, it also creates an atmosphere, re-creates a period.

"Warners was pressed for a release, so we decided to remake *The Strawberry Blonde* as a musical," recalls Raoul Walsh, who also directed the 1948 Technicolor version of James Hagan's play, which reverted back to its original title—*One Sunday Afternoon*.

"We shot the picture in about three weeks or thereabouts. It was a big mistake. The songs weren't that good and, frankly, neither was the film."

With the exception of dropping the character of Biff Grimes's father, Robert L. Richards's screenplay made no significant departures from the Epstein brothers' 1941 revised story line. Dennis Morgan took over the role of Biff, Janis Paige was Virginia, Don DeFore

The Strawberry Blonde: **James Cagney and Olivia DeHavilland.**

The Strawberry Blonde: **Jack Carson and James Cagney.**

One Sunday Afternoon (1948): **Alan Hale, Jr., Don DeFore, Dennis Morgan, and Ben Blue.**

One Sunday Afternoon (1948): **Dorothy Malone, Dennis Morgan, and players.**

played Hugo, and Dorothy Malone did Amy. Ben Blue was seen as Biff's loyal friend—essayed in earlier versions by Roscoe Karns and George Tobias respectively. Producer Jerry Wald unwisely allowed too much screen time for the comedian to perform some of his classic routines, which, although amusing, slowed the film considerably.

The musical score by Ralph Blane was pleasant, but forgettable.

In sum, *One Sunday Afternoon* was a weak programmer. According to the *New York Times*: "Raoul Walsh . . . seems to have slackened the directorial reins this time. And the cast, with the exception of Miss Malone, who is genuinely appealing, never fully projects the flavor of the people or the period. Theirs is a lackadaisical and uninspired jaunt down memory lane."

Walsh had made a near-perfect picture with *The Strawberry Blonde*. He should have quit when he was ahead.

One Sunday Afternoon

FILMOGRAPHY

1933: (Par/Stephen Roberts) Gary Cooper.
1941: *Strawberry Blonde, The* (WB/Raoul Walsh) James Cagney.
1948: (WB/Raoul Walsh) Dennis Morgan.

21
The Phantom of the Opera

As an interpreter of the macabre during the movies' silent era, Lon Chaney had no equal. His adeptness with makeup gave the screen a long line of gruesome creatures, mad doctors, and other outcasts of society. *London After Midnight* was an eerie film, as were *The Unknown* and *A Blind Bargain*. But, undoubtedly, the actor's most famous excursion into the horror genre was as Erik—*The Phantom of the Opera*.

Universal's Carl Laemmle, inspired by the box-office success of *The Hunchback of Notre Dame*, obtained the rights to Gaston LeRoux's novel about a disfigured recluse who haunts the Paris Opera House. Budgeting the melodrama at one million dollars, the executive hired Rupert Julian to direct a scenario by Raymond Schrock and Elliott J. Clawson. The first shooting stage ever erected on a structural steel framework was built for the replica of the Opera House. Additionally, the two-color Technicolor process was utilized for certain sequences.

The 1925 release, which follows the book fairly religiously, is set in 1880. Erik, the phantom, falls in love with Christine (Mary Philbin), an aspiring singer in the Paris Opera Company. Keeping his face hidden, he trains the young woman to become an exceptional singer, then begins a reign of terror in the Opera House to coerce the management into making his protégée their prima donna. When his warnings are ignored, the phantom cuts loose a huge chandelier from the ceiling of the auditorium, killing several members of the audience.

Erik subsequently abducts Christine and takes her to his secret headquarters, located in the subcellars beneath the Opera House. There, the girl unmasks his skeletonlike face and promptly faints.

Christine is rescued by Raoul de Chagny (Norman Kerry) and Ledoux (Arthur Edmund Carewe), a member of the secret police. The phantom escapes, but is hunted down and killed by a mob.

Chaney's skeletal face was covered throughout the first four reels of *Phantom* and, so that the shock value of the unmasking scene would be heightened, no publicity photographs of the actor in makeup were published for some time after the picture's initial release.

That release, however, was delayed considerably. After a rough cut of the production was assembled, it was decided to lengthen, as well as rearrange, the climactic chase scene. The original material had had the phantom drowning in his subterranean lake, rather than in the Seine, as was the case in the final version.

More editing—the picture was still not right. New sequences were shot, then eliminated, before the general public finally saw the finished film, which officially premiered in New York on September 6, 1925.

The *New York Times* reported: "*The Phantom of the Opera* is an ultra fantastic melodrama, an ambitious production in which there is much to marvel at

The Phantom of the Opera (**1925**): **Lon Chaney and players.**

The Phantom of the Opera (1925): **Lon Chaney and Mary Philbin.**

in the scenic effects. . . . This is a well-dressed thriller, with a capable acting by the villain, a stiff and stilted hero and an insipid heroine. So far as the story is concerned, it looks as if too many cooks had rather spoiled the broth, which was served up in novel form by Gaston LeRoux."

Despite mixed reviews, the uneven Universal production was a huge financial success. Five years later the studio re-released it as a talkie. They had reshot some of the opera sequences with sound, then added music and effects throughout. About a third of this 1930 version had dialogue, but it was an actor other than Chaney whose voice was heard from the screen.

LeRoux's novel described Erik as being a "freak" from birth. He traveled around Europe with gypsies and various fairs—learning magic and ventriloquism at the same time. While helping to build the Paris

Opera House, he decided to construct himself a secret hideout beneath the edifice.

Conversely, Chaney's film explained its title character as being a self-educated musician, who was declared criminally insane and sent to Devil's Island. Following his escape, he took up residence under the Opera House.

There were two remakes of the horror classic—1943 and 1962. Essentially, the plot lines of the films differed in three areas: the origin/motivation of the phantom; the extent of sympathy he evoked from the audience; and the specifics of the denouement.

Whereas Chaney's Erik was a madman and almost total villain (his only redeeming feature being the twisted affection he felt for Christine), the phantoms of the succeeding versions were progressively more

The Phantom of the Opera (1943: **Frank Puglia and Claude Rains.**

"likable." In fact, the characterization in the 1962 film seemed nearly heroic.

Claude Rains was the second actor to play the phantom. The accomplished character star, hired after Boris Karloff proved unavailable, was billed third in Universal's 1943 Technicolor rendition of the LeRoux work, which co-starred Nelson Eddy as Anatole Carron, an opera singer, Susanna Foster as Christine, and Edgar Barrier as police inspector Raoul de Chagny. Arthur Lubin directed the lavishly mounted production from a screenplay by Eric Taylor and Samuel Hoffenstein.

Rains played Enrique Claudin, a violinist with the Paris Opera Company, who is dismissed after an arthritic hand affects his ability to play. When a music publisher attempts to pirate Claudin's life work, a piano concerto, the composer strangles him, whereupon the dead man's mistress throws a pan of sulphuric

The Phantom of the Opera (1943): **Claude Rains and Susanna Foster.**

acid into his face. Escaping the scene of his crime, Claudin descends into a manhole and ultimately winds up beneath the Opera House.

In the ensuing months, Claudin, wearing a mask to hide his burn scars, terrorizes the Opera Company. He wants the management to make his protégée, Christine, their prima donna. Kidnapping the girl from the stage one night, he takes her to the catacombs beneath the Opera House. She unmasks this mysterious phantom, then is rescued by her two suitors, Anatole and Raoul. Claudin is killed in a cave-in and Christine goes on to become a popular opera star.

Although it was never actually stated, the screenplay hinted strongly that Claudin was Christine's father, whom she had never known. Prior to his being fired from the orchestra, the musician had spent his entire savings for the girl's singing lessons. Christine was unaware of this gift, thinking that her instructor was so impressed with her potential that he was donating his services. Unlike the lecherous intentions of Chaney, once Claudin became the phantom, his attitude toward the girl was strictly a paternal one. His only desire was for her to become successful—no matter what the cost in human life.

Unfortunately, the 1943 release was more of a musical than a horror film. Director Arthur Lubin recalls the reasons: "Claude Rains insisted that the phantom be played as a sympathetic character. He didn't want to do the entire picture with a scarred face, as he considered himself to be a 'romantic' character actor and that a pure monster role, such as was played by Chaney, would harm his future career. We compromised by having him wear a mask until the final scene . . . and then he would only allow the make-up people to apply a minimum amount of 'scaring' to his face.

"In the original script, it was made quite clear that Susanna Foster was Rains' illegitimate daughter. Again, Claude insisted on changes and we, therefore, only hinted at the relationship."

Certainly, Rains's ideas weakened the production's shock potential. The ninety-five minute effort was blessed with beautiful music, settings, and color, yet too much footage was spent on the opera numbers, as well as the "amusing" romantic scenes between Foster, Eddy, and Barrier, rather than with the phantom and his evil deeds. The final result was, according to the *Hollywood Reporter,* "a rare musical treat, an arresting beautiful spectacle," but it was *not* a very thrilling melodrama, which is what audiences had expected it to be.

The Phantom of the Opera (1962): Michael Gough and
Herbert Lom.

The Phantom of the Opera (1962): Herbert Lom and Heather Sears.

The weakest filming of *The Phantom of the Opera* was in 1962 by England's Hammer Productions for Universal release. Shot in Eastmancolor, the project starred Herbert Lom as the phantom (Cary Grant had, at one time, been rumored for the part). Terence Fisher directed John Elder's screenplay—moving the story setting to London.

Midway through this version, the phantom's origins were revealed via a flashback—a device which would have also worked well in the 1943 rendition had it been employed, as Rains would then have been an unknown and more frightening figure. To the detriment of that earlier film, Eddy, Barrier, and the audience were quite aware of the phantom's identity—almost from his first appearance.

The *Los Angeles Citizen-News* described Lom's character as "a lovable ol' English phantom who goes around doing good."

Indeed, the phantom's former identity in the Hammer film was one Professor Pietre, a musical genius, who, cheated out of his composition by the nasty Lord Ambrose D'Arcy (Michael Gough), is disfigured by fire when he attempts to destroy the sheet music that should bear his name. He takes refuge in an underground grotto near the Opera House. Aided by a demented hunchback (Ian Wilson), the masked paranoic attempts to halt the presentation of his opera, which is now signed by D'Arcy.

Pietre abducts Christine (Heather Sears), a young singer. He plans to train her to properly perform the leading role in his opera. After explaining his reasons for seeking vengeance against D'Arcy to the frightened girl and her sweetheart, who has found his way into the subterranean sanctuary, the couple agree to go along with him.

Christine's debut is a triumph, but Pietre sacrifices his life to save his protégée from death by a falling chandelier that has been accidentally released by the hunchback.

This unimaginative version of *The Phantom of the Opera* was lumbered with a silly story line, paltry sets, inadequate performances, and virtually no atmosphere of suspense whatsoever. Conspicuously missing was the famous unmasking scene. The finished film, in fact, seemed like a patchwork. For example, two recurring characters—a police inspector and a representative of the Opera House—seem to have been added to the story following the completion of principal photography, as they do nothing but comment on the action in the rest of the picture and *never* appear in a scene with a key character.

The *New York Times* said: "The only shock—a mild one—is that the British, who could have had a field day with this antique, have simply wafted it back with a lick and a promise. Coming from Hammer Productions, a suspense unit specializing in eerie atmosphere, especially in the color and music departments, the new Universal release is a real disappointment. . . .

"Mr. Chaney's ghost and picture still lead the opera hit parade. The Hollywood color package for the excellent Mr. Rains at least was somewhat stylized. Mr. Lom and company play it in neutral."

A 1964 Mexican production, *Santo Against the Strangler,* also claimed to have been inspired by Gaston LeRoux's book. Then, in 1974, 20th Century-Fox's rock-musical horror satire, *Phantom of the Paradise* was released, with William Finley in the title role. Written and directed by Brian DePalma, the film *did not* acknowledge a relationship to the LeRoux material, but was obviously based on it. *Paradise* concerned a disfigured novice songwriter, who haunts a rock palace owned by the entrepreneur responsible for

Phantom of the Paradise: **William Finley.**

stealing his musical compositions.[1] Paul Williams played the twisted record mogul, while Jessica Harper was the young singer the phantom was smitten with. The *Hollywood Reporter* called the color picture "a campy, aggressive audio-visual super-hype."

In any case, it was certainly a far cry from Lon Chaney and the Paris Opera House.

---

[1] Instead of playing an organ like his predecessors, this modern phantom was adept at the Moog synthesizer.

The Phantom of the Opera

FILMOGRAPHY

1925: (U/Rupert Julian) Lon Chaney.
1943: (U/Arthur Lubin) Claude Rains.
1962: (British/Terence Fisher) Herbert Lom.
1974: *Phantom of the Paradise* (Fox/Brian DePalma) William Finley.

22
The Philadelphia Story

The Philadelphia Story, Philip Barry's sophisticated comedy about the complexities of life among the upper classes, did for Katharine Hepburn what *Destry Rides Again* did for Marlene Dietrich.

Labeled "box-office poison" in 1938 by the Independent Theatre Owners of America, Miss Hepburn had fled Hollywood—vowing not to return until she was offered a "good" picture. She remained inactive for some time and even refused a very lucrative movie contract, which did *not* allow her script approval. It was Mr. Barry who finally brought her back into the limelight.

The leading character in Barry's new play had been fashioned with Hepburn in mind, and, after reading the script, the actress knew that *this* was the vehicle she'd been waiting for. To get the play on the boards, Hepburn agreed to put up twenty-five percent of the production cost and waived her salary in favor of ten percent of the gross profits from the New York run and twelve and one-half percent from the road company. She also purchased the motion picture rights.

Opening at the Shubert Theater in New York on March 28, 1939, *The Philadelphia Story* boasted a cast that included Joseph Cotton, Van Heflin, Shirley Booth, and a teenage Anne Baxter. It was both a critical and commercial success, playing a total of 415 performances on Broadway, as well as an additional 254 on the road.

On the eve of her marriage to stuffed-shirt George Kittredge, Tracy Lord, a priggish and demanding Philadelphia society girl, is visited by her first husband, the wealthy and likable sportsman, C. K. Dexter Haven. Dexter has arranged for reporter, Macaulay "Mike" Connor, and a photographer, Liz Imbrie, of

Spy Magazine to cover the wedding. The usually unapproachable Miss Lord agrees to let the members of the press stay in her household, only after she learns that, otherwise, their periodical will print a scandalous story about her father's illicit affair with an actress.

Tracy is forced to take a good look at herself during the next twenty-four hours. Confrontations with Dexter and her father make her realize that she is, in fact, a rather cold woman and has failed as both a wife and a daughter.

But it is cynical reporter Connor who has the greatest effect on her. Mutually infatuated with each other, the couple get drunk on champagne and go for a moonlight swim in the nude. When Kittredge learns of his fiancée's indiscretion, he demands an explanation. However, the incident has made Tracy realize that she is indeed fallible and not the "goddess on a

The Philadelphia Story: **John Howard, Cary Grant, Katharine Hepburn,** and **James Stewart.**

145

The Philadelphia Story: **John Howard and Katharine Hepburn.**

The Philadelphia Story: **James Stewart, John Howard, and Katharine Hepburn.**

pedestal," as men had always pictured her. She breaks her engagement with Kittredge, refuses Connor's proposal of marriage, then proceeds with the wedding—the new groom being her ex-husband, C. K. Dexter Haven.

Miss Hepburn sold the film rights to *The Philadelphia Story* to Metro-Goldwyn-Mayer for $250,000. The deal called for her to re-create the role of Tracy, and she was also given her choice of a director, co-stars, and reasonable script supervision.

The motion picture was released in 1940. George Cukor directed Donald Ogden Stewart's faithful adaptation of the Philip Barry play. A first-rate cast included Cary Grant as Dexter; James Stewart doing Connor; Ruth Hussey as Liz; John Howard as Kittredge; John Halliday essaying Tracy's father; and Roland Young as Uncle Willie.

Of the production, the *Hollywood Reporter* said: "Great in entertainment, great in production, great in performance, and great in direction and writing. There are not enough superlatives in picture jargon to sufficiently appreciate this show."

Regarding Hepburn's Tracy Lord, the paper continued: "She is sensational. Her love scenes, her emotional moments; her movements, the toss of the head; her laughter and tears; her banter of words, the fire in her eyes, the twists of her luscious mouth, cause about as much excitement as any performance that has ever been given in a screen presentation."

A tremendous hit, the film garnered six Academy Award nominations, including Best Picture, Best Actress (Hepburn), Best Actor (Stewart), Best Supporting Actress (Hussey), Best Screenplay (Donald Ogden Stewart), and Best Director (Cukor). Both of the Stewarts won.

Though talky and even somewhat dated by today's standards, *The Philadelphia Story* with its ideas of an American aristocracy has managed to maintain much of its charm through the years, due primarily to the ensemble performances of its brilliant cast working under Mr. Cukor's sensitive guidance.

The fact that Mr. Barry's witty, if rather synthetic, story demanded *exceptional* actors in its principal roles became quite apparent when Metro decided to film the play again in 1956. The idea for the project had been conceived by producer Sol C. Siegel: "I'd always considered *The Philadelphia Story* to be a perfect picture and felt that the only way we could remake it was as a musical."

Siegel's plan was to get his friend Cole Porter to

High Society: **Bing Crosby and Louis Armstrong.**

compose a score, writer John Patrick (*Teahouse of the August Moon*) to create a new screenplay, and Grace Kelly, Bing Crosby, and Frank Sinatra to do the roles originally played by Hepburn, Grant, and Stewart respectively. Being a superior salesman, as well as a veteran showman, Siegel talked the studio into going along with him, then, over a period of several months, proceeded to put his package together.

His task was a relatively easy one. There was no question that all five talents wanted to participate in the project, and Siegel found that the only major obstacle he faced was in working his picture into their individual schedules. It took a bit of doing, but the job was finally accomplished.

Rounding out the cast of this Technicolor/Vista-Vision production were Celeste Holm as Liz, John Lund as Kittredge, Louis Calhern as Uncle Willie, and Sidney Blackmer as the father. Jazz great Louis Armstrong was also present—functioning as a musical "Greek chorus." Charles Walters directed.

High Society, as the Barry play was retitled, still told the story of "the privileged class enjoying their privileges," but, aside from retaining the principal characters and general plot outline, little of the playwright's original material remained. In the first place, the locale of the story was switched to Newport, Rhode

High Society: **Grace Kelly and Bing Crosby.**

High Society: **Celeste Holm and Frank Sinatra.**

Island. To accommodate the musical requirements of the project, Dexter became a popular song writer involved with the Newport Jazz Festival. On the other hand, the reporters from *Spy Magazine* now came to the wedding through the arrangements of Uncle Willie, rather than Dexter. Veritably, the entire scandal magazine subplot was underplayed in this version and utilized only as a script device to get the reporters into the story. These elements had been far more important in the 1940 picture.

Unlike the original, Connor does not propose to Tracy on the morning after the moonlight swim but, instead, asks Liz to be his bride.

The best part of *High Society* was Cole Porter's score, as performed by Messrs. Crosby, Sinatra, and Armstrong. Highlights included: "Well Did You

Evah?," a Crosby/Sinatra duet, spoofing the haughty and blasé; "True Love," "You're Sensational," and another duet, this time with Bing and Satchmo, "Now You Has Jazz."

Certainly, the principal problem with Siegel's picture was its casting. Bing Crosby (too old to be playing opposite Grace Kelly) and Frank Sinatra did little more than "walk through" their assignments, contributing only their well-established and superficial screen personalities to a story that required much more shaded characterizations, as had been supplied by Mr. Grant and Mr. Stewart. Of Kelly's interpretation of the pivotal role, the *New York Times* said: "The part was obviously written to be acted with a sharp cutting-edge. Miss Kelly makes the trenchant lady no more than a petulant wistful girl."

Such miscasting may have been justifiable from the standpoint of box office, but it definitely destroyed whatever depth or humor remained from Philip Barry's social comedy after writer Patrick had finished neutralizing it. The final result was rather dull—and it became a long wait between musical numbers.

The Philadelphia Story

FILMOGRAPHY

1940: (MGM/George Cukor) Katharine Hepburn.
1956: *High Society* (MGM/Charles Walters) Grace Kelly.

23
The Prisoner of Zenda

"Uniform" might be the best word to describe the screen history of *The Prisoner of Zenda*. Anthony Hope's famous novel of swashbuckling and court intrigue has been filmed on four different occasions, yet, unlike many often-made properties, none of the versions varied significantly from the author's original story in either character or incident.

Set near the end of the last century, *Zenda* deals with British-born Rudolf Rassendyll, "unacknowledged" descendant of the royal Elphberg line of Ruritania (a fictional mid-European kingdom), who happens to be an exact double of King Rudolf V. When the King is drugged on the night prior to his coronation, Rassendyll is drafted by the loyal Colonel Sapt and Fritz von Torlenheim to "stand-in" for the future monarch at the ceremony.

The villains of the tale are the king's half-brother, Prince Michael—the aspirant to the throne and the man who ordered the wine drugged—and his chief conspirator, Rupert of Hentzau. It was the prince's hope that when the usually undependable potentate failed to appear at the coronation, he, Michael, would be offered the crown.

With Rassendyll assuming the guise of the king, the ceremony takes place without incident. Later, the Englishman meets Princess Flavia, the future Queen of Ruritania, and it is love at first sight.

Rassendyll and Sapt return to the hunting lodge where the unconscious sovereign has been hidden, to find the king missing—presumably kidnapped by Rupert and Michael.

Forced to continue his masquerade until the real monarch can be rescued, Rassendyll receives aid from Antoinette de Mauban, Michael's mistress, who realizes that, should the prince gain the throne, he would marry Flavia instead of her. The woman informs the bogus potentate that the king is being held captive in Black Michael's castle at Zenda.

While Sapt and a small group of trusted soldiers wait outside the castle, the Britisher swims the moat in order to lower the drawbridge and protect his royal cousin from assassination.

Rupert slays Michael in a dispute over Antoinette's affections, then, discovering Rassendyll in the castle, engages him in a duel with sabres. The conspirator escapes when Sapt and his men cross the drawbridge to rescue their ruler.

Realizing that their love can never be consummated, Rassendyll and Flavia part—she to marry the king and he to return to his native England.

Hope's book, published in 1896, was first brought to the screen in 1913 by producers Adolph Zukor and Daniel Frohman. The Famous Players production was directed by Edwin S. Porter and starred James K. Hackett in the dual role of Rassendyll and the king. Hackett was no stranger to the parts, having essayed them several times on the stage. The supporting cast included Beatrice Beckley as Flavia, David Torrence as Black Michael, and Alan Hale as Rupert of Hentzau.

The picture was well received by the critics of that time. W. Stephen Bush in the *Moving Picture World* reported: "With this four-act film drama the producers have leaped to the pinnacle of moving picture fame at one gigantic bound. *The Prisoner of Zenda* . . . bears a message of hope and cheer to every friend of the motion picture and vindicates, beyond all cavil, American supremacy in the world of films. We have seen a new standard in dramatic architecture for screen

The Prisoner of Zenda (1922): **Robert Edeson, Lewis Stone, Alice Terry, and player.**

The Prisoner of Zenda (1922): **Ramon Novarro and Lewis Stone.**

The Prisoner of Zenda (1922): **Ramon Novarro, Stuart Holmes, and Barbara La-Marr.**

purposes and we have witnessed an ensemble of American artists, in whom this debut in the new art called forth the very best that was in them."

Working from a scenario by Mary O'Hara, director Rex Ingram remade the adventure story for Metro Pictures in 1922. It starred Lewis Stone as Rassendyll/ King Rudolf, Alice Terry as Flavia, Stuart Holmes as Black Michael, and Ramon Novarro as Rupert.

Like its 1913 predecessor, this film followed the Hope classic quite closely. The *New York Times* gave it a mixed notice: "Mr. Ingram individualizes his scenes. He makes telling use of facial expressions. He stamps his people with meaning, even when they are only flitting through the action. . . . But because it is Mr. Ingram's, and because it offers itself as something exceptional, it cannot be compared to the average. It must be compared to other exceptional films. And in this comparison one sees faults. For instance, it is needlessly talky, sometimes its action is not clear, its story runs roughly in spots, a number of its efforts at comedy are crude, and at times it lacks dash and go such a romantic yarn should have . . . the chief fault with the picture is that it lacks consistency."

In 1937, David O. Selznick decided to film *Zenda* as a vehicle for Ronald Colman. Initially, the producer and star were unsure as to whether Colman should play *both* Rassendyll and the king or, whether it would be better if another actor assumed the latter role. Ultimately, it was decided that tradition would be followed and Colman accepted the dual assignment.

Selznick also ruled that the old-fashioned style of dialogue, as well as the black-or-white nature of Hope's characters, must be retained in the picture to give it the quality of nobility that was necessary to the believability of the piece. Attempts at modernization were kept at a minimum.

John Cromwell directed the screenplay by John L. Balderson, which was based on an adaptation by Wells Root of Edward Rose's 1897 stage dramatization of the Hope novel. A well-chosen supporting cast for the exciting melodrama included Madeleine Carroll as Flavia, Douglas Fairbanks, Jr., as Rupert, Mary Astor as Antoinette, Raymond Massey as Michael, and David Niven as Fritz.

The United Artists release was a class production— expertly acted, splendidly photographed, carefully directed, and extravagantly mounted. The *New York Times* said: "Here is the most pleasing film that has come along in ages."

The picture has become one of the most beloved romantic swashbucklers in film history.

Stewart Granger had recently finished starring in a good production of *Scaramouche* at MGM and the studio was seeking a comparable follow-up vehicle for their British contract player. A new Technicolor version of *The Prisoner of Zenda* seemed like the logical choice.

Believing that one shouldn't argue with success, Metro purchased John Balderson's 1937 screenplay from Selznick-International and set writer Noel Langley to make a few minor adjustments in dialogue. Their cast, of course, was a new one—Deborah Kerr as Flavia, James Mason as Rupert, Robert Douglas as Michael, Jane Greer as Antoinette, and Lewis Stone, star of the 1922 rendition, as the Cardinal.

Characters were portrayed along the same lines as the earlier film, with one exception. Mason's Rupert came across much more villainous than had Fairbanks's, who'd played the part with a roguish appeal.

The finished picture that Metro released in 1952 was virtually a shot-by-shot recreation of the Ronald Colman film. In fact, to further ensure the project's success, the producers even reused the 1937 musical score by Alfred Newman.

Richard Thorpe, a MGM contract director, was assigned to the production. He recalls that he had "a wonderful cast," but that the film was "just routine work."

Although the 1952 version of *Zenda* was, according to *Variety,* "an entertaining remake" and had a "highly polished production," it was inferior to its immediate predecessor. Absent from the Granger film were the elaborate crowd scenes, rich production values, and meticulous care that were the trademarks of all Selznick's work.

The one improvement that Thorpe did make over the 1937 picture was in the staging of the final duel between Rassendyll and Rupert. Whereas the Colman/ Fairbanks encounter had been rather tame and was even refilmed after editing had failed to inject it with much dash, Thorpe, an expert at action sequences of this type, created an exciting scene that many swashbuckling aficionados consider to be one of the better displays of movie swordsmanship.

Most recently, *The Prisoner of Zenda* was spoofed in the 1965 Blake Edwards chase comedy, *The Great Race.* The latter portion of this sometimes-hilarious piece of slapstick borrowed freely from the Anthony

The Prisoner of Zenda (1937): **Ronald Colman and Madeleine Carroll.**

The Prisoner of Zenda (1937): **David Niven, C. Aubrey Smith, and Ronald Colman.**

The Prisoner of Zenda (1937): **Douglas Fairbanks, Jr., and Ronald Colman.**

The Prisoner of Zenda (1952): **Robert Coote, Louis Calhern, and Stewart Granger.**

The Prisoner of Zenda (1952): **Stewart Granger and James Mason.**

Hope adventure, with Jack Lemmon playing the dual role of the film's dastardly, if incompetent, villain, as well as the imbecile king of a mythical kingdom. Ross Martin was the counterpart to Rupert, while hero Tony Curtis, garbed all in white, saved the day in this Warner Brothers release.

Romantics who were unhappy that Rassendyll and Flavia parted at the end of *Zenda*, will be heartened to learn that Anthony Hope wrote a little-known sequel to his famous novel in 1898. Titled *Rupert of Hentzau*, it was filmed twice—the most recent version by Selznick Pictures in 1923. That offering starred Bert Lytell as the brave Englishman, Elaine Hammerstein as Flavia, and Lew Cody in the title role.

The story tells how Rupert returns to Ruritania and assassinates the king, after intercepting a love letter from Flavia to Rassendyll, who is in England. Rassendyll eventually kills the villain in a duel, then refuses an offer of the Ruritanian crown. Flavia abdicates and follows the man she loves back to his native country.

Since there have been no sound versions of *Rupert of Hentzau*, it would seem that producers felt the sadder, but nobler, conclusion of *The Prisoner of Zenda* was more dramatically correct than an idyllic ending.

The Prisoner of Zenda

FILMOGRAPHY

1913: (Famous Players/Edwin S. Porter) James K. Hackett.
1922: (Metro/Rex Ingram) Lewis Stone.
1937: (Selznick/John Cromwell) Ronald Colman.
1952: (MGM/Richard Thorpe) Stewart Granger.
1976: Remake announced.

The Prisoner of Zenda (1952): **Stewart Granger meets Stewart Granger.**

24
Rain

One of the most colorful women in modern literature is Sadie Thompson, the carefree young hooker created by W. Somerset Maugham for his 1921 short story, *Miss Thompson,* and dramatized a year later by John B. Colton and Clemence Randolph in the successful stage play, *Rain,* which starred Jeanne Eagels.

Set during the rainy season on the tropical island of Pago Pago, the story tells of an odd assortment of travelers, delayed on their journey to Apia due to a ship quarantine. Among the group are Sadie Thompson, an attractive woman of "questionable" reputation, the Reverend Alfred Davidson and his wife, and Dr. and Mrs. McPhail.

The stranded passengers are quartered at the general store and hotel, run by trader Joe Horn. Almost immediately, Sadie throws a party for several of the Marines stationed on the island and Davidson, a religious fanatic, objects to such disrespectful conduct on the Sabbath. After he is ejected from her room by Sergeant O'Hara, the reverend complains to the governor, who orders Sadie deported back to the United States.

The desperate Miss Thompson begs Davidson not to have her sent back, since she is wanted for a crime in San Francisco that she did not commit and faces a three-year prison sentence if she returns. The missionary, in turn, replies that she must go back to prove she is worthy of God's mercy.

A few days of praying with Davidson results in a completely subdued Sadie, the preacher having entranced her with promises of redemption. Even a proposal of marriage from O'Hara does not sway her from her intention to return to San Francisco and face punishment.

The night before her boat leaves, Davidson, consumed by his lust for the girl, rapes her, then, guilt-ridden, takes his own life. In the morning, Sadie is back to her old self—disillusioned with Davidson's teachings. She departs for Sydney, Australia, to wait for O'Hara, who plans to join her in a few weeks when his enlistment is up.

Although Maugham's story has been filmed a total of three times, the initial version, a 1928 silent picture entitled *Sadie Thompson,* was the most satisfying.

Directed by Raoul Walsh, who also did the scenario, the United Artists release was produced by and starred Gloria Swanson. Walsh, himself, played O'Hara. The Reverend Davidson role, rechristened Alfred Atkinson, was adjusted to avoid censorship problems. Ergo, Lionel Barrymore was presented in the part as a self-styled reformer, rather than an ordained minister.

It was a well-received film. The *New York Times* called it "a stirring pictorial drama with shrewd development of the plot and admirable characterization."

Of Miss Swanson, the paper said: ". . . while this actress may have given clever performances in some of her pictures, she displays more genuine ability and imagination in this present production."

In 1932, Joseph M. Schenek produced a talkie version of the story for United Artists—this time, under the title of *Rain.* Joan Crawford was borrowed from MGM to essay the part of Sadie Thompson, while William Gargan was set for O'Hara. Walter Huston played the preacher role, which, in this picture, retained its original moniker of Reverend Alfred Davidson. Lewis Milestone directed the screenplay by Maxwell Anderson, following the source material quite closely.

A play featuring a prostitute heroine and a lecherous minister may have shocked theater audiences a decade

Sadie Thompson: **Gloria Swanson and Lionel Barrymore.**

Sadie Thompson: **Raoul Walsh and Gloria Swanson.**

Rain: **Joan Crawford and William Gargan.**

Rain: **Walter Huston and Joan Crawford.**

earlier, but, by 1932, most of the novelty had worn thin. Instead of a powerful drama, moviegoers found the film talky and, in some spots, even laughable. According to *Variety*: "Milestone tried to achieve action with the camera, but wears the witnesses down with words."

Performances from Joan Crawford and Mr. Huston were less than competent. Of the lady, the aforementioned trade paper said: "It turns out to be a mistake to have assigned the Sadie Thompson role to Miss Crawford. It shows her off unfavorably. The dramatic significance of it all is beyond her range."

Regarding the character actor, the *New York Times* commented: "Mr. Huston is at his worst as the Rev. Davidson, the bigoted preacher. He walks as if he had spent years as a private in the Prussian Army. . . ."

Possibly the most memorable aspect of Milestone's film was the almost impressionistic handling of the incessant rain, which he employed to create an atmosphere of gloomy confinement at the trading post.

Adding songs to *Rain* was *not* an original idea with producer Jerry Wald,[1] who filmed such a treatment of the play in 1953, under the title *Miss Sadie Thompson*. Released by Columbia, the 3-D Technicolor production was directed by Curtis Bernhardt from a screenplay by Harry Kleiner. Rita Hayworth was cast as Sadie Thompson, Jose Ferrer essayed Davidson, and Aldo Ray inherited the role of O'Hara. Lester Lee, Ned Washington, and Allan Roberts composed several songs for the film, none of which were particularly memorable.

Updated to take place after the Second World War, Kleiner's screenplay presented Miss Thompson, not as a prostitute (her profession had only been hinted at in the earlier versions), but as a happy-go-lucky girl who had worked only as a singer in a Honolulu bawdy house in order to earn a living. Davidson, on the other hand, was no longer a minister, but a traveling chairman of a missions board.

Director Bernhardt reflects on the project: "I felt that the film should have been played straight . . . without music . . . or, at least, not as much music as we finally used. But Jerry Wald was a forceful man and the thing was his 'baby.' He wanted the songs, so that's the way we did it."

The use of music in the picture was, indeed, a mis-take. Miss Hayworth did little more than sing during the first half of the film, which gave the impression that the Maugham story was only there to serve as a frame for her activities, rather than *her* being an integral part of the action. One such scene, in which she sang a gay, Disney-like tune ("Hear No Evil, See No Evil") to a group of children, was completely out of place in what was intended to be a strong melodrama.

The rain in this version, which seemed to follow the plot of its predecessors fairly closely, came down only occasionally, since the producer wanted the cameras to take full advantage of the scenic beauty of the film's Hawaiian locations.

References to Sadie's supposedly lurid background were handled in a rather naive fashion—even for the only *somewhat* sophisticated audiences of the early 1950s. One found it hard to believe that a tough and worldly wise sergeant like O'Hara would be as shocked upon learning of his intended bride's previous indiscretions as Aldo Ray so indicated in his interpretation. That response would have been far more believable coming from William Gargan, who played the Marine with much more innocence in the 1932 filming.

The best performance in the piece was, surprisingly, delivered by Miss Hayworth, of whom *Variety* said: "She catches the feel of the title character well, even to braving completely deglamorizing makeup, costuming and photography to fit her physical appearance to that of the bawdy, shady lady that was Sadie Thompson."

Conversely, Jose Ferrer (hired after Henry Fonda proved unavailable) seemed completely out of his element as Davidson. The actor's monotone voice made one sense that he was totally bored with what he was doing. According to the same trade paper: "Less effective is Jose Ferrer's Alfred Davidson, no longer a minister, but a straight layman bigot. Missing under the change is the religious fanaticism that motivated and made understandable the original character. In this version, he is just a narrow evil man."

And, in summing up the film itself, the *New York Times* commented: "What has happened here, briefly, is that the Sadie and the Reverend Davidson of *Rain* have been washed right out of *Miss Sadie Thompson* and right out of Miss Hayworth's hair. And all that is left is glitter and the unmistakable evidence of a shampoo."

[1] June Havoc had done a musical rendition on Broadway in 1944.

Miss Sadie Thompson: **Rita Hayworth and Jose Ferrer.**

Miss Sadie Thompson: **Aldo Ray and Rita Hayworth.**

On the surface, the characters of Sadie Thompson and Reverend Davidson appear to be two juicy roles, which many performers would like to sink their teeth into. Regretfully, neither the parts, nor the moral attitudes inherent in Maugham's story, have withstood the test of time and it would perhaps be better if *Rain* were let alone to take its proper place in theatrical history.

Rain

FILMOGRAPHY

1928: *Sadie Thompson* (UA/Raoul Walsh) Gloria Swanson.
1932: *Rain* (UA/Lewis Milestone) Joan Crawford.
1953: *Miss Sadie Thompson* (Col/Curtis Bernhardt) Rita Hayworth.

25
Red Dust

If any romantic screen team of the thirties symbolized raw sex, it was Gable and Harlow. These two diverse personalities brought to their love scenes a light and earthy quality—delighting audiences, but making the censors blush. Together, the lusty beefcake and the platinum blonde cheesecake were good box office. Metro knew it and paired them on six different occasions.

Their most engaging encounter took place in *Red Dust,* a 1932 release. It was the couple's second film together (both had supported Wallace Beery a year earlier in *The Secret Six*) and is best remembered for its mildly erotic moments.

John Lee Mahin based his script on a play by Wilson Collison. He recalls: "The original gave me just the bare beginnings for my screenplay. It was a heavy, turgid drama . . . nothing like we finally wound up with."

Directed by Victor Fleming, the picture takes place on a rubber plantation in a remote area of Indochina. Dennis Carson (Gable) and his two assistants, Guidon (Donald Crisp) and McQuarg (Tully Marshall), are in charge of the operation. Vantine (Harlow), a hooker escaping the law, arrives on a boat from Saigon. Carson reluctantly allows her to stay until the next boat comes, but, in the meantime, he succumbs to her charms. They have an amorous week together and she is quite hurt that he gives her money when it is time for her to depart.

The boat brings a married couple, Gary and Barbara Willis (Gene Raymond and Mary Astor) to the outpost. Gary, an engineer hired by Carson, comes down with jungle fever and his employer nurses him back to health.

Vantine returns to the plantation because the boat has broken down. However, Dennis pays scant attention to her, since he and the ladylike Barbara have become lovers.

Carson likes Gary and, eventually, his conscience gets the better of him. To break off his romance with Barbara, he openly makes a play for Vantine. Furious, Barbara shoots Dennis. Willis enters and Vantine covers for Barbara by claiming that Carson had made advances toward her.

Gary quits his job, leaving the plantation with Barbara. Vantine cuts the bullet out of Carson, then stays with him while he recovers. As entertainment for the bedded tough guy, the blonde reads him children's nursery stories. Naturally, Dennis comes to realize that Vantine is the girl for him.

Red Dust was a popular picture and garnered impressive reviews—not so much for its story, but for the performances of its stars. *Variety*: "Sure-fire box-office. Familiar plot stuff but done so expertly it almost overcomes the basic script shortcomings. With Harlow and Gable it's an exhibs delight and a cinch for fancy takings. . . . It'll also do much for the pair of players, as they acquit themselves handily, despite the now familiar hot-love-in-the-isolated-tropics theme."

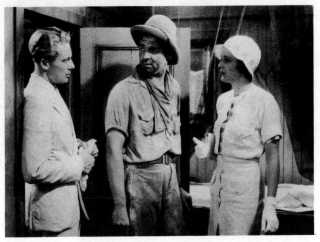

Red Dust: **Gene Raymond, Clark Gable,** and **Mary Astor.**

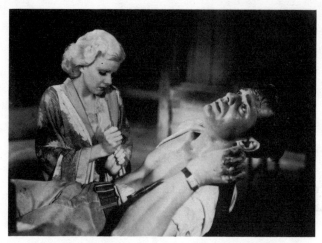

Red Dust: **Jean Harlow and Clark Gable.**

Red Dust: **Clark Gable and Jean Harlow.**

Clark Gable, incidentally, was not the original choice for the leading assignment. That role was to go to silent star John Gilbert until John Lee Mahin spotted the future "King" in a Warner Brothers feature, *Night Nurse,* and suggested him for the part.

Writer Mary McCall, Jr., freely adapted Wilson Collison's original material for *Congo Maisie,* an episode in the popular film series that starred Ann Sothern as a wise-cracking good-natured vaudeville performer. Directed by H. C. Potter, the 1940 programmer had John Carroll playing a doctor in the African jungle (the Gable counterpart) and Rita Johnson and Shepperd Strudwick as the married couple. Miss Sothern, of course, stood in for Jean Harlow—with the story line being adjusted to fit her already established character of "Maisie."

The *New York Times* said: "In his direction, H. C. Potter has followed a fine line between solemnity and farce. You can literally take your pick. And Ann Sothern, well heeled with gags, plays the bedizened Maisie with just enough flounce and impudence to keep her fixit role from going gummy. Altogether this corner sees it as a nice bit of harmless fun."

Congo Maisie: **John Carroll and Ann Sothern.**

According to John Lee Mahin, Sam Zimbalist called him into his MGM office one day in 1952 and said: "Let's do *Red Dust* in Africa." The producer had had a successful film in *King Solomon's Mines* a couple of years previously and wanted to go back to the Dark Continent for another picture.

"We'll go on safari," continued Zimbalist, "do some gorillas, and generally update the thing. It'll be fun."

Mahin was enthusiastic about the project: "It gave me the opportunity to fix my mistakes . . . to 'polish' what I'd done on the first version. Actually, I think the story worked better in this new situation than in the 1932 film."

The men decided that the picture could not go unless Gable would agree to repeat his original role, so, before any commitments were made, the star was approached and he promised to participate. Signed to direct was John Ford.

Mogambo, released in 1953, had Gable playing a white hunter/trapper in Africa, who leads safaris and captures wild animals for zoos. Ava Gardner, inheriting the Harlow part, wasn't a prostitute, but, simply, a not-too-bright showgirl with a tragic past. She's come to Africa to join a maharaja for a fun-filled safari, but, unfortunately, her boyfriend has been called back to his country on urgent business.

The young marrieds were portrayed by Grace Kelly and Donald Sinden. Instead of an engineer, the husband became an anthropologist in this version—interested in studying the family life of gorillas.

Aside from the fact that the love scenes in the highly successful ($5.2 million—domestic) Technicolor entertainment were toned down considerably (i.e., the audience is never completely *sure* if Gable is actually sleeping with Gardner and/or Kelly in this rendition or just doing some heavy necking), there were no other significant changes from the original.

The *Hollywood Reporter* commented: "Ford's direction is his usual masterful style, keeping the tension high and drawing topknotch performances from a fine cast.

"Gable plays the hunter with a mixture of quizzical humor and toughness which is highly effective. Miss Gardner hits her acting peak to date, deftly combining a hoydenish and a hard-boiled quality, somehow emerging as an appealingly gallant figure."

Indeed, *most* critics agreed that the actress "stole" the film from Gable. The Academy of Motion Picture Arts and Sciences did also, and voted her an Oscar nomination for the performance.

Mahin: "Gable came up to me one day while we

Mogambo: **Ava Gardner, Clark Gable, and Grace Kelly.**

Mogambo: **Clark Gable and players.**

were on location and said, 'You son-of-a-bitch, you gave Ava all the funny lines.'

"I thought for a second, then explained, 'But, Clark, the audience won't laugh until they see your reaction.'

"He pondered that, smiled, and replied, 'You know, you're absolutely right.'

"And I was right!"

Red Dust

FILMOGRAPHY

1932: (MGM/Victor Fleming) Clark Gable.
1940: *Congo Maisie* (MGM/H. C. Potter) Ann Sothern.
1953: *Mogambo* (MGM/John Ford) Clark Gable.

26
Rio Bravo

Rio Bravo is not a *great* western, but it is a very good one. Producer/director Howard Hawks considers it his answer to *High Noon,* a film that he didn't particularly care for: "Gary Cooper wasn't a good marshal in that picture. If he had been, he wouldn't have asked the *townspeople* to help him fight the killers. They were inexperienced with guns and would have only gotten in his way. Cooper was better off going up against the gang alone.

"In *Rio Bravo,* John Wayne asked only *capable* people to help him."

Warner Brothers' 1959 release was written by Jules Furthman and Leigh Brackett from a short story by B. H. McCampbell. The simple, traditional western tells of Sheriff John T. Chance's (Wayne) efforts to hold killer Joe Burdette (Claude Akins) in jail on a murder charge until the United States Marshal arrives. The peace officer enlists the help of his former deputy, Dude (Dean Martin), who is now, because of an unhappy love affair, a seemingly hopeless drunk. Also on call is Colorado (Ricky Nelson), an easy-going youth, and Stumpy (Walter Brennan), a crippled old man. These four must face an army of professional gunfighters, hired by Nathan Burdette (John Russell) to free his wayward brother. After several futile attempts to get Chance out of the way, Burdette's men abduct Dude and offer to free him in exchange for Joe. A final gun battle takes place at the rendezvous point, resulting in the lawmen capturing the troublemakers. The film concludes with bachelor Chance taking up with Feathers (Angie Dickinson), a lady gambler he has recently met.

Emphasizing characterization as usual, Hawks took 141 minutes to relate his uncomplicated saga: "We were telling the story of a friendship between a sheriff and his drunken deputy and how the deputy is rehabilitated."

The *New York Times* commented: "Mr. Hawks, abetted by a script that on occasion is more polished than the action, makes the most of his somewhat sparse plot. And he is also aided more than somewhat by the performance of John Wayne as the man of the law who, after all these years of riding the studios' ranges, is satisfyingly laconic and fast with a six-shooter and a rifle. Credit him with major assets, however, from Dean Martin, as the alcoholic who conquers the demon rum and regains his self-respect under fire, and Walter Brennan, as the garrulous and truly funny old crippled deputy, who is as quick on the riposte as he is on the draw."

As is the case with most John Wayne pictures, the color western was very popular with the public and became a major box-office success.

Astute moviegoers had little trouble recognizing that the second half of the 1966 Hawks/Wayne western, *El Dorado,* was, basically, an inferior rehash of *Rio Bravo.* The characters were almost identical (except for names and the actors portraying them) to those in the earlier film, as was the general plot structure.

Hawks and writer Leigh Brackett had started out on the project by adapting *The Stars in Their Courses,* a novel by Harry Brown, into screenplay form. But, unhappy with what they were winding up with, the director pulled out his notes from *Rio Bravo* and decided to incorporate many of the same elements (with slight variations) into this new production for Paramount.

El Dorado presented John Wayne as Cole Thornton, a gunfighter and good friend of Sheriff J. P. Harrah (Robert Mitchum). After refusing an offer from rancher Bart Jason (Edward Asner) to take his side in a range war, Thornton is partially responsible for a tragic mistake, which costs the life of Luke (Johnny

Rio Bravo: **Walter Brennan and John Wayne.**

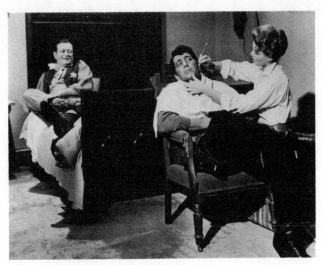

Rio Bravo: **John Wayne, Dean Martin, and Angie Dickinson.**

El Dorado: **John Wayne, Christopher George, and Edward Asner.**

El Dorado: **John Wayne, Robert Mitchum, and Arthur Hunnicutt.**

Crawford), young son of Jason's rival, Kevin Mac-Donald (R. G. Armstrong). Angered, the dead boy's sister (Michele Carey) ambushes Cole, dropping him with a rifle bullet in the back.

Thornton survives the shooting, but the slug remains dangerously close to his spine. He refuses surgery and, when he is well enough to travel, having been nursed back to health by saloon owner Maudie (Charlene Holt), leaves town.

Months later, Thornton meets a young man, nick-named Mississippi (James Caan), who is expert with a knife, yet completely inexperienced with guns. Cole becomes friends with the lad and the pair head back to visit Harrah.

They find that the sheriff has, as the result of an ill-fated romance, become a hopeless drunk. His deputy, Bull Thomas (Arthur Hunnicutt), a cantankerous sort, has been unable to force Harrah into performing his duties properly at a time when strong law and order are needed. The range feud, it seems, is about to come to a head, since Jason was successful in hiring professional gunslingers, led by Dan McLeod(Christopher George).

With Thornton's help, Harrah takes hold of himself and returns to duty. The sheriff proves that he is still capable when, following a gunfight in which one of the MacDonald sons is wounded, he arrests and jails Jason.

McLeod and his men make several unsuccessful attempts to free Jason from the town jail, guarded by Thornton, Harrah, Bull, and Mississippi. They are eventually able to capture Cole when the bullet next to his spine temporarily paralyzes his arm.

Thornton is released in exchange for Jason's freedom. Nevertheless, Harrah and company go after the dastardly rancher and his henchmen in the saloon and, of course, are victorious.

Mitchum's role in *El Dorado* was the counterpart of Dean Martin's in *Rio Bravo*, as was James Caan's to Ricky Nelson's, Arthur Hunnicutt's to Walter Brennan's, and Charlene Holt's to Angie Dickinson's. Hawks had varied the characters only minimally— Wayne was a gunfighter, instead of a sheriff; Caan, unlike Nelson, was *not* proficient with a gun; and so forth. In fact, the director instructed Miss Holt to deliver her lines utilizing the same speech patterns that had been *naturally* employed by her predecessor. The actress recalls: "I knew he was directing me to play 'Angie Dickinson,' but he likes that kind of woman and I wanted to give him what he wanted."

One sequence that had played quite effectively in *Rio Bravo* was repeated practically verbatim in the

1966 production. The episode had Wayne and Martin/Mitchum going into a saloon filled with members of the "enemy camp," in order to capture a killer. Whereas the earlier film had the hunted man hiding in the rafters, the Paramount release moved him downstairs behind a piano. Otherwise, the scenes were identical. Explains Hawks: "I'll often repeat a scene that I think worked well in another picture."

While *El Dorado* may have lacked the polish of the Wayne/Martin starrer, it was still a well-acted and entertaining western that was enhanced by beautiful Technicolor photography. The *Hollywood Reporter* called the film Hawks's "best since *Rio Bravo* . . . at all times, Hawks' direction is evident in the taste and flow of the action and in a pervading point of view, which composes but does not intrude upon the story on view."

Released in 1970 by Cinema Center Films, Hawks's *Rio Lobo,* from a screenplay by Leigh Brackett and Burton Wohl, again employed many of the components that had previously been used in both *Rio Bravo* and *El Dorado.* However, the plot for this new Technicolor western, which shared with its forerunners the director's favorite basic themes of friendship and loyalty, was substantially original.

This time, Wayne was Cord McNally, a former colonel in the Union Army. Together with ex-Confederate Pierre Cordova (Mexico's Jorge Riviro), salty old Phillips (Jack Elam), and young Tuscarora (Chris Mitchum), as well as the lovely Shasta (Jennifer O'Neill), he tracks down the two traitors, who, during the Civil War, were responsible for the death of one of his junior officers. Coincidentally, these men now reside in the town of Rio Lobo, stealing water rights from local ranchers.

Wayne and his followers capture one of the villains (Victor French), then barricade themselves in the jail. A shootout at dawn regains the town for the honest citizens.

Again, Riviro, Elam, Miss O'Neill, and Chris Mitchum were the counterparts to Martin/Robert Mitchum, Brennan/Hunnicutt, Dickinson/Holt, and Nelson/Caan respectively. Only John Wayne remained constant. The new actors' plot functions were similar to those of their predecessors, save for characterizations, which were not as well developed. Rivera did not share the drinking problem of Martin/ Mitchum, but, instead, was just a straight two-dimensional leading man. Young Mitchum, on the other hand, did little but decorate the background. Only Wayne and Elam delivered notable performances.

Interestingly enough, the final gun battle was filmed on a locale that looked very similar to the exterior on which its counterpart scene in *Rio Bravo* was staged.

Most critics reported that the production was one of its creator's lesser efforts. Said *Variety*: "Hawks' direction is as tired as the plot, without style or vitality. Except for the ingenuity of the opening train robbery, staged by second-unit director Yakima Canutt, the action is ho-hum. In the attempts at lightness, the lines fall curiously flat.

". . . all of the acting and speech have a curious flatness, as if Hawks meant the whole film to be a sort of put-on that doesn't come off."

Hawks disputes observers who claim that both *El Dorado* and *Rio Lobo* are little more than "switched-around" versions of *Rio Bravo*: "I don't consider them to be remakes. There were many story differences.

Rio Lobo: **John Wayne, Jorge Riviro, and Jack Elam.**

"Frankly, in making a film, I don't care that much about the story. I believe in making good scenes. Of course similar characters were used in all three pictures. But, they were *good* characters and, I think they worked well every time."

The legendary director chuckles when he recalls that, upon completing *Rio Lobo,* John Wayne said to him: "Next time . . . I'll play the drunk."

Rio Lobo: **John Wayne and Chris Mitchum.**

Rio Bravo

FILMOGRAPHY

1959: (WB/Howard Hawks) John Wayne.
1966: *El Dorado* (Par/Howard Hawks) John Wayne.
1970: *Rio Lobo* (CCF/Howard Hawks) John Wayne.

27
The Sea Hawk

Michael Curtiz's 1940 version of *The Sea Hawk* might best be termed as a *non*remake. That is, while the original intent of Warner Brothers had been to redo Rafael Sabatini's classic swashbuckling tale, what finally wound up on the screen certainly bore little resemblance to either the novel or the 1924 First National picture of the same name, ergo, a *non*remake.

Sabatini's story tells of Sir Oliver Tressilian, a Cornish gentleman, who, at the instigation of his half-brother Lionel, is shanghaied by freebooter Jasper Leigh. Following his disappearance, Oliver is blamed for the death of Peter Godolphin, brother of his fiancée, Rosamund. Actually, it was Lionel who'd killed Godolphin in a duel.

Captured by Spaniards at sea, Oliver is made a galley slave, but he later escapes with the help of the Moors. To these barbarians, he becomes Sakr-el-Bahr—the scourge of Christendom—the Sea Hawk.

Oliver learns of Rosamund's impending marriage to Lionel and, on their wedding day, he and his men kidnap them both. To prevent the woman he loves from becoming a member of the Basha of Algiers' harem, the buccaneer surrenders to a British ship. Rosamund helps Oliver to clear his name and, after the sacrificial death of Lionel, the couple are wed.

Frank Lloyd both produced and directed the 1924 release of *The Sea Hawk,* which, through an excellent scenario by J. G. Hawks, stayed very close to Sabatini's 1915 novel. The cast was headed by Milton Sills, one of the silent screen's most popular matinee idols. Other major roles were filled by Lloyd Hughes (Lionel), Enid Bennett (Rosamund), and Wallace Beery (Jasper Leigh).

Both audiences and critics enjoyed the high-adventure drama. The *New York Times* called it "the best sea story that has ever been brought to the screen and

we doubt if anybody who sees the scenes of the galley slaves will forget them. They are utterly different from any others presented in a film. Frank Lloyd, who started picture work as an 'extra' himself, is to be congratulated on this film masterpiece of the sea."

The release of *Captain Blood* in 1935 made Errol Flynn an overnight sensation and Warners immediately set forth to find other swashbuckling vehicles for their new star. A natural choice was Sabatini's *The Sea Hawk,* the rights to which the Burbank-based studio

The Sea Hawk (1924): **Milton Sills and Enid Bennett.**

The Sea Hawk (1924): **Wallace Beery and Milton Sills.**

had acquired when they took over the entire First National company in 1929–30. Writer Delmer Daves was assigned to the project, completing his screenplay in 1936. However, the studio was already keeping Flynn busy with such epics as *The Charge of the Light Brigade, The Adventures of Robin Hood,* and *The Private Lives of Elizabeth and Essex,* so Daves's script was tabeled indefinitely.

A while later, Seton I. Miller sold an original story to the studio entitled *Beggars of the Sea,* which dealt with a character suggested by Sir Francis Drake. Warners liked the story, since it seemed to contain many of the elements that they felt were responsible for the successes of *Robin Hood, Elizabeth and Essex,* and *Captain Blood.*

Finally, in 1939, the studio decided to produce *The Sea Hawk,* but instead of utilizing Sabatini's original story, substituted the treatment by Miller, which had been revised by Howard Koch. The feeling among the producers was that Miller's material would be more popular with a 1940 audience than a rehash of the earlier film.

The new picture, directed by Michael Curtiz, with a splendid score by Erich Wolfgang Korngold, had Flynn playing Captain Geoffrey Thorpe, a privateer or "sea hawk," in the service of Queen Elizabeth (Flora Robson), who preys on Spanish shipping during the late sixteenth century.

On an ill-fated expedition to steal Spanish treasure in Panama, Thorpe and his men are captured and sentenced to serve as galley slaves. He, of course, escapes on a commandeered ship, then returns to England in time to kill Lord Wolfingham (Henry Daniell), a traitor to the Crown, and warn the Queen that the Spanish are sending an Armada to destroy England. The picture ends with Thorpe reunited with his true love, Dona Maria (Brenda Marshall), and Elizabeth giving a double-edged patriotic speech about destroying foreign invaders, which, in fact, seemed to be the studio's method of commenting on the then-contemporary activities of Nazi Germany.

Budgeted at approximately $1,750,000, the production was enhanced with large sets, a sweeping sea battle, and a lavish display of extras. It remains one of the best pictures of Flynn's career.

Nevertheless, *Variety* commented: *"The Sea Hawk* retains all of the bold and swashbuckling adventure and excitement of its predecessor. . . . But the screenplay of the new version is expanded to include endless episodes of court intrigue . . . that tend to diminish the effect of the epic sweep of the high seas dramatics."

Warners' original intent was to bill the Flynn picture as "Rafael Sabatini's *The Sea Hawk.*" But, sometime prior to its release, either the author or the Writers Guild of America voiced a strong objection to the plan and the film went out sans Sabatini's name.

Ultimately, the protests were in vain because, even though the production credits clearly list the screenplay as being original, many pseudomovie aficionados still believe that the 1940 motion picture is indeed a remake of the old Milton Sills swashbuckling classic.

The Sea Hawk

FILMOGRAPHY

1924: (FN/Frank Lloyd) Milton Sills.
1940: (WB/Michael Curtiz) Errol Flynn.

The Sea Hawk (1940): **Claude Rains and Brenda Marshall.**

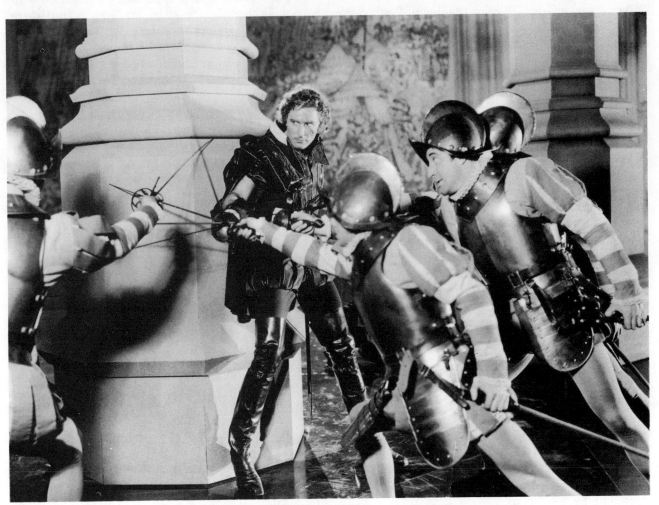

The Sea Hawk (1940): **Errol Flynn and players.**

28
The Sea Wolf

Narratives about the sea have spawned many cruel ships' masters—Ahab, Bligh, and, possibly the most brutal of all, Wolf Larsen, the Nietzschean "superman" created in 1904 by Jack London for his book *The Sea Wolf*.

As captain of the *Ghost,* a seal-hunting schooner out of San Francisco, Larsen rules his crew with an iron hand. Savage beatings are a common occurrence aboard the ship.

Literary critic Humphrey Van Weyden is rescued by the crew of the *Ghost* after the ship upon which he was a passenger is wrecked off the California coast. Larsen refuses to put the gentleman ashore, forcing him to become the schooner's cabin boy.

Wolf takes an interest in his new hand and often invites him to his cabin for an exchange of ideas. Van Weyden learns that the captain is a mystic and a well-read philosopher. He is also on the verge of madness—a manic-depressive who suffers from crippling headaches. In time, the critic becomes an able seaman and, following an attempted mutiny, Larsen gives him the job of first mate.

The sole female survivor from another tragedy at sea—Maud Brewster, a wealthy poet—is picked up by the *Ghost.* She is almost immediately shocked at Larsen when he deliberately lets Leach and Johnson, two deserters from his crew, drown.

Maud and Van Weyden are attracted to each other. The captain resents this and, as an outlet for his anger, decides to give Mugridge, the *Ghost*'s cowardly cook, a bath by towing him behind the ship. The cruel prank results in the cook losing his right foot to a shark.

Larsen fears only one man—his brother, Death Larsen, captain of the *Macedonia.* The two ships encounter each other during the voyage, but the *Ghost* escapes into a fog bank.

When Wolf attempts to force himself on Maud, Van Weyden rescues her by stabbing the captain in the shoulder. Subsequently, another of Larsen's headaches overcome him—this time, resulting in blindness. The two lovers seize the opportunity to steal away in a small boat and, ultimately, reach an island where they find the wreck of the *Ghost.* Wolf is still aboard, the crew having deserted to the *Macedonia.*

Several days later, Larsen dies from a stroke and is buried at sea. Maud and Van Weyden are rescued by a ship that returns them to civilization.

The Sea Wolf is powerful drama and, not surprisingly, has been filmed eight times, including one adaptation to the western genre. It is also a saga that allows its leading man an acting tour de force.

Silent screen character star Hobart Bosworth was

The Sea Wolf (1913): Herbert Rawlinson and Hobart Bosworth.

the first to tackle the difficult role of Wolf Larsen. The 1913 seven-reeler from Bosworth, Inc., followed London's novel very carefully. Indeed, so faithful was the adaptation that it became a basis for criticism on the picture, since many reviewers felt the film should have eliminated some of the plot's secondary sequences and thereby strengthen the overall action. Otherwise, the notices were mixed. The *Moving Picture World* said: "No praise can be too high for the settings and for the photography. The spirit of the ocean, which London conjures with such enviable ease, is on the screen and travels from the screen to the delighted audience. . . ."

Regarding the star, the publication reported: "Mr. Bosworth had the physique and the artistic size required by the part, though in the characterization he was not quite as strong as in the 'straight' acting. He seemed in the early part of the story not quite certain of his ground, but as the action advanced to the great dramatic moments he electrified the audience by his masterly portrayals."

Bosworth was supported by Herbert Rawlinson and Viola Barry, playing Van Weyden and Maud respectively.

The Sea Wolf (1920): **Tom Forman and Noah Beery.**

In 1920, George Melford directed a *Sea Wolf* scenario, penned by Will Richey. This time, Noah Beery was Larsen, with Tom Forman and Julienne Scott essaying the hero and heroine. The Paramount-Artcraft release made a couple of minor changes from the original text:

At the film's start, Maud and Van Weyden are already engaged to be married and are both rescued by the *Ghost* after a ferryboat collision. There is also a climactic scene that has Wolf and Death Larsen clashing in a bloody fistfight. Otherwise, it was an honest rendition.

Photoplay: "*The Sea Wolf* is another picture that

The Sea Wolf (1925): **Ralph Ince and Snitz Edwards.**

is forced to hold its audience by the picturesque quality of its scenes rather than the plausible grip of its story. . . . But as an exhibition of picturesque brutality, George Melford has accomplished wonders with the picture. . . .

"The individual performances are excellent. . . . Noah Beery was a fine, upstanding brute in the titular role. . . ."

Ralph Ince produced, directed, and starred as Wolf Larsen in the 1925 version of *The Sea Wolf,* released through Producers Distributing Corporation. It costarred Claire Adams as Maud Brewster, Theodore von Eltz as Van Weyden, and Snitz Edwards as Mugridge.

J. Grubb Alexander's script had Van Weyden and Maud meeting aboard the ill-fated ferry, dressed in masquerade costumes. Because of her attire, the crew of the *Ghost* initially take Maud for a boy. The truth becomes known and Larsen saves the woman from Mugridge by announcing he will marry her. Luckily,

The Sea Wolf (1930): **Jane Keith and Milton Sills.**

The Sea Wolf (1930): **Jane Keith and Raymond Hackett.**

the wedding is interrupted when the crew decides to mutiny. Maud and Van Weyden escape the vessel after it is set afire—an act that eventually results in the captain's death.

The first "talkie" version of Jack London's novel starred Milton Sills in what proved to be his final film appearance. Directed by Alfred Santell from a screenplay by Ralph Block and S. N. Behrman, the 1930 Fox Film Corporation release featured the silent movie idol as Larsen, with Jane Keith and Raymond Hackett doing counterparts to Maud and Van Weyden.

This dramatization of the famous sea saga has Larsen meeting prostitute Lorna Marsh (Keith) in a Japanese port and inviting her to join him on the *Ghost*. Refusing the offer, she, nevertheless, goes aboard the schooner when Allen Rand (Hackett), a gentle man she has become infatuated with, is shanghaied along with some of Death Larsen's sailors.

Initially, Wolf, who is guided by the philosophy "big fish eat little fish," considers Rand to be a weakling. However, after the man saves his life during a mutiny, the captain promotes him to first mate. Later, Wolf attempts to seduce Lorna, but she escapes with Allen when the *Macedonia* overtakes the *Ghost*.

Mugridge, not headaches, is the cause of Larsen's blindness in this 1930 picture. Seeking revenge for the shark's mutilation of his foot, the cook puts out the captain's eyes with a hot poker and, of course, the mutiny ensues.

The *New York Times* reported: "The flavor of Jack London's sea swept tale permeates *The Sea Wolf* . . . in which Milton Sills, as Wolf Larsen, gives an incisive performance. . . . The direction of Alfred Santell is excellent."

Warner Brothers originally planned to produce *The Sea Wolf* as a vehicle for Paul Muni, but when the gifted character actor refused the part of Wolf Larsen, that assignment was inherited by Edward G. Robinson.

Henry Blanke, associate producer for the 1941 release, recalls that it took writer Robert Rossen twenty weeks to come up with the finished screenplay: "One day, Jack Warner came across a magazine item that said Jack London wrote *The Sea Wolf* within a two week period. He showed me the clipping and asked, 'If London could do it in that short of time, why can't Rossen?' He was only *half*-serious."

Rossen made some rather interesting improvements on the original material. First, he divided the plot function of Van Weyden between two separate characters. Alexander Knox was excellent in his portrayal

The Sea Wolf (1941): **Barry Fitzgerald, Alexander Knox, and Edward G. Robinson.**

of the novelist (as opposed to a literary critic), who matches wits with the brutal Larsen. John Garfield, on the other hand, supplied the romantic interest. As George Leach, he joined the crew of the *Ghost* to escape the "long arm of the law." He falls in love with *escaped convict* Ruth Webster (Ida Lupino), another victim of the ferryboat accident that had brought Van Weyden aboard the cursed vessel.

The picture's climax has the novelist sacrificing his life by staying aboard the sinking *Ghost* with a blind and half-crazed Larsen, while Ruth and Leach, who'd been one of the leaders of an earlier mutiny, escape to a nearby island.

Whereas Death Larsen in this version is often discussed in the most frightening terms, he is *never* seen by the audience. Yet, it is the attack of the *Macedonia* that incites the decisive mutiny on the *Ghost*.

Finally, via the several scenes between Van Weyden and Wolf in the latter's cabin, Rossen explored the deep psychological aspects of the captain's character—moreso than any previous dramatization of London's tale. Veritably, 1941 critics found Robinson's megalomania akin to that of Hitler's. Larsen's motto for this filming: "Better to reign in hell than to serve in heaven."

Directed by Michael Curtiz, *The Sea Wolf* was a splendid production (in spite of the fact that all exteriors were shot on a sound stage)—certainly, the best rendition of London's work to date. Although some critics felt that the scenes between Larsen and Van Weyden were excessively "talky" and slowed the action, most of the comment was favorable. The *New York Times:* "When *The Sea Wolf* is topside . . . it rolls along ruthlessly and draws a forbidding picture of oppressive life at sea, of a captain who rules his

The Sea Wolf (1941): **Ida Lupino and John Garfield.**

The Sea Wolf (1941): **Edward G. Robinson, Gene Lockhart, and John Garfield.**

Barricade: **Robert Douglas and Raymond Massey.**

Barricade: **Dane Clark and Ruth Roman.**

men without mercy and without heart. Some of it is too heavily drenched with theatrical villainy, and Mr. Robinson occasionally overacts his part. But, on the whole, the slapping and cuffing are done with impressive virility and in a manner distinctive to Warner films."

Writer William Sackheim recalls how the Rossen screenplay became the basis for a 1950 Warner Brothers western: "Saul Elkins had a low budget production unit on the lot and it was his idea to turn *The Sea Wolf* into a western. I was assigned to do the script. They ran the Robinson film for me, then announced that the project would be titled *Barricade*. To this day, I have no idea what that title meant."

Sackheim found his most difficult problem with the adaptation was in isolating his characters so that there could be no escape from Wolf Larsen's (or his counterpart's) absolute rule. Naturally, that kind of situation was easier to come by on a boat, but Sackheim solved his dilemma by casting his "captain," known as "Boss" Kruger, as the owner of a gold mine that utilized slave labor. The dastardly Kruger, well-played by Raymond Massey, got his just deserts when the men revolted and beat him to death.

Peter Godfrey directed the color feature, which had Ruth Roman and Dane Clark as the fugitive lovers and Robert Douglas doing the Van Weyden opposite. The *New York Times* dismissed the programmer with ". . . a calm observer of the passing events in this film can find little other reason for it than a glorification of mayhem."

Dane Clark remembers the picture as "a painful experience. I'd just come off suspension at the time and the studio assigned me to this as punishment."

Wolf Larsen, the most recent American filming of Jack London's book, was, at one time, a pet project of actor Sterling Hayden and writer Turnley Walker, who penned the first version of the screenplay. Walker reflects: "In previous movies of *The Sea Wolf,* Larsen had been played as a 'gangster.' But, we saw him as a kind of 'misplaced angel' . . . a 'Nordic god' . . . 'pure-of-heart' and always testing people.

"Sterling owned a hundred-foot schooner, the *Gracie* S, that had been built in 1893. It was our plan to shoot the entire film out on the ocean on that boat and to use *our* interpretation of Larsen, which, I felt, had been London's original intent for the character in the first place.

"Unfortunately, about the time we were to go into production, John Huston's *Moby Dick* came out and

Wolf Larsen: **Barry Sullivan.**

bombed at the boxoffice. So, the producers got a little frightened and insisted that we go back to a tried-and-true formula for the story."

The producer for the 1958 Allied Artists release was Lindsley Parsons: "Sterling Hayden brought the project to me, but the way *he* wanted to film it would have been too expensive. He thought we should take his boat out and play the sea sequences for real. That is, shoot film in actual storms and so forth. That would have been fine, however our two hundred thousand dollar budget made 'faking' these sequences mandatory."

Rather than compromise, the actor withdrew from the project. Parsons then hired writer Jack DeWitt to come in and rework Walker's screenplay, after which Harmon Jones was signed to direct. Although he was no longer associated with the film, Hayden allowed

Wolf Larsen: **Barry Sullivan, Gita Hall, and Peter Graves.**

Parsons the use of the *Gracie S* for the picture's ten-day shooting schedule.

Barry Sullivan played a more subdued, less flamboyant, Larsen than his predecessors. Peter Graves was Van Weyden and, once again, this role assumed its romantic duties with the movie's heroine, Gita Hall, who entered the action late in the footage. The melodrama began, incidentally, with Graves floating in the water. Obviously, the low budget would not allow for an on-screen shipwreck.

The script attempted to follow the novel as much as possible, but there were a couple of differences:

Death Larsen was eliminated from the story completely.

Wolf goes blind as he is about to rape the film's heroine—a dancer in this rendition. He is later shot and killed by a crew member.

Parson's film was sluggishly directed and suffered from a script full of ornate dialogue. It had a generally mediocre reception from both audiences and the press and, for the most part, played the lower half of double bills.

The *Hollywood Reporter*: "Barry Sullivan does his best, under severe handicaps, to be Wolf . . . . Considerable effort has been made to modernize the leading feminine role for Gita Hall (who plays it well). But Larsen's going blind just as he's about to have his wicked will with her smacks a little too much of 'heaven will protect the working girl'. . . . As an adventure classic, *Wolf Larsen* rates just fair."

Larsen: Wolf of the Seven Seas: **Chuck Connors.**

Although it cries out for updating, *The Sea Wolf* remains an exciting melodrama and will certainly provide excellent material for future remakes. In fact, as we go to press, an eighth version of the story—made on Malta and in Rome by director Giuseppe Vari and starring Chuck Connors—is awaiting release.

The Sea Wolf

FILMOGRAPHY

1913: (Bosworth) Hobart Bosworth.
1920: (Par/George Melford) Noah Beery.
1925: (PDC/Ralph Ince) Ralph Ince.
1930: (Fox/Alfred Santell) Milton Sills.
1941: (WB/Michael Curtiz) Edward G. Robinson.
1950: *Barricade* (WB/Peter Godfrey) Raymond Massey.
1958: *Wolf Larsen* (AA/Harmon Jones) Barry Sullivan.
1975: *Larsen: Wolf of the Seven Seas* (Italian/Giuseppe Vari) Chuck Connors.

29
Show Boat

The plots from Edna Ferber's best-known novels usually cover a span of decades and, in some cases, generations. Her principal characters are, invariably, three in number, although one of them might stay removed from the primary action, while still having a strong influence upon it. *Cimarron* meets these criteria, as do *So Big, Giant, Ice Palace,* and, of course, *Show Boat,* which was first published in 1926 and, a year later, became the basis for an immortal Broadway operetta by Oscar Hammerstein II and Jerome Kern. That production introduced to the American stage a new kind of musical play—one in which the songs flowed naturally from the story's action—and preceeded by sixteen years the history-making Rogers and Hammerstein string of musicals, beginning with *Oklahoma* in 1943.

Miss Ferber's novel centers around Magnolia Hawks, daughter of Captain Andy and his shrewish wife, Parthy Ann, the owners of a Mississippi showboat, the *Cotton Blossom.* Growing up on the river, Magnolia feels her strongest bonds of affection for her father and Julie Dozier LaVerne, the company's leading actress. Julie encourages the girl's theatrical interest and gives her the warmth and understanding she is unable to evoke from her mother. Magnolia is heartbroken after Julie, who has Negro blood, and her white husband are accused of miscegenation and forced to leave the boat.

When she is older, Miss Hawks becomes the company's star. Later, gambler Gaylord Ravenal is hired to play opposite her. It is love at first sight between the two and they subsequently run off to be married. Andy is happy about the union, but Parthy Ann has no respect for her son-in-law. Not even the birth of Kim, her granddaughter, can change the woman's attitude.

Captain Andy is swept overboard one night and drowns. Despite his efforts to get along with his mother-in-law, who now runs the *Cotton Blossom,* Gaylord eventually tells Magnolia that she must choose between him and Parthy Ann. Naturally, she takes Kim and leaves with her husband.

The life of a professional gambler is not easy. One day Ravenal and his family will live in luxury—the next they are broke. To obtain a stake, he borrows a thousand dollars from the owner of a notorious Chicago brothel. When Magnolia goes to pay the madam back (Gaylord had doubled the money), she realizes that this woman is her beloved Julie.

Continued bad luck forces Magnolia to seek work in vaudeville, singing the songs of the Mississippi. Upon returning home one afternoon, she finds a note from her husband. He has deserted his family and

Show Boat (1929): **Joseph Schildkraut and Otis Harlan.**

Show Boat (1929): **Joseph Schildkraut and Laura LaPlante.**

later dies alone in San Francisco. Magnolia becomes well-known for her Negro spirituals. Kim grows up, gains fame as an actress also, and, eventually, marries.

Following the death of Parthy Ann, who had lived to see ninety, Magnolia decides to stay where her roots are—on the *Cotton Blossom.*

Of the three motion picture versions of *Show Boat,* only the first remained essentially true to the novel, rather than to the Flo Ziegfeld stage production. Unlike the later filmings, the 1929 release includes scenes of Magnolia as a child and retains the deaths of both Captain Andy and Parthy. However, as per the other dramatizations, it has a happy ending in that Magnolia and Gaylord are reunited, subsequent to her return to the showboat.

The twelve-reel Universal production was only a fifty percent talkie. It had songs, although most of the Hammerstein/Kern numbers were performed by members of the Broadway company (Helen Morgan, Jules Bledsoe, and Aunt Jemima) in an eighteen-minute prologue. New tunes by other composers were added to the story portion of the picture.

Harry Pollard directed the Carl Laemmle project, which, for some unknown reason, changed the name of the showboat to the *Cotton Palace.* Scenario was by Charles Kenyon, Tom Reed, and Mr. Pollard. The cast included Laura LaPlante as Magnolia, Joseph Schildkraut as Ravenal, Otis Harlan as Captain Andy, Emily Fitzroy as Parthenia, Stepin Fechit as Joe, and Alma Rubens as the tragic Julie—the third corner of Miss Ferber's triangle.

Reviews for the production were mixed. The *New York Times* reported: "The melodies in this well-staged lachrymose tale are so fine that they atone for some of the prolonged melodramatic stretches . . . . Harry Pollard, producer of Carl Laemmle's version of *Uncle Tom's Cabin*, is responsible for the direction of the picture. It is a pity that he has such a passion for pathos, for he does not realize where misfortunes on the screen become tedious to the onlooker."

Allan Jones, who essayed the part of Ravenal in Universal's 1936 remake of *Show Boat*, recalls the production: "Most of the cast had done the play before. In fact, Charles Winninger [Captain Andy] and Helen Morgan [Julie] were in the original New York company.

"I think that our picture was the best of the three. We may not have had color like the 1951 version did,

but James Whale certainly created a realistic Southern atmosphere. Natchez really looked like a town of that period—not something that was on a studio backlot."

Oscar Hammerstein II wrote the screenplay, following closely the plot line of his stage production, which had compressed the story's major events into a relatively short time span. Only the ending underwent major alterations. Gaining inspiration from the Ferber novel, Hammerstein traced the lives of his principal characters for another decade or so—to the point where Kim Ravenal, now an adult, achieves fame as a singing star. On one of her opening nights, her aged parents are, unknown to each other, both in attendance. Before the evening is over, Gaylord and Magnolia are happily reunited.

The circumstances surrounding Julie's reappearance into the story were "borrowed" from the play and differ from both the novel and the 1929 filming. After

Show Boat (1936): **Donald Cook, Helen Morgan, Charles Middleton, Helen Westley, Irene Dunne, and Charles Winninger.**

Show Boat (1936): **Irene Dunne and Allan Jones.**

Show Boat (1936): **Paul Robeson.**

Show Boat (1951): **Kathryn Grayson and Howard Keel.**

Ravenal leaves a pregnant Magnolia in Chicago, the unhappy heroine applies for a job as a nightclub singer. She gets the position when a now-alcoholic Julie, the star at the club, spots her and, wanting to give her former protegée a break, quits. Magnolia begins work on New Year's Eve. Her father, Captain Andy, is in the audience and he takes his grateful daughter back to the *Cotton Blossom.*

The cast for the 1936 picture was a fine one. Aside from those previously mentioned, it featured Irene Dunne as Magnolia, Helen Westley as Parthy, and Paul Robeson as Joe, the roustabout who stops the show with "Ol' Man River." James Whale directed.

Said *Variety*: "*Show Boat,* Universal's second talkerized version, is a smash film-musical . . . Irene Dunne and Allan Jones are superb . . . . Charles Winninger in his original Captain Andy role is, as ever, engaging. . . . Helen Morgan looks as good as she did 15 years ago and troupes her half-caste role in a

manner that suggests much cinematic promise . . . . Robeson's rendition and the cinemagraphic treatment of 'Ol' Man River' is perhaps the single song production highlight . . . ."

The most enduring version of *Show Boat* was filmed by Metro-Goldwyn-Mayer in 1951. That Arthur Freed-Technicolor production, directed by George Sidney, had for its cast: Kathryn Grayson as Magnolia; Ava Gardner as Julie; Howard Keel as Gaylord ("I didn't really want to do the film because I always thought Ravenal was rather bland—a bit of a shnook. But, I must admit that the writer, John Mahin, *did* get into the character and made him more interesting."); Joe E. Brown as Captain Andy; Agnes Moorehead as Parthy; and William Warfield as Joe.

George Sidney: "MGM didn't want to buy *Show Boat* from Universal. But, back in 1938, there were two other stories that Metro wanted from that studio

Show Boat (1951): Robert Sterling, Ava Gardner, and
Kathryn Grayson.

Show Boat (1951): Kathryn Grayson, Joe E. Brown, and Howard Keel.

and they were forced to take the Kern/Hammerstein musical as part of a package. The property lay around for years until Arthur Freed decided that he wanted to do it.

"We did very little to the play—just streamlined the main incidents somewhat and freshened the dialogue."

Writer John Lee Mahin: "My long contract at MGM had expired, but Arthur Freed asked me to come back to do this script. I'd always thought that Julie was the best part in the story. Arthur agreed and we decided that the role should be built-up. For example, in our film, Ravenal goes back to Magnolia as a direct result of an accidental encounter with Julie, who informs him that he has a daughter. [Gaylord, in this rendition, had been ignorant of that fact.]

"I also thought it was wrong to keep the lovers apart for such a long period of time, so I reunited them on the showboat after about five years."

The picture received uniformly excellent reviews. *Variety* said: "All the flamboyancy of the original Kern-Oscar Hammerstein II musical play is captured in John Lee Mahin's deft and moving screenplay, a skillfully woven depiction of the showboat on the Mississippi and the drama unfolding there. . . . Sidney's smooth and sensitive direction endows film with beauty and tantalizing charm which capitalizes on every scene. Both in his handling of musical sequences and the more intimate aspects of the story, his innate good taste and showmanship are always apparent and highest credit accrues to him for once again delivering to Metro and the public a top musical entertainment."

Show Boat was truly a splendid presentation—certainly one of the best pictures to come from MGM during their "Golden Age of Musicals." It is unlikely that the essence of Edna Ferber's story, or the Kern/Hammerstein songs—"Bill," "Make Believe," "Can't Help Lovin' That Man," and, of course, "Ol' Man River"—will ever find a more perfect production to preserve their brilliance for posterity.

Show Boat

FILMOGRAPHY

1929: (U/Harry Pollard) Joseph Schildkraut.
1936: (U/James Whale) Allan Jones.
1951: (MGM/George Sidney) Howard Keel.

30
The Spoilers

While none of its five film versions ever achieved the stature of such westerns as *Red River* or *High Noon*, Rex Beach's *The Spoilers* must still be ranked as a minor classic of that genre, due primarily to the story's brutal climactic fight scene. Initially staged by William Farnum and Tom Santschi for the Selig Polyscope Company in 1914, the no-holds-barred saloon brawl has become the prototype for all succeeding screen fisticuffs.

Beach's novel of the Alaskan gold rush was first published in 1906. Being an astute businessman, the author never sold the story outright to the movies, but, each time a film company wished to produce it, licensed the rights for a seven-year period. That practice enabled him to continue to reap the rewards from his work for many years.

The basic plot line of the book, as well as the Selig production, concerns Roy Glenister (Farnum) and Bill Dextry (Frank Clark), owners of the rich Midas gold mine, located outside of Nome. Trouble begins for the partners, as well as the other miners, when "law and order" arrives in the Yukon in the persons of Judge Stillman (Norvel MacGregor) and Gold Commissioner Alex McNamara (Santschi), two crooked politicians who plan to steal mine claims through a corrupted court process. Glenister had met and fallen in love with the judge's niece, Helen Chester (Bessie Eyton), on a boat trip from Seattle.

Appointed receiver for the mines whose titles are clouded, McNamara takes the opportunity to steal ten thousand dollars in gold from the Midas owners, who, in turn, send their attorney to San Francisco to summon Federal marshals.

A short, sharp battle results in Glenister, Dextry, and the other sourdoughs seizing their mines back from McNamara's men. Then, the following morning,

Glenister confronts the gold commissioner in the latter's office and the two fight it out—with the miner emerging the victor after he breaks McNamara's arm.

The U.S. Marshals arrive to arrest Stillman, McNamara, and their cohorts. Upon learning that Helen was not a party to her uncle's evil schemes, Glenister renews his romantic relationship with her.

There were two other important, if secondary, characters in Beach's novel: Cherry Malotte (played in 1914 by Kathlyn Williams), a woman of questionable reputation who loves Glenister, and the Bronco Kid (Wheeler Oakman), a shady gambler and long-lost brother of Helen Chester. Both of these roles became more important in the later screen versions of *The Spoilers*.

The Spoilers (1914): **William Farnum, Tom Santschi, Kathlyn Williams, and players.**

The Spoilers (1923): **Anna Q. Nilsson, Robert Edeson, and Milton Sills.**

The Spoilers (1923): **Milton Sills and Barbara Bedford.**

Colin Campbell directed the Selig motion picture, which, though primitive in its production techniques, was acclaimed by all who first saw it. Said the *Moving Picture World*: ". . . the story is a great one, and it has been filmed in a way that is also great—great in direction, acting and photography."

The battle royal between Farnum and Santschi has, of course, become a screen legend. Working sans trained stuntmen and breakaway props, the actors pulled no punches and, although the fight may appear rather tame and unexciting by today's standards, the blood and bruises on the screen were the real thing. In an interview years later, Farnum discussed the embroilment, in which Santschi's first swing broke his nose: "I am ashamed to say that I thought he hit me on purpose. So, I waited for an opening, and then I let him have it. After that, we were both punch drunk. . . . He caught me over the left eye and I spurted blood like a stuck pig.

". . . I've never been quite the same man since that fight. Besides the broken nose, I had two bent ribs and a crushed sinus in my cheek that gave me fainting spells for years. At the end, I got a good shoulder lock on Tom and bent him back and back and back until I heard him groan, 'For God's sake, Bill!' Then I had enough sense to let go. When it was all over, messy and bloody as we were, Tom and I went to a Turkish bath and stayed for three days."

The nine-reel feature, comprised of three acts and a prologue, which depicted explanatory scenes such as Glenister's renunciation of Cherry and McNamara's plotting in Washington to rob the miners, was the most successful film in Selig's history.

Jesse D. Hampton shot a second silent version of *The Spoilers* in 1923. Directed by Lambert Hillyer, from an essentially faithful adaptation by Fred Kennedy Myton, Elliott Clawson, and Hope Loring, the Goldwyn release starred Milton Sills (Glenister), Anna Q. Nilsson (Cherry), Barbara Bedford (Helen), Robert Edeson (Dextry), Noah Beery (McNamara), Wallace MacDonald (Bronco), and Sam DeGrasse (Stillman).

Production techniques were first-rate and director Hillyer did well in conveying the atmosphere of the turn-of-the-century Yukon, portraying his town as a line of ugly shacks and dirt thoroughfares. The *New York Times* called the picture "a splendid fighting film . . . this production has action, force, good acting, suspense, but no subtlety."

The climactic battle between Sills and Beery was no disappointment to those who recalled the Farnum/

Santschi slug-fest nine years previously. The *Times* labeled it "one of the most realistic fights ever depicted."

With the coming of sound, Beach's basic story changed slightly. The first "talkie" version of *The Spoilers* was produced in 1930 by Paramount, under the direction of Edwin Carewe. Agnes Brand Lehy did the screenplay from an adaptation by Bartlett Cormack. The cast had Gary Cooper playing Glenister, Kay Johnson as Helen, Betty Compson as Cherry, William "Stage" Boyd essaying McNamara, James Kirkwood as Dextry, Lloyd Ingraham doing Stillman, and Slim Summerville as Slapjack Simms, a *third* partner in the Midas mine. Jack Trent played the Bronco Kid, who was no longer the brother of Helen.

Of the production, *Variety* reported: "There are plenty of fights, realistic sets and locales, but the action is not as closely knit nor has the story been as well adapted to the talker as it might be."

The *New York Times* called it "a muddled piece of work with some absurdly melodramatic dialogue."

Yet, as with both the 1914 and 1923 versions, the saving grace of Paramount's remake was the fight, which began upstairs in the saloon, continued down a

The Spoilers (1930): Betty Compson and Gary Cooper.

The Spoilers (1930): **William "Stage" Boyd and Gary Cooper.**

staircase, and wound up in the street with the townspeople gathered around. The trade paper said: "This sequence is worth all of the others, especially to the fans who have been longing during the past year for less drawing room stuff, and a return of action."

Universal purchased *The Spoilers* in the early 1940s as a proposed vehicle for Marlene Dietrich. The actress's tremendous success as the saloon hostess in the 1939 comedy/western *Destry Rides Again* had inspired the studio to seek similar roles for her.

Since Dietrich was to play the cynical but tender Cherry Malotte, owner of Nome's most popular saloon, Beach's story was considerably reworked to build up her role—almost to the point where it overshadowed both Glenister and McNamara. In previous versions, Cherry had been a relatively minor, unsympathetic character—a Faro dealer, whose main plot function was to mislead Glenister into believing that Helen was involved in McNamara's scheme.

To restructure the story, writers Lawrence Hazard and Tom Reed emphasized the romance between Cherry and Glenister (played by John Wayne), while making Roy's relationship with Helen Chester (Margaret Lindsay) a brief flirtation—at least on his part.

Helen, on the other hand, falls in love with the strapping miner, but realizes that her feelings are destined for frustration, since she is, in fact, working as a decoy for her uncle (Samuel S. Hinds). At the film's conclusion, Helen goes to jail, while Cherry gets Glenister.

Again, the Bronco Kid (Richard Barthelmess) is not related to Helen, but works for Cherry as a Faro dealer. Jealous of Glenister because he himself is in love with Cherry, the gambler attempts to kill Roy while the latter is trying to steal his safe, filled with gold and legal papers, back from McNamara (Randolph Scott). But, it is the sheriff who accidentally stops Bronco's bullet, with Roy being accused and jailed for the murder.

Unlike the earlier films, McNamara is *not* infatuated by Helen, but, instead, pursues Cherry. When Roy breaks jail to go with Dextry (Harry Carey) and the other miners to reclaim the Midas, the enchanting woman lures McNamara up to her apartment above the saloon, so that he will not suspect what her "lover" is up to.

It is in Cherry's rooms that the fight starts—moving downstairs through the saloon and out into the muddy street. As *Variety* said: "It is a terrific melee—brutally ferocious, ceaseless in its battering onrush and also a bit preposterous if its gargantuan unreality is subjected to reasonable reflection. . . ."

The 1942 Frank Lloyd production was directed by Ray Enright. Most observers felt it was the best version of *The Spoilers* to date. Certainly its cast—Dietrich, Scott, and Wayne—was a powerful one and, as the *Variety* review continued: "Ray Enright . . . turns in

The Spoilers (1942): **Richard Barthelmess and Marlene Dietrich.**

The Spoilers (1942): **John Wayne, Randolph Scott, and Samuel S. Hinds.**

The Spoilers (1942): **John Wayne and Randolph Scott.**

The Spoilers (1955): **Anne Baxter and Barbara Britton.**

The Spoilers (1955): **Jeff Chandler and John McIntire.**

a capital piece of direction, telling his narrative vigorously, giving his top players their head for best results, blending big sweeps of action and the violence of gun and fistic battle with sharply pointed detail in a style perfectly fitted for melodrama."

William Farnum, incidentally, also appeared in the movie, playing Glenister's attorney.

Filmed in 1955 by Universal-International, the most recent version of Beach's novel followed the altered story line of the 1942 remake quite closely. The cast in this rather sterile and unatmospheric Technicolor epic had Anne Baxter as Cherry, Jeff Chandler as Glenister, and Rory Calhoun as McNamara. Supporting players included Ray Danton as Bronco (rechristened "Blackie" here), Barbara Britton as Helen, John McIntire as Dextry, and Carl Benton Reid as Judge Stillman. Screenplay was by Oscar Brodney and Charles Hoffman.

Director Jesse Hibbs recalls why he was unhappy with his picture: "I'd rather have had Dietrich, Wayne, and Scott for my cast, rather than the players I was saddled with. They were, for the most part, good actors, but none of them had the 'personality' that made the earlier performances so great.

"The female lead had already been built-up for Dietrich several years before, but Ross Hunter, who was the producer, insisted on enlarging it even further. Obviously, the men [Chandler and Calhoun] weren't too happy with that.

"It was a middle job."

The basic problem with the movie was the producer's approach to it. Ross Hunter has a reputation in the motion picture industry for making glossy films containing magnificent sets and beautiful costumes. Such a practice is fine for projects like *Magnificent Obsession* or *Airport,* but these production values were definitely out of place in what was supposed to be a

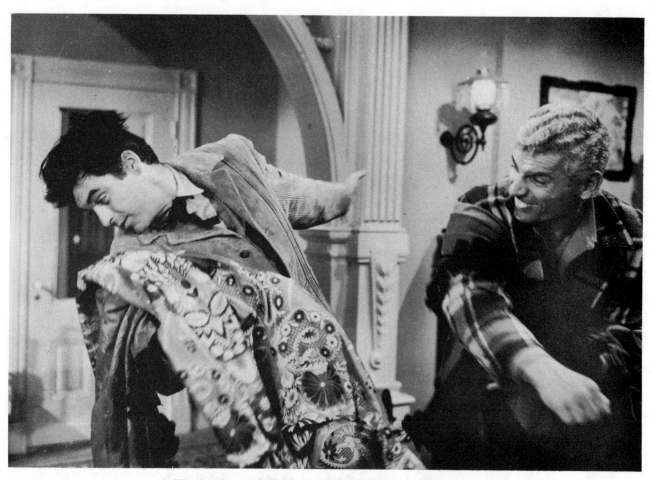

The Spoilers (1955): **Rory Calhoun and Jeff Chandler.**

gutsy action melodrama, set in a dirty Alaskan gold town.

Additionally, by concentrating on the character of Cherry and making her less hard-bitten and more understanding than she'd previously been played, Hunter went a long way toward turning *The Spoilers* into a "woman's picture."

Although it followed the same basic choreography as the Wayne/Scott battle, the fight in this 1955 film was, in comparison, quite subdued. The action appeared to lack any spontaneity whatsoever, with the two actors seeming to go through their motions "by the numbers."

Few critics could get very excited about the Universal programmer. The *Hollywood Reporter* summed the whole thing up by saying: "All in all, it's a smooth job." And that was one of the more enthusiastic remarks.

As years pass, audiences seem to forget the story details of even the best films. Yet, specific sequences—particularly those involving violent action—remain vivid in their memories. *Bullitt* and *The French Connection* have their wild automobile chases—*Ben-Hur* has its chariot race—*Psycho* has the shower murder. But, unlike the others, *The Spoilers* created a tradition —a fight sequence that moviemakers have tried to surpass for more than sixty years. It hasn't been an easy job.

The Spoilers

FILMOGRAPHY

1914: (Selig/Colin Campbell) William Farnum.
1923: (Goldwyn/Lambert Hillyer) Milton Sills.
1930: (Par/Edwin Carewe) Gary Cooper.
1942: (U/Ray Enright) John Wayne.
1955: (U/Jesse Hibbs) Jeff Chandler.

31
Stagecoach

The words of praise that have been written about John Ford's 1939 production of *Stagecoach* are seemingly endless. Its literate screenplay by Dudley Nichols; vivid characterizations from a carefully chosen cast; the sweeping grandeur of Monument Valley; an unconventional use of background music; and the exciting chase sequence—the elements meshed together perfectly to form the first film that successfully combined the mythical aspects of the old West with pure and simple entertainment values.

According to star Claire Trevor: "*Stagecoach* was the only thing I've ever done that couldn't have been done in another medium. Up to that time, it was the only sound film that used the medium of motion pictures to its full extent."

Unfortunately, by current standards, *Stagecoach* is somewhat of a museum piece. Whereas one can still appreciate the picture's performances and photography, as well as many of its production techniques, which were innovative back in 1939, the film as a whole has *not* aged gracefully. Nichols's once viable script is badly dated and the snail-paced direction of John Ford has a lethargic effect. Today, even the well-executed Indian attack on the coach is not enough to make the classic western anything but a chore to watch.

Based on a story by Ernest Haycox, *Stage to Lordsburg,* which in turn had its origins in de Maupassant's "Boule de Suif," the Walter Wanger production for United Artists release dealt with eight Overland stage passengers, traveling through dangerous Apache country from Tonto to Lordsburg. Although essentially stereotypes, the characters are quite believable and form the basic strength of the piece: Dallas (Claire Trevor), the prostitute with a "heart"; the Ringo Kid (John Wayne in the role that made him a star), an escaped convict out to get the man who framed him;

Buck (Andy Devine), the rough-and-ready stage driver; Hatfield (John Carradine), a gambler and scion of a wealthy Southern family; Doc Boone (Thomas Mitchell in his Oscar-winning portrayal), the jaded man of medicine; Lucy Mallory (Louise Platt), the pregnant wife of a cavalry officer; Curley Wilcox (George Bancroft), the dutiful marshal; Mr. Gatewood (Berton Churchill), an embezzling banker; and Mr. Peacock (Donald Meek), a timid whiskey drummer.

The trek across the desert is not without incident—a romance between Dallas and Ringo; the birth of Mrs. Mallory's baby at a station stop; and, of course, the attack on the coach by Geronimo's braves, which is thwarted by the arrival of the U.S. Cavalry. At journey's end, Hatfield has been killed, Peacock wounded, and Gatewood arrested for absconding with bank funds. Ringo kills his enemy, Luke Plummer (Tom Tyler), in the streets of Lordsburg, then is released by Curley to start a new life with Dallas.

Of *Stagecoach,* the *New York Times* commented: "In one superbly expansive gesture . . . John Ford has swept aside ten years of artifice and talkie compromise and has made a motion picture that sings a song of camera. . . . Here, in a sentence, is a movie of the grand old school, a genuine rib-thumper and a beautiful sight to see."

Considering the lofty reputation of Ford's picture, producer Martin Rackin's decision to remake *Stagecoach* in the mid-1960s was a rather daring one. He'd become interested in the property shortly after leaving Paramount in 1964, where he'd been executive in charge of production. Then, after securing the rights to Nichols's script, Rackin arranged for 20th Century-Fox to finance the project.

Stagecoach (1939): Claire Trevor and John Wayne.

Stagecoach (1939): John Carradine, Donald Meek, and
Thomas Mitchell.

Stagecoach (1939): **George Bancroft, John Wayne, Andy Devine, and player.**

In a 1965 interview with the *Los Angeles Times*, the producer discussed his version in relation to Ford's: "In the old picture, there's a murder and a fight over a scarlet woman (Claire Trevor), so the women's league march her and also a drunken doctor (Mitchell) out of town—and let twenty other women like her stay. Another boffo moment is that in which Ringo gallantly announces of the scarlet woman, 'This is a lady!'

"*Stagecoach* was a classic because everyone was going to the movies three times a week. Nobody of this generation ever saw it except for snatches in roundups of old movies and in local TV telecasts, all chopped up. Its never been shown on network TV because it isn't good enough, and never on TV abroad. And I'm not depreciating John Ford, because if he made it today he wouldn't make it that way.

"I'm not remaking it, either. If I were, I'd use Dudley Nichols' script and go back to Monument Valley. I'm making my version because I believe the western is the bread and butter of our industry—and they're being shot all over the world but here. Nichols' script was very dated; we've altered it, tightened it, given it greater depth, greater purpose. And because we were able to look at the original over and over

again, we had the greatest chance to see where Ford made his mistakes by modern standards."

Rackin's 1966 color production was written by Joseph Landon and directed by Gordon Douglas. The cast, for the most part, was an impressive one: Dallas (Ann-Margret), Mr. Peacock (Red Buttons), Hatfield (Mike Connors), Ringo (Alex Cord—instead of first choice, James Coburn), Doc Boone (Bing Crosby), Mr. Gatewood (Bob Cummings), Curley (Van Heflin), Buck (Slim Pickens), Mrs. Mallory (Stefanie Powers), and Luke Plummer (Keenan Wynn). With the exception of Ann-Margret and the Messrs. Cord and Conners, who all seemed to be rather miscast in their assignments, the performances were solid—none of them suffering when compared to their 1939 counterparts.

The remake, which filmed most of its exteriors in the Colorado Rockies, did, in fact, make some valid changes in the handling of specific scenes and characters. First, Rackin ordered that, during the Indian attack, the coach be turned over: "In the original, thirty indians chase the stagecoach till they are alongside. Why didn't one of them shoot the lead horse? That would have ended the chase."

Adaptations were also made with the characters. Bob Cummings's Gatewood became the son-in-law of a banker, who runs off with funds in order to rid himself of, among other things, his unattractive wife. A prior amorous relationship with Dallas was also hinted at. On the other hand, the Ringo Kid of Alex Cord was less naive about Dallas's "profession" than John Wayne had been. It was also rather amusing that where Carradine's gambler had been dressed all-in-black, Mike Connors was garbed in white.

Stagecoach (1966): **Alex Cord and Ann-Margret.**

Stagecoach (1966): **Van Heflin and Bing Crosby.**

Stagecoach (1966): **Bing Crosby, Red Buttons, and Ann-Margret.**

The final shoot-out between Ringo and Plummer, as staged by Rackin/Douglas, was completely different from what had taken place in the Ford film. In that earlier production, Gatewood is arrested as he gets off the stage by the local law officials, then Curley lets Ringo go to meet his two-dimensional enemies in a partially off-screen showdown, which takes place in the middle of the street.

However, the 1966 filmmakers had Keenan Wynn endow Plummer with a colorful personality—that of a maniacal Bible-spouting killer—and stationed him with his sons in the local saloon to await Ringo. Upon his arrival in Lordsburg, Gatewood goes to Plummer seeking sanctuary, offering him a portion of the stolen bank money. Plummer decides to keep all the loot for himself, so he shoots down the embezzler. Next, Curley attempts to convince the murderous patriarch to call off his feud with Ringo, but the marshal gets a bullet in the leg for his trouble. Ergo, it is Ringo who must ultimately confront the Plummers.

Although none of the reviews for Rackin's production claimed that the movie came anywhere near the milestone achievements of its predecessor, many indicated that the film was, in itself, a good piece of entertainment. Said *Variety*: "New version of *Stagecoach* is loaded with box office appeal. Ten stars, repping a wide spectrum of audience interest, an absorbing script about diverse characters thrown together by fate, plus fine direction and performances are all wrapped up in a handsomely mounted Martin Rackin produc-

tion. Comedy and action complement the basic human drama which, although set in the old U. S. West, is timeless."

Sadly, the picture was *not* a solid box-office contender. As to the reasons, director Gordon Douglas speculates: "Frankly, the story wasn't strong enough to be remade. Also, in many areas, the casting was weak . . . especially Ann-Margret, who didn't look like a hooker, and Alex Cord, who . . . well, recasting John Wayne is a hard thing to do."

Martin Rackin cites a much simpler reason for the failure: "If I were to do it again, I'd change the title . . . call it *Ringo* . . . anything but *Stagecoach*. We were fighting the memory of a film that didn't really exist.

"There are just so many dramatic situations. *Stagecoach* has been made dozens of times . . . *The High and the Mighty* . . . *Airport* . . . *The Poseiden Adventure*—all of them were about a group of people caught in a tense situation. Ford's film just came early enough to be considered innovative."

Stagecoach

FILMOGRAPHY

1939: (UA/John Ford) John Wayne.
1966: (Fox/Gordon Douglas) Alex Cord.

32
The Ten Commandments

Cecil B. DeMille, Hollywood's master showman, achieved his greatest commercial success by remaking simply the prologue from his 1923 silent feature, *The Ten Commandments*. The new and expanded version of the Old Testament saga was released through Paramount in 1956 and has, to date, garnered a domestic gross of forty-three million dollars.

The original *Ten Commandments*[1] was produced as the result of a national contest DeMille had sponsored in which the public wrote in their ideas for the director's next picture. In going over the entries, DeMille noted that a great number of them suggested that he do a movie that employed a religious theme. Eight of the letters were even more specific, recommending that a picture be made about Moses and the Ten Commandments.

DeMille decided to film the story of Moses as a relatively short prologue to a more modern tale, which would parallel the biblical one. Produced on a budget of 1.5 million dollars, the epic feature thrilled audiences with its spectacle and special effects, especially the parting of the Red Sea—at that time, the most striking scene ever committed to celluloid.

The scenario was adapted from the Book of Exodus by Jeannie MacPherson, who was also responsible for devising the modern and longer portion of the film.

Photographed in color, the prologue concerns the efforts of Moses (Theodore Roberts) to gain the freedom of the Children of Israel from bondage under the Egyptian Pharaoh Rameses (Charles de Roche). Moses, with the help of God, brings forth a series of plagues on the Egyptians, after which Rameses allows the Hebrews to depart.

The remaining action in the first section involves the exodus from Egypt, the parting of the Red Sea, and, of course, Moses' receiving the Ten Commandments from the Lord on the top of Mount Sinai.

As contrast, DeMille shot the modern portion of the Paramount release in black and white. The allegory concerned two brothers—John (Richard Dix) and Dan (Rod La Rocque) McTavish. Dan, the younger of the pair, breaks many of God's Commandments (he is involved in graft, commits adultery, etc.), which, ultimately, leads to the death of both his mother (Edythe Chapman) and himself, although he does not succumb until after he has contracted leprosy. John, on the other hand, is both law-abiding and God-fearing, and it is through his faith and prayer that Dan's good wife, Mary (Leatrice Joy), is able to rid herself of the dreaded disease that her husband had exposed her to.

In general, critics were impressed with the first portion of DeMille's production, but didn't like the modern tale. The *New York Times* reported: "It is probable that no more wonderful spectacle has ever been put before the public in shadow-form than the greatly heralded prelude to Cecil B. DeMille's costly film. . . . It is built in two sections, the spectacle and the melodrama. Two men might have directed the feature, as it goes from the sublime to the out-and-out movie. Not that the latter part is bad, but that almost any melodramatic picture would have fitted into the second section of this photodrama."

Following the successful release of his *Samson and Delilah* (1949), DeMille began to receive numerous requests from moviegoers to remake the first portion of *The Ten Commandments*. He was enthusiastic about the idea, but selling the powers at Paramount, to whom he was under contract, was another matter. Despite the huge grosses (11.5 million—domestic)

[1] *The Life of Moses,* a Vitagraph product, had been directed by J. Stuart Blackton in 1909.

The Ten Commandments (1923): Theodore Roberts, Charles DeRoche, and Pat Moore.

The Ten Commandments (1923): Richard Dix, Rod LaRocque, and Leatrice Joy.

from *Samson*, the executives were not convinced that another biblical picture would make money.

Yet, DeMille finally won his case and was given an initial budget of eight million (the costs later went beyond thirteen million) to create what was to become his masterpiece.

The screenplay for the lavish 219-minute spectacle was written over a three-year period by Aeneas MacKenzie, Jesse L. Lasky, Jr., Jack Gariss, and Frederic M. Frank. It dealt entirely with the story of Moses: from his infancy when his mother sent him floating down the Nile in a cradle of bulrushes, so that he might escape the wrath of the Pharoah, who had condemned all newborn Hebrew males to death; through his adoption by the Pharaoh's daughter; and, finally, through his discovery of his true origins, which lead to his banishment to the desert and, eventually, his freeing of the Children of Israel, as per the Old Testament.

Charlton Heston, whose film credits up to that point boasted little more than leading roles in such Paramount programmers as *Pony Express* and *The Savage*, was chosen by DeMille to star as Moses. The producer/director felt that the actor bore an uncanny resemblance to Michaelangelo's famous statue of the Lawgiver.

Supporting Heston was an all-star cast: Yul Brynner as Rameses, Anne Baxter, Edward G. Robinson, Yvonne DeCarlo as Sephora, Moses' wife, Sir Cedric Hardwicke, John Derek as Joshua, Debra Paget, Nina Foch, Vincent Price, Martha Scott, Judith Anderson, and John Carradine.

The Technicolor/VistaVision production took more than seven months to shoot, including three months in Egypt with a cast of twenty thousand extras. It was during this location filming that DeMille suffered a massive heart attack, but in spite of warnings from his physicians, decided to carry on with his picture—even if the pace killed him.

The Ten Commandments (1956): **Vincent Price, Charlton Heston, and player.**

The Ten Commandments (1956): Henry Wilcoxon and Edward G. Robinson.

The Ten Commandments (1956): Anne Baxter, Eugene Mazzola, and Yul Brynner.

The Ten Commandments (1956): John Derek, Debra Paget, Yvonne DeCarlo, Charlton Heston, and players.

Back in Hollywood, the company took over twelve of the eighteen sound stages at Paramount and, in order to construct a three-hundred-thousand-gallon tank for use in the Red Sea sequences, later spread out to the neighboring RKO lot.

The finished film received mixed reviews from the nation's critics. Whereas virtually all of the reporters were impressed by the remarkable settings, decor, and scope of the project, many said that they were disappointed with the special effects. The *New York Times* commented: "The parting of the Red Sea is an obvious piece of camera trickery in which two churning walls of water frame a course as smooth and dry as a race track. And the striking off of the Ten Commandments by successive thunderbolts, while a deep voice intones their contents, is disconcertingly mechanical."

Other papers insisted that, although quite inspiring, the mammoth production was too long and would have benefited if an hour's worth of footage were removed from the earlier sequences dealing with Moses' years as the adopted grandson of the Pharaoh and his romance with Princess Nefretiri (Anne Baxter).

Heston's performance was praised by most of the press, but other members of the ensemble did not fare as well. Writing in the *Los Angeles Mirror-News,* Dick Williams said: "The supporting cast is generally satis-factory, if not outstanding. Yul Brynner, looking much as he did in *The King and I,* makes a virile Pharaoh who inherits the throne and battles Moses. . . . Less effective are the heavies. Villains, under DeMille's characteristic flowery approach, inevitably become unbelievable blackguards of an old and outdated school of melodrama. Edward G. Robinson as the evil Hebrew informer, Dathan, looks ludicrously like Little Caesar in a turban. Vincent Price as the effete, whip-cracking, master builder Baka, is equally overdone."

Had Cecil B. DeMille's talent for staging "a big show" included a keener sense of good dialogue, believable characterization, and tight story construction, then his production of *The Ten Commandments,* as well as most of his earlier film efforts, would be remembered today, not only as spectacular entertainments, but as fine dramatic motion pictures as well.

The Ten Commandments

FILMOGRAPHY

1923: (Par/Cecil B. DeMille) Theodore Roberts.
1956: (Par/Cecil B. DeMille) Charlton Heston.

33
Wuthering Heights

"Translating Emily Bronte's novel to the screen became more a matter of establishing and maintaining a mood, rather than telling a story," reflected director Robert Fuest, shortly after he'd completed filming on the 1970 American-International remake of *Wuthering Heights*.

"The characters Miss Bronte created are so powerful and their state of mind so important, that her story line becomes merely a vehicle which brings them together and the result is an atmosphere charged with fascinating drama."

The haunting love story of Heathcliff and Cathy was written in 1847. Mr. Earnshaw retrieves a young waif from the streets of London, brings him home to Wuthering Heights, his farmhouse on the Yorkshire moors, and dubs the lad Heathcliff. Earnshaw's daughter, Catherine, becomes a constant playmate of the orphan, but son Hindley detests him for stealing his father's affections. Following the death of the master, Hindley returns from college with a wife and kicks Heathcliff out of the house, forcing him to become a servant. However, Cathy remains loyal to the youth, vowing to stay with him in their fantasy world on the moors.

Time passes and Cathy matures. She meets gentle Edgar Linton of Thrushcross Grange, a neighboring estate, and eventually falls in love with him. One night, the confused girl confesses to her housekeeper, Nelly Dean, that she really feels more spiritually akin to Heathcliff than Edgar, in that they have the same wild temperament. Yet, she reflects, it would almost be degrading to marry him.

Heathcliff has listened in on this last remark. Hurt and angry, he runs away—not hearing Cathy say that she would only marry Edgar in order to help her childhood lover escape the brutality of Hindley, now a widower and the father of an emotionally dependent son, Hareton.

After recovering from the shock of Heathcliff's departure, Cathy marries Edgar. They are happy for a time—until Heathcliff returns, having gained wealth and polish. The ex-ruffian purchases Hindley's gambling debts and thereby the title to Wuthering Heights. Nevertheless, to enjoy his revenge, he allows the drunken Hindley and his son to continue to live on the premises.

To spite Cathy, who still loves him, a bitter Heathcliff courts Isabella Linton, later eloping with the girl against her brother Edgar's wishes. Isabella's life at Wuthering Heights is an unhappy one, since her husband treats her miserably.

Cathy dies in childbirth, but not before she sees Heathcliff a final time, with both professing their love for each other. Distraught, Heathcliff beats his head against a tree and cries out for Cathy's ghost to haunt him.

Isabella flees to London where she has a son, Linton. Following her death several years later, Heathcliff brings his sickly son home where he terrorizes him into slavery. He also arranges a marriage between the boy and Catherine, the daughter of Edgar and his late wife. Shortly thereafter, both Edgar and Linton die and the Grange, subsequently, becomes the property of Heathcliff—as per his son's will.

More years go by. Heathcliff, always the tortured soul, dies in bed, after which young Catherine wins over the uneducated Hareton—who'd lived his life under Heathcliff's thumb—and they plan to marry.

The narrative, incidentally, was told entirely in flashbacks by Nelly Dean. The housekeeper related the tale to Mr. Lockwood, present-day owner of Thrushcross Grange, after he'd seen the ghost of Catherine Earnshaw Linton.

Wuthering Heights has been filmed four times[1] with varying degrees of success. Interestingly, it was the first edition, made in 1920 by Ideal, a British company, that remained closest to Miss Bronte's tale, in that it went into the third generation of characters. Though running a scant sixty-five minutes, the photoplay, directed by A. V. Bramble from Eliot Stannard's scenario, included most of the original story line, eliminating only the parts of Mr. Lockwood, Isabella, and Linton Heathcliff, the latter's story function being assumed by the Hareton Earnshaw role.

[1] After extensive investigation, I was unable to *verify* claims of additional versions made prior to 1920.

In the Ideal production, Hareton and the young Catherine meet and, ultimately, marry. It is, in fact, a union of love, despite the efforts of Heathcliff, who remains a bachelor throughout the picture, to use the couple to humiliate Edgar. The film ends with Heathcliff's death.

According to the *Exhibitor's Trade Review*: "Strong emotional situations, a genuine sympathy for the gypsy hero, splendid settings of the Yorkshire moors and a fine acting cast should make the picture acceptable. Milton Rosmer, one of the most reliable of English artists, scores quite a triumph by his ruthless and consistent reading of the character of Heathcliff. Cathy is well taken by Annie Trevor, and Warwick Ward is excellent as Hindley Earnshaw."

Undoubtedly, the most enduring version of *Wuthering Heights* came from Samuel Goldwyn Productions

Wuthering Heights (1939): **Laurence Olivier and Merle Oberon.**

Wuthering Heights (1939): Geraldine Fitzgerald,
Laurence Olivier, Leo G. Carroll,
and Flora Robson.

in 1939, under the direction of William Wyler. The
screenplay by Ben Hecht and Charles MacArthur was
originally commissioned by Walter Wanger as a vehicle
for two of his contractees, Charles Boyer and Sylvia
Sidney, but when the actress refused the assignment
because she felt the casting was wrong, the producer
became quite amiable to Wyler's expressed interest in
obtaining the property.

Goldwyn, hesitant at first, since he didn't like movies
with unhappy endings, eventually agreed to finance
Wyler's project—after the director informed him that
Jack Warner wanted to do it with Bette Davis as
Cathy. The fact that another studio was interested in
making the picture had, of course, convinced Goldwyn
that the Hecht/MacArthur script would indeed be a
desirable one to produce himself.

Cast in the leading roles were Laurence Olivier as
Heathcliff and Merle Oberon as Cathy.

The carefully written screenplay successfully adapted
Miss Bronte's nineteenth-century melodrama to the
tastes of 1939 audiences. A most obvious change in
the plot was the elimination of the third-generation
characters—Hareton, Linton, and young Catherine,
as well as Hindley's wife. Heathcliff's and especially
Cathy's wild natures were toned down to a certain
extent, but, on the other hand, the once gentle Lin-
tons—Edgar and Isabelle—became a bit more coarse.

The film, utilizing flashback technique as per the
novel, concentrated almost entirely on the fierce passionate romance between the two principals. It only
returned to the present after Cathy's death and Heathcliff's pleas for her to haunt him.

When Lockwood, an uninvited house guest at Wuth-

ering Heights, views the mournful spirit of Cathy outside his bedroom window, Heathcliff rushes out of the
house into a blinding blizzard and is later found fro-
zen to death on the moors—at the same spot where
he and Cathy use to play together. A final shot (filmed
later over Wyler's objections and without his co-opera-
tion) shows the two lovers, young again, walking
hand-in-hand through the clouds.

Considered today to be an all-time cinema classic,
Wuthering Heights was not a box-office success when
it was initially released. However, a reissue during the
1950s put the production into the black.

Said the New York Times: "It is Goldwyn at his
best, and better still, Emily Bronte at hers. Out of her
strange tale of a tortured romance Mr. Goldwyn and
his troupe have fashioned a strong and somber film,
poetically written as the novel not always was, sinister
and wild as it was meant to be, far more compact
dramatically than Miss Bronte had made it."

The leading performances were also highly praised
by the press, including the Times: "Laurence Olivier's
Heathcliff is the man. He has Heathcliff's broad lowering brow, his scowl, the churlishness, the wild ten-
derness, the bearing, speech and manner of the demon-
possessed.

". . . and Merle Oberon as Cathy has matched the
brilliance of his characterization with hers. She has
perfectly caught the restless, changing spirit of the
Bronte heroine who knew she was not meant for heaven and broke her heart and Heathcliff's in the synthetic paradise of her marriage with gentle Edgar Linton [David Niven]."

Music by Alfred Newman and photography by
Gregg Toland were definite assets to the production.

1953: Mexico's Luis Buñuel adapted the Bronte
story to a Spanish setting, changing character names
to accommodate the new locale. Titled Cumbres Borrascosas (aka Abismos de Pasion), the poorly cast production starred Irasema Dilian, Jorge Mistral, and
Lilia Prado.

Producers Samuel Z. Arkoff and James H. Nicholson, who, since the mid-1950s, managed to build—
through the production of a successful series of inex-
pensive motorcycle, beach party, and horror movies—
their American-International Pictures from a small
exploitation film company into a multimillion-dollar
concern, decided early in 1970 that the time was right
for another remake of Wuthering Heights—one that
would appeal to the youth market. The recent phe-
nomenal box-office grosses of Zeffirelli's Romeo and

Wuthering Heights (1970): **Timothy Dalton and Anna Calder-Marshall.**

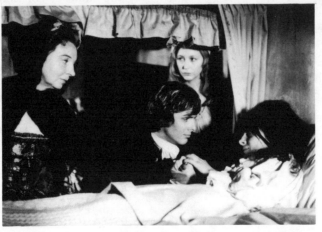

Wuthering Heights (1970): **Pamela Browne, Ian Ogilvy, Judy Cornwall, and Anna Calder-Marshall.**

Wuthering Heights (1970): **Timothy Dalton and Anna Calder-Marshall.**

Juliet had convinced them that literary classics, designed for such an audience, could make big money.

Feeling that the story was so well known that it did not require major stars for its principal roles, the producers cast British performers Timothy Dalton (bearing a striking resemblance to Laurence Olivier) and Anna Calder-Marshall as Heathcliff and Cathy. Both had achieved a certain amount of success in their previous screen efforts and were capable actors, but neither, in any sense of the word, could be considered a "star."

It was decided that the two-million-dollar production, shot in color on the Yorkshire moors, would remain as faithful as possible to the book, although, once again, the third generation characters were dropped. Also, the story, though told in a flashback, did without Mr. Lockwood.

Writer Patrick Tilley explains why he and director Robert Fuest felt that Heathcliff's origins, virtually ignored in Miss Bronte's novel, should be brought out in the new dramatization: "For purposes of the film we felt some explanation should be offered as to why an uncharitable man like Earnshaw (Harry Andrews)[2] should have picked up this boy and taken him home to be brought up alongside his own children. So we hinted in the script, as Somerset Maugham, Thomas Moser

---

[2] Cecil Kellaway's Earnshaw in the Goldwyn version was much more benevolent.

and other literary authorities have done, that Heathcliff was probably Earnshaw's illegitimate son.

"Of course, it's only a theory, but if the theory is correct, it would make Heathcliff the half-brother of Catherine, and this would put their love affair on an incestuous footing.

"It would also account for the strange intensity of their relationship, and, more importantly, explain why their ill-fated love has built-in factors for its own destruction."

The 1970 release enlarged the role of Nelly, the housekeeper, considerably and had pretty actress Judy Cornwall play it much younger than Flora Robson had done in the Wyler film when the part was called Ellen. Miss Cornwell spent much of her screen time pining away for Hindley's affections.

It is Hindley (Julian Glover), incidentally, who kills Heathcliff in this version. Following Cathy's funeral, her drunken brother, at Isabella's (Hilary Dwyer) urging, shoots the new master of the Yorkshire estate. Heathcliff then makes his way back to the cemetery and dies next to the grave of his beloved Cathy, whose ghost appears before him.

Variety: "American-International Pictures' *Wuthering Heights* is a nice *Wuthering Heights* but not a great *Wuthering Heights*. It is a competent, tasteful, frequently even lovely readaptation of Emily Bronte's Gothic, mystical love story. But the brooding tension, the electric passion of two lovers compelled to an inevitable tragedy is not generated. . . . Miss Calder-Marshall and Dalton simply fail to generate the chemistry that gave the Merle Oberon-Laurence Olivier romance its haunting power."

The production was, without doubt, entertaining— one that easily held audience interest. However, *moving* the audience emotionally was another matter altogether, and in that department, the 1970 remake was a failure.

Wuthering Heights

FILMOGRAPHY

1920: (British/A. V. Bramble) Milton Rosmer.
1939: (Goldwyn/William Wyler) Laurence Olivier.
1953: *Cumbres Borrascosas* (Mexican/Luis Buñuel) Jorge Mistral.
1970: (AIP/Robert Fuest) Timothy Dalton.

Compendium of Film Remakes

The more than five hundred entries on the following pages are only a partial listing of the many literary properties that have been filmed on multiple occasions. They have been selected to appeal to the interests of the general reader, rather than film scholars, and some have been edited to eliminate less important filmings of the story material.

Every film title is cross-referenced so that the detailed listing of all versions appears under the title of the earliest *verified* production of that particular work. If no basic literary source (i.e., novel, play, poem, etc.) is mentioned, then it may be assumed that the movie was based on an original screenplay.

Each production recorded under a master heading includes the year of release, the title (if different from that of the initial rendition), then, in parentheses, the producer, distributor, or country of origin of the picture, followed by the director's name. Finally, if known, the star is identified.

In the majority of instances, production and distribution organizations have been abbreviated. Below is a key to the less obvious abridgments:

AA	Allied Artists
AIP	American-International
AP	Associated Producers
APD	Allied Producers and Distributors
Aud	Audubon
Bio	Biograph
BRI	Briskin
BV	Buena Vista
CCF	Cinema Center Films
CMPC	California Motion Picture Corporation
Col	Columbia

Cos	Cosmopolitan
CW	Commonwealth
Edu	Educational
EL	Eagle Lion
Ess	Essanay
FBO	Film Booking Offices of America
FN	First National
Fox	Fox Films *or* Twentieth Century-Fox
GRI	Griffith
GPSC	General Publicity and Sales Company
HEH	Hemisphere
HOD	Hodkinson
Lip	Lippert
MGM	Metro-Goldwyn-Mayer
Mon	Monogram
Par	Paramount
PDC	Producers Distributing Corporation
PRC	Producers Releasing Corporation
RC	Robertson-Cole
Rep	Republic
SE	Select
SG	Screen Guild
SHU	Sherman-United
Tif	Tiffany
20th	Twentieth Century
U	Universal
UA	United Artists
Vit	Vitagraph
WB	Warner Brothers
WW	World Wide Pictures

Abie's Irish Rose
—from a play by Anne Nichols.
1928: (Par/Victor Fleming) Jean Hersholt.
1946: (UA/A. Edward Sutherland) Michael Chekov.

About Face
See *Brother Rat.*

Accent on Youth
—from a play by Samson Raphaelson.
1935: (Par/Wesley Ruggles) Herbert Marshall.
1950: *Mr. Music* (Par/ Richard Haydn) Bing Crosby.
1959: *But Not for Me* (Par/Walter Lang) Clark Gable.

Across to Singapore
See *All the Brothers Were Valiant.*

Admirable Crichton, The
—from a play by James M. Barrie.
1918: (British/G. B. Samuelson) Basil Gill.
1919: *Male and Female* (Par/Cecil B. DeMille) Thomas
Meighan.
1934: *We're Not Dressing* (Par/Norman Taurog) Bing
Crosby.
1957: *Paradise Lagoon* (British/Lewis Gilbert) Kenneth
More.

Adventure in Iraq
See *Green Goddess, The.*

Adventure in Manhattan
See *Three Hours.*

Adventure Island
See *Ebb Tide.*

Adventures of Don Juan
See *Don Juan.*

Adventures of Huckleberry Finn, The
See *Huckleberry Finn.*

Adventures of Martin Eden, The
See *Martin Eden.*

Adventures of Robin Hood, The
See *Robin Hood and His Merry Men.*

Adventures of Robinson Crusoe
See *Robinson Crusoe.*

Adventures of Scaramouche, The
See *Scaramouche.*

Adventures of Tom Sawyer, The
See *Tom Sawyer.*

Affair To Remember, An
See *Love Affair.*

After Many Years
—from "Enoch Arden," a poem by Alfred Tennyson.
1908: (Bio/D. W. Griffith) Florence Lawrence.
1911: *Enoch Arden* (Biograph/D. W. Griffith) Wilfred
Lucas.
1914: *Enoch Arden* (British/Percy Nash) Gerald Lawrence.
1915: *Enoch Arden* (Majestic/Christy Cabanne) Wallace
Reid.

Against All Flags
1953: (U/George Sherman) Errol Flynn.
1967: *King's Pirate, The* (U/Don Weis) Doug McClure.

Ah, Wilderness
—from a play by Engene O'Neill.
1935: (MGM/Clarence Brown) Wallace Beery.
1948: *Summer Holiday* (MGM/Rouben Mamoulian) Walter
Huston.

Alaska Seas
See *Spawn of the North.*

Algiers
See *Pepé Le Moko.*

Alias Jimmy Valentine
—from a play by Paul Armstrong.
1915: (World)
1920: (Metro/Maxwell Karger) Bert Lytell.
1929: (MGM/Jack Conway) William Haines.

Alice Adams
—from the novel by Booth Tarkington.
1923: (Encore/Rowland V. Lee) Florence Vidor.
1935: (RKO/George Stevens) Katharine Hepburn.

Alice in Wonderland
—from the novel by Lewis Carroll.
1903: (British/Cecil Hepworth, Percy Stow) May Clark.
1910: *Alice's Adventures in Wonderland* (Edison).
1921: (U.S./W. W. Young).
1931: (U.S./Bud Pollard) Ruth Gilbert.
1933: (Par/Norman McLeod) Charlotte Henry.
1951: (Disney/Animation).
1951: (French/Dallas Bower) Carol Marsh.
1972: *Alice's Adventures in Wonderland* (British/William
Sterling) Fiona Fullerton.

Alice's Adventures in Wonderland
See *Alice in Wonderland.*

All the Brothers Were Valiant
—from the novel by Ben Ames Williams.
1923: (MGM/Irvin V. Willat) Lon Chaney.
1928: *Across to Singapore* (MGM/William Nigh) Ramon
Novarro.
1953: (MGM/Richard Thorpe) Robert Taylor.

Almost Human
  —from "The Bar Sinister," a story by Richard Harding
Davis.
1927: (Pathé/Frank Urson) Vera Reynolds.
1955: *It's a Dog's Life* (MGM/Herman Hoffman)
  Jeff Richards.

Aloma of the South Seas
  —from the play by John B. Hymer and Leroy Clemens.
1926: (Par/Maurice Tourneur) Gilda Gray.
1941: (Par/Alfred Santell) Dorothy Lamour.

Always in My Heart
  See *Daughters Courageous.*

And Then There Were None
  —from the novel by Agatha Christie.
1945: (Fox/Rene Clair) Louis Hayward.
1965: *Ten Little Indians* (British/George Pollock) Hugh
  O'Brian.

1975: *Ten Little Indians* (Talia/Peter Collinson) Oliver
  Reed.

Angel from Texas, An
  See *Butter and Egg Man, The.*

Angel Street
  —from a play by Patrick Hamilton.
1940: (British/Thorold Dickinson) Anton Walbrook.
1944: *Gaslight* (MGM/George Cukor) Charles Boyer.

Animal Kingdom, The
  —from a play by Philip Barry.
1932: (RKO/Edward H. Griffith) Leslie Howard.
1946: *One More Tomorrow* (WB/Peter Godfrey) Ann
  Sheridan.

Anna and the King of Siam
  —from a book by Margaret Landon.
1946: (Fox/John Cromwell) Irene Dunne.
1956: *King and I, The* (Fox/Walter Lang) Yul Brynner.

Anything Goes (1936): Bing Crosby and Ethel Merman. Crosby also starred in
the 1956 version.

Anna Christie
—from a play by Eugene O'Neill.
1923: (FN/John G. Wray) Blanche Sweet.
1930: (MGM/Clarence Brown) Greta Garbo.

Anna Karenina
—from the novel by Leo Tolstoy.
1911: (French)
1911: (French)
1914: (Russian)
1915: (Fox/J. Gordon Edwards)
1928: *Love* (MGM/Edmund Goulding) Greta Garbo.
1934: (French)
1935: (MGM/Clarence Brown) Greta Garbo.
1948: (Fox/Julien Duvivier) Vivien Leigh.
1971: (Russian/Alexander Zarkhi) Tatyana Samoilova.
1976: Remake announced to star Sophia Loren.

Anna Lucasta
—from a play by Philip Yordan.
1949: (Col/Irving Rapper) Paulette Goddard.
1958: (UA/Arnold Laven) Eartha Kitt.

Anne of Green Gables
—from a novel by L. M. Montgomery.
1919: (Realart/Wm. Desmond Taylor) Mary Miles Minter.
1934: (RKO/George Nicholls, Jr.) Anne Shirley.

Anything Goes
—from a play by Howard Lindsay and Russel Crouse.
1936: (Par/Lewis Milestone) Bing Crosby.
1956: (Par/Robert Lewis) Bing Crosby.

Apache Trail
—from "Stage Station," a story by Ernest Haycox.
1942: (MGM/Richard Thorpe) Lloyd Nolan.
1952: *Apache War Smoke* (MGM/Harold F. Kress) Gilbert Roland.

Apache War Smoke
See *Apache Trail.*

April Love
See *Home in Indiana.*

Arab, The
—from a play by Edgar Selwyn.
1915: (Par/Cecil B. DeMille) Edgar Selwyn.
1924: (MGM/Rex Ingram) Ramon Novarro.
1933: *Barbarian, The* (MGM/Sam Wood) Ramon Novarro.

Arms and the Man
See *Chocolate Soldier, The* (1).

Arsene Lupin
—from a play by Maurice Le Blanc and Francis de Crosset.

1916: (British/George L. Tucker) Gerald Ames.
1917: (Vit/Paul Scardon) Earle Williams.
1932: (MGM/Jack Conway) John Barrymore.

As No Man Has Loved
See *Man Without a Country, The.*

Asphalt Jungle, The
—from a novel by W. R. Burnett.
1950: (MGM/John Huston) Sterling Hayden.
1958: *Badlanders, The* (MGM/Delmer Daves) Alan Ladd.
1962: *Cairo* (MGM/Wolf Rilla) George Sanders.

As You Like It
—from the play by William Shakespeare.
1908: (Kalem).
1912: (Vit) Maurice Costello.
1915: *Love in a Wood* (British/Maurice Elvey) Elizabeth Risdon.
1936: (British/Paul Czinner) Laurence Olivier.

Auntie Mame
—from a play by Jerome Lawrence and Robert E. Lee, adapted from the novel by Patrick Dennis.
1958: (WB/Morton DaCosta) Rosalind Russell.
1974: *Mame* (WB/Gene Saks) Lucille Ball.

Avenging Conscience, The
—from "The Tell-Tale Heart," a story by Edgar Allan Poe.
1914: (Mutual/D. W. Griffith) Henry B. Walthall.
1934: *Bucket of Blood* (British/Brian Desmond Hurst) Norman Dryden.
1941: *Tell-Tale Heart, The* (MGM short/Jules Dassin) Joseph Schildkraut.
1953: *Tell-Tale Heart, The* (British short/J. B. Williams) Stanley Baker.
1960: *Tell-Tale Heart, The* (British/Ernest Morris) Laurence Payne.

Awful Truth, The
—from a play by Arthur Richman.
1925: (PDC/Paul Powell) Warner Baxter.
1929: (Pathé/Marshall Neilan) Ina Claire.
1937: (Col/Leo McCarey) Cary Grant.
1953: *Let's Do It Again* (Col/Alexander Hall) Ray Milland.

Babbitt
—from the book by Sinclair Lewis.
1924: (WB/Harry Beaumont) Willard Louis.
1934: (FN/William Keighley) Guy Kibbee.

Babes in Toyland
—from the operetta by Victor Herbert.
1934: (MGM/Gus Meins, Charles R. Rogers) Laurel and Hardy.
1961: (Disney/Jack Donohue) Ray Bolger.

Baby Mine
—from a play by Margaret Mayo.
1917: (MGM/John S. Robertson, Hugo Ballin) Madge Kennedy.
1928: (MGM/Robert Z. Leonard) Karl Dane.

Bachelor Mother
1939: (RKO/Garson Kanin) Ginger Rogers.
1956: *Bundle of Joy* (RKO/Norman Taurog) Debbie Reynolds.

Back from Eternity
See *Five Came Back.*

Back Street
—from a novel by Fannie Hurst.
1932: (U/John M. Stahl) Irene Dunne.
1941: (U/Robert Stevenson) Charles Boyer.
1961: (U/David Miller) Susan Hayward.

Back to God's Country
—from the story by James Oliver Curwood.

1919: (FN/David M. Hartford) Nell Shipman.
1927: (U/Irvin Willat) Renee Adoreé
1953: (U/Joseph Pevney) Rock Hudson.

Bad Day at Black Rock
—from "Bad Time at Hondo," a story by Howard Breslin.
1954: (MGM/John Sturges) Spencer Tracy.
1960: *Platinum High School* (MGM/Charles Haas) Mickey Rooney.

Badlanders, The
See *Asphalt Jungle, The.*

Bad Man, The
—from the story by Porter Emerson Brown and C. H. Towne.
1923: (FN/Edwin Carewe) Enid Bennett.
1930: (FN/Clarence Badger) Walter Huston.
1937: *West of Shanghai* (FN/John Farrow) Boris Karloff.
1941: (MGM/Richard Thorpe) Wallace Beery.

Ballet of Romeo and Juliet, The
See *Romeo and Juliet.*

The Barretts of Wimpole Street (**1934**): **Fredric March and Norma Shearer.**

Ball of Fire
1941: (RKO/Howard Hawks) Gary Cooper.
1948: *Song Is Born, A* (RKO/Howard Hawks) Danny Kaye.

Barbarian, The
See *Arab, The.*

Barker, The
—from a play by John Kenyon Nicholson.
1928: (FN/George Fitzmaurice) Milton Sills.
1933: *Hoop-La* (Fox/Frank Lloyd) Clara Bow.
1945: *Billy Rose's Diamond Horseshoe* (Fox/George Seaton) Betty Grable.

Barretts of Wimpole Street, The
—from a play by Rudolph Besier.
1934: (MGM/Sidney Franklin) Norma Shearer.
1957: (MGM/Sidney Franklin) Jennifer Jones.

Bat, The
See *Circular Staircase, The.*

Bat Whispers, The
See *Circular Staircase, The.*

Beachcomber, The
—from "Vessel of Wrath," a story by W. Somerset Maugham.
1938: (Par/Erich Pommer) Charles Laughton.
1955: (UA/Muriel Box) Robert Newton.

Beau Brummell
—from a play by Clyde Fitch.
1924: (WB/Harry Beaumont) John Barrymore.
1954: (MGM/Curtis Bernhardt) Stewart Granger.

Beau Geste
—from a novel by P. C. Wren.
1926: (Par/Herbert Brenon) Ronald Colman.
1939: (Par/William Wellman) Gary Cooper.
1966: (U/Douglas Hayes) Guy Stockwell.

Becky Sharp
See *Vanity Fair.*

Beggar's Opera, The
See *Dreigroschenoper, Die.*

Bel Ami
—from a story by Guy de Maupassant.
1938: (German/Willi Forst) Olga Techechowa.
1947: *Private Affairs of Bel Ami, The* (UA/Albert Lewin) George Sanders.

Beloved Vagabond, The
—from a novel by William J. Locke.
1916: (French)

1923: (British/Fred Leroy Granville) Carlyle Blackwell.
1936: (Col/Kurt Bernhardt) Maurice Chevalier.

Berkeley Square
—from a play by John Balderston.
1933: (Fox/Frank Lloyd) Leslie Howard.
1951: *I'll Never Forget You* (Fox/Roy Baker) Tyrone Power.

Best Man Wins, The
See *Jumping Frog, The.*

Between Two Worlds
See *Outward Bound.*

Big Operator, The
See *Joe Smith, American.*

Bill of Divorcement, A
—from the play by Clemence Dane.
1922: (British/Denison Clift) Fay Compton.
1932: (RKO/George Cukor) John Barrymore.
1940: (RKO/John Farrow) Maureen O'Hara.

Billy's Rose's Diamond Horseshoe
See *Barker, The.*

Billy the Kid
—from *The Saga of Billy the Kid,* a novel by Walter Noble Burns.
1930: (MGM/King Vidor) Wallace Beery.
1941: (MGM/David Miller) Robert Taylor.

Bird of Paradise
1932: (RKO/King Vidor) Joel McCrea.
1951: (RKO/Delmer Daves) Louis Jourdan.

Birds and the Bees, The
See *Lady Eve, The.*

Biscuit Eater, The
—from a story by James Street.
1940: (Par/Stuart Heisler) Billy Lee.
1972: (Disney/Vincent McEveety) Earl Holliman.

Bittersweet
—from an operetta by Noel Coward.
1933: (British/Herbert Wilcox) Anna Neagle.
1940: (MGM/W. S. Van Dyke II) Nelson Eddy.

Black Arrow, The
—from the novel by Robert Louis Stevenson.
1912: (Edison).
1948: (Col/Gordon Douglas) Louis Hayward.

Black Beauty
—from the novel by Anna Sewell.
1906: (British/Lewin Fitzhamon) Lewin Fitzhamon.

Blind Alley (1939): **Ralph Bellamy, Chester Morris, and Ann Dvorak.**

The Dark Past (1948): **William Holden and Lee J. Cobb.**

1910: (British/Lewin Fitzhamon) Lewin Fitzhamon.

1917: *Your Obedient Servant* (Edison/Edward H. Griffith)

1921: (Vit/David Smith) Jean Paige.

1933: (Mon/Phil Rosen) Esther Ralston.

1946: (Fox/Max Nosseck) Mona Freeman.

1957: *Courage of Black Beauty* (Fox/Harold Schuster) John Crawford.

1971: (Par/James Hill) Mark Lester.

Black Cat, The
See *Living Dead, The.*

Black Watch, The
—from *King of the Khyber Rifles,* a novel by Talbot Mundy.

1929: (Fox/John Ford) Victor McLaglen.

1953: *King of the Khyber Rifles* (Fox/Henry King) Tyrone Power.

Blind Alley
—from a play by James Warwick.

1939: (Col/Charles Vidor) Chester Morris.

1948: *Dark Past, The* (Col/Rudolph Mate) William Holden.

Blonde Trouble
See *June Moon.*

Blood and Sand
—from a novel by Vicente Blasco-Ibanez.

1922: (Par/Fred Niblo) Rudolph Valentino.

1941: (Fox/Rouben Mamoulian) Tyrone Power.

Blowing Wild
See *Bordertown.*

Bluebeard
1901: (France).

1909: (Edison).

1944: (PRC/Edgar G. Ulmer) John Carradine.

1960: *Bluebeard's Ten Honeymoons* (AA/Lee Wilder) George Sanders.

1963: (French/Claude Chabrol) Charles Denner.

1972: (Cinerama/Edward Dmytryk) Richard Burton.

Bluebeard's Eighth Wife
—from a play by Alfred Savoir.

1923: (Par/Sam Wood) Gloria Swanson.

1938: (Par/Ernst Lubitsch) Gary Cooper.

Bluebeard's Ten Honeymoons
See *Bluebeard.*

Blue Bird, The
—from a play by Maurice Maeterlinck.

1910: (British) Pauline Gilmer.

1918: (Par/Maurice Tourneur) Tula Belle.

1940: (Fox/Walter Lang) Shirley Temple.

1976: (Fox/George Cukor) Elizabeth Taylor.

Body and Soul
1947: (UA/Robert Rossen) John Garfield.

1975: (Par) Remake announced.

Border Legion, The
—from a novel by Zane Grey.

1919: (Goldwyn/T. Hayes Hunter) Hobart Bosworth.

1924: (Par/William K. Howard) Antonio Moreno.

1930: (Par/Otto Brower, Edwin H. Knopf) Richard Arlen.

1934: *Last Round-Up, The* (Par/Henry Hathaway) Randolph Scott.

1940: (Rep/Joseph Kane) Roy Rogers.

Bordertown
1935: (WB/Archie Mayo) Paul Muni.

1940: *They Drive by Night* (WB/Raoul Walsh) George Raft.

1953: *Blowing Wild* (WB/Hugo Fregonese) Gary Cooper.

Born to the West
—from a novel by Zane Grey.

1926: (Par/John Waters) Jack Holt.

1937: (Par/Charles Barton) John Wayne.

Boy of Flanders, A
—from *A Dog of Flanders,* a novel by Ouida.

1924: (MGM/Victor Schertzinger) Jackie Coogan.

1935: *Dog of Flanders, A* (RKO/Edward Sloman) Frankie Thomas.

1959: *Dog of Flanders, A* (Fox/James B. Clark) David Ladd.

Brain, The
See *Lady and the Monster, The.*

Brasher Doubloon, The
See *Time To Kill.*

Breaking Point, The
See *To Have and Have Not.*

Breath of Scandal, A
See *His Glorious Night.*

Brewster's Millions
—from a novel by George Barr McCutcheon and a play by Winchell Smith and Byron Ongley.

1914: (Par/Oscar C. Apfel) Edward Abeles.

1921: (Par/Joseph Henabery) Fatty Arbuckle.

1926: *Miss Brewster's Millions* (Par/Clarence Badger) Bebe Daniels.

1935: (British/Thornton Freeland) Jack Buchanan.

1945: (UA/Allan Dwan) Dennis O'Keefe.

1961: *Three on a Spree* (British/Sidney J. Furie) Jack Watling.

Bridge of San Luis Rey, The
—from the novel by Thornton Wilder.

1929: (MGM/Charles Brabin) Lily Damita.

1944: (UA/Rowland V. Lee) Lynn Bari.

British Intelligence
See *Three Faces East*.

Broadway
—from a play by Philip Dunning and George Abbott.
1929: (U/Paul Fejos) Glenn Tryon.
1942: (U/William A. Seiter) George Raft.

Broadway Bill
—from a story by Mark Hellinger.
1934: (Col/Frank Capra) Warner Baxter.
1950: *Riding High* (Par/Frank Capra) Bing Crosby.

Broken Blossoms
—from "The Chink and the Child," a story by Thomas Burke.
1919: (GRI/D. W. Griffith) Richard Barthelmess.
1936: (British/Hans Brahm) Emlyn Williams.

Broncho Billy and the Baby
—from the story by Peter B. Kyne.
1909: (Ess) G. M. Anderson.
1916: *Three Godfathers* (Bluebird/Edward J. LeSaint) Harry Carey.
1920: *Marked Men* (U/John Ford) Harry Carey.
1929: *Hell's Heroes* (U/William Wyler) Charles Bickford.
1936: *Three Godfathers* (MGM/Richard Boleslawski) Chester Morris.
1948: *Three Godfathers* (MGM/John Ford) John Wayne.

Brother Rat
—from a play by Fred Finklehoff and John Monks.
1938: (WB/William Keighley) Wayne Morris.
1952: *About Face* (WB/Roy Del Ruth) Gordon MacRae.

Brothers Karamazov, The
See *Karamazov*.

Buccaneer, The
—from *Lafitte, the Pirate*, a novel by Lyle Saxon.
1938: (Par/Cecil B. DeMille) Fredric March.
1958: (Par/Anthony Quinn) Yul Brynner.

Bucket of Blood
See *Avenging Conscience, The*.

Bulldog Drummond
—from a play by Sapper.
1923: (British/Oscar Apfel) Carlyle Blackwell.
1929: (Goldwyn/F. Richard Jones) Ronald Colman.

Bulldog Drummond's Peril
See *Bulldog Drummond's Third Round*.

Bulldog Drummond's Third Round
—from *The Third Round*, a novel by Sapper.
1925: (British/Sidney Morgan) Jack Buchanan.

1938: *Bulldog Drummond's Peril* (Par/James Hogan) John Barrymore.

Bulldog Drummond Strikes Back
—from a novel by Sapper.
1934: (UA/Roy Del Ruth) Ronald Colman.
1947: (Col/Frank McDonald) Ron Randell.

Bullets for O'Hara
See *Public Enemy's Wife*.

Bundle of Joy
See *Bachelor Mother*.

Burlesque on Carmen
See *Carmen*.

But Not for Me
See *Accent on Youth*.

Butter and Egg Man, The
—from a play by George S. Kaufman.
1928: (FN/Richard Wallace) Jack Mulhall.
1932: *Tenderfoot, The* (FN/Ray Enright) Joe E. Brown.
1937: *Dance, Charlie, Dance* (FN/Frank McDonald) Stuart Erwin.
1940: *Angel from Texas, An* (FN/Ray Enright) Eddie Albert.
1953: *Three Sailors and a Girl* (WB/Roy Del Ruth) Gordon MacRae.

Cabaret
See *I Am a Camera*.

Cabinet of Caligari, The
See *Cabinet of Doctor Caligari, The*.

Cabinet of Doctor Caligari, The
1919: (German/Robert Wiene) Conrad Veidt.
1962: *Cabinet of Caligari, The* (Fox/Roger Kay) Dan O'Herlihy.

Caged
—from "Women Without Men," a story by Virginia Kellogg and Bernard Schoenfeld.
1950: (WB/John Cromwell) Eleanor Parker.
1962: *House of Women* (WB/Walter Doniger) Shirley Knight.

Cain and Mabel
See *Great White Way, The*.

Cairo
See *Asphalt Jungle, The*.

Calling Philo Vance
See *Kennel Murder Case, The*.

Call of the North, The
—from *Conjuror's House,* a novel by Stewart Edward White.
1914: (Par/Cecil B. DeMille) Robert Edeson.
1921: (Par/Joseph Henabery) Jack Holt.

Call of the Wild, The
—from the novel by Jack London.
1923: (Pathé/Fred Jackman) Jack Mulhall.
1935: (UA/William Wellman) Clark Gable.

Cameo Kirby
—from a play by Booth Tarkington and Harry Leon Wilson.
1914: (Par) Dustin Farnum.
1923: (Fox/John Ford) John Gilbert.
1930: (Fox/Irving Cummings) J. Harold Murray.

Cameraman, The
1928: (MGM/Edward Sedgwick) Buster Keaton.
1950: *Watch the Birdie* (MGM/Jack Donohue) Red Skelton.

Camille
See *Lady with the Camellias, The.*

Camille 2000
See *Lady with the Camellias, The.*

Captain Applejack
See *Strangers of the Night.*

Captain Blood
—from the novel by Rafael Sabatini.
1924: (Vit/David Smith) J. Warren Kerrigan.
1935: (FN/Michael Curtiz) Errol Flynn.
1950: *Fortunes of Captain Blood* (Col/Gordon Douglas) Louis Hayward.
1975: (UA) Remake announced.

Cameo Kirby (1923): Alan Hale and John Gilbert.

Cardboard Lover, The
—from a play by Jacques Deval.
1928: (MGM/Robert Z. Leonard) Marion Davies.
1932: *Passionate Plumber, The* (MGM/Edward Sedgwick) Buster Keaton.
1942: *Her Cardboard Lover* (MGM/George Cukor) Norma Shearer.

Cardinal Richelieu
See *Richelieu.*

Cardinal's Edict, The
See *Richelieu.*

Carmen
—from a story by Prosper Mérimée.
1910: (Spanish) MIle. Victoria Lepanto.
1912: (Feature Film Sales).
1913: (Monopol) Marion Leonard.
1914: (Spanish).
1915: (Fox/Raoul Walsh) Theda Bara.
1915: (Par/Cecil B. DeMille) Geraldine Farrar.
1916: *Burlesque on Carmen* (Ess/Charles Chaplin) Charlie Chaplin.
1918: *Gypsy Blood* (German/Ernst Lubitsch) Pola Negri.
1922: (British/George Wynn) Patricia Fitzgerald.
1926: (France).
1927: *Loves of Carmen, The* (Fox/Raoul Walsh) Dolores del Rio.
1927: (British/H. B. Parkinson) Zeda Pascha.
1931: (British/Cecil Lewis) Marguerite Namara.
1932: *Idol of Seville, The* (Edu/Howard Higgin)
1933: (German animation/Lotte Reiniger).
1940: (Spanish).
1942: (French/Christian Jaque) Vivianne Romance.

Cameo Kirby (1914): Dustin Farnum.

1948: *Loves of Carmen, The* (Col/Charles Vidor) Rita Hayworth.
1954: *Carmen Jones* (Fox/Otto Preminger) Dorothy Dandridge.
1967: *Carmen Baby* (Aud/Radley Metzger) Uta Levka.

Carmen Baby
　See *Carmen.*

Carmen Jones
　See *Carmen.*

Carousel
　See *Trip to Paradise, A.*

Casbah
　See *Pepé Le Moko.*

Castle on the Hudson
　See *Twenty-Thousand Years in Sing Sing.*

Cat and the Canary, The
　—from a play by John Willard.
1927: (U/Paul Leni) Laura La Plante.
1930: *Cat Creeps, The* (U/Rupert Julian) Helen Twelvetrees.
1939: (Par/Elliott Nugent) Bob Hope.

Cat Creeps, The
　See *Cat and the Canary, The.*

Ceiling Zero
　—from a play by Frank Wead.
1936: (FN/Howard Hawks) James Cagney.
1941: *International Squadron* (WB/Lothar Mendes) Ronald Reagan.

Challenge to Lassie
　—from *Greyfriars Bobby,* a novel by Eleanor Atkinson.
1949: (MGM/Richard Thorpe) Edmund Gwenn.
1961: *Greyfriars Bobby* (Disney/Don Chaffey) Donald Crisp.

Charge of the Light Brigade, The
　—from the poem by Alfred Tennyson.
1912: (Edison/J. Searle Dawley).
1936: (WB/Michael Curtiz) Errol Flynn.
1968: (British/Tony Richardson) David Hemmings.

Charley's Aunt
　—from the play by Brandon Thomas.
1925: (PDC/Scott Sidney) Sydney Chaplin.
1930: (Col/Al Christie) Charles Ruggles.
1940: (British/Walter Forde) Arthur Askey.
1941: (Fox/Archie Mayo) Jack Benny.
1951: *Where's Charley* (WB/David Butler) Ray Bolger.
1956: (German).

Cheat, The
1915: (Par/Cecil B. DeMille) Fannie Ward.
1923: (Par/George Fitzmaurice) Pola Negri.
1931: (Par/George Abbott) Tallulah Bankhead.
1937: (French/Marcel L'Herbier).

Cheating Cheaters
　—from the play by Max Marcin.
1919: (SE/Allan Dwan) Clara Kimball Young.
1927: (U/Edward Laemmle) Betty Compson.
1934: (U/Richard Thorpe) Fay Wray.

Chicago
　—from a play by Maurine Watkins.
1927: (Pathé/Frank Urson) Phyllis Haver.
1942: *Roxie Hart* (Fox/William Wellman) Ginger Rogers.

Child Is Born, A
　See *Life Begins.*

Children's Hour, The
　See *These Three.*

Chocolate Soldier, The (1)
　—from *Arms and the Man,* a play by G. B. Shaw.
1914: (U.S./Walter Morton).
1932: *Arms and the Man* (British/Cecil Lewis) Barry Jones.
1938: *Arms and the Man* (German).
1962: *Arms and the Man.* (German/Franz Peter Wirth) O. W. Fischer.

Chocolate Soldier, The (2)
　See *Guardsman, The.*

Christian, The
　—from the novel by Hall Caine.
1914: (Vit/Frederick Thomson) Earle Williams.
1923: (Goldwyn/Maurice Tourneur) Richard Dix.

Christmas Carol, A
　See *Scrooge.*

Cimarron
　—from a novel by Edna Ferber.
1931: (RKO/Wesley Ruggles) Richard Dix.
1960: (MGM/Anthony Mann) Glenn Ford.

Cinderella
　See *Cinderella and the Fairy Godmother.*

Cinderella and the Fairy Godmother
　—from the fairy tale by the Brothers Grimm.
1898: (British/G. A. Smith) Laura Bayley.
1899: *Cinderella* (French).
1907: *Cinderella* (British/Lewin Fitzhamon) Dolly Lupone.
1909: *Cinderella* (Italian).

1911: *Cinderella* (Selig/Colin Campbell) Mabel Taliaferro.
1911: *Cinderella* (Thanhouser).
1914: *Cinderella* (Par/James Kirkwood) Mary Pickford.
1918: *Cinderella and the Magic Slipper* (Wholesome).
1923: *Verlorene Schuh, Der* (German/Ludwig Berger) Mady Christians.
1949: *Cinderella* (Disney/Animation).
1955: *Glass Slipper, The* (MGM/Charles Walters) Leslie Caron.
1960: *Cinderfella* (Par/Frank Tashlin) Jerry Lewis.
1960: *Cinderella* (Russian) Bolshoi Ballet.
1976: Remake announced.

Cinderella and the Magic Slipper
See *Cinderella and the Fairy Godmother*.

Cinderfella
See *Cinderella and the Fairy Godmother*.

Circular Staircase, The
—from a novel by Mary Roberts Rinehart.
1915: (Selig/Edward J. Le Saint).
1926: *Bat, The* (Feature/Roland West) Louise Fazenda.
1930: *Bat Whispers, The* (Art/Roland West) Chester Morris.
1959: *Bat, The* (AA/Crane Wilbur) Vincent Price.

Circus Days
—from *Toby Tyler*, a novel by James Otis Kaler.
1923: (FN/Eddie Cline) Jackie Coogan.
1960: *Toby Tyler* (Disney/Charles Barton) Kevin Corcoran.

Claw, The
—from a book by Cynthia Stockley.
1918: (SE/Robert G. Vignola) Milton Sills.
1927: (U/Sidney Olcott) Norman Kerry.

Cleopatra
1912: (Gardner/Charles Gaskill) Helen Gardner.
1917: (Fox/J. Gordon Edwards) Theda Bara.
1934: (Par/Cecil B. DeMille) Claudette Colbert.
1963: (Fox/Joseph E. Mankiewicz) Elizabeth Taylor.

Climax, The
—from a play by Edward Locke.
1930: (U/Renaud Hoffman) Jean Hersholt.
1944: (U/George Waggner) Boris Karloff.

Code of the West
—from the novel by Zane Grey.
1925: (Par/William K. Howard) Owen Moore.
1934: *Home on the Range* (Par/Arthur Jacobson) Randolph Scott.
1947: (RKO/William Berke) James Warren.

Cleopatra (1917): Fritz Leiber and Theda Bara.

Cleopatra (1934): Henry Wilcoxon and Claudette Colbert.

Cleopatra (1963): Richard Burton and Elizabeth Taylor.

College Widow, The
  —from a play by George Ade.
1915: (Lubin) Ethel Clayton.
1927: (WB/John F. Dillon) Dolores Costello.
1936: *Freshman Love* (WB/William McGann) Frank Mc-
    Hugh.

Color Me Dead
  See *D. O. A.*

Common Clay
  —from a play by Cleves Kinkead.
1919: (Pathé/George Fitzmaurice) Fannie Ward.
1930: (Fox/Victor Fleming) Lew Ayres.
1936: *Private Number* (Fox/Roy Del Ruth) Robert Taylor.

Conde de Monte Cristo, El
  See *Count of Monte Cristo, The.*

Coney Island
1943   (Fox/Walter Lang) Betty Grable.
1950: *Wabash Avenue* (Fox/Henry Koster) Betty Grable.

Connecticut Yankee, A
  See *Connecticut Yankee in King Arthur's Court, A.*

Connecticut Yankee in King Arthur's Court, A
  —from the novel by Mark Twain.
1921: (Fox/Emmett J. Flynn) Harry Myers.
1931: *Connecticut Yankee, A* (Fox/David Butler) Will
    Rogers.
1949: *Connecticut Yankee, A* (Par/Tay Garnett) Bing
    Crosby.

Constant Nymph, The
  —from the novel by Margaret Kennedy.
1928: (British/Adrian Brunel) Ivor Novello.
1934: (British/Basil Dean) Brian Aherne.
1943: (WB/Edmund Goulding) Charles Boyer.

Convicted
  See *Criminal Code, The.*

Cool Mikado, The
  See *Fan-Fan.*

Corbeau, Le
1948: (French/H. G. Clouzot) Pierre Fresnay.
1951: *Thirteenth Letter, The* (Fox/Otto Preminger) Linda
    Darnell.

Corsican Brothers, The
  —from the novel by Alexandre Dumas.
1898: (British/G. A. Smith).
1902: (British/Dicky Winslow) A. W. Fitzgerald.
1908: (U.S.).
1912: (Edison).

1915: (U) King Baggot.
1919: (United) Dustin Farnum.
1941: (UA/Gregory Ratoff) Douglas Fairbanks, Jr.
1960: (French) Geoffrey Horne.
1976: Remake announced.

Count Dracula
  See *Nosferatu.*

Count of Monte Cristo, The
  —from the novel by Alexandre Dumas.
1908: (Selig/Francis Boggs).
1910: (Challenge).
1911: (Powers).
1912: (Selig/Colin Campbell) Hobart Bosworth.
1912: (Par/Edwin S. Porter) James O'Neill.
1915: (Italian).
1917: *Monte Cristo* (French).
1922: *Monte Cristo* (Fox/Emmett J. Flynn) John Gilbert.
1934: (UA/Rowland V. Lee) Robert Donat.
1943: *Conde de Monte Cristo, El* (Mexican/Chano Urueta)
    Arturo de Cordova.
1954: (French/Robert Vernay) Jean Marais.
1955: (French) Pierre Wilm.
1961: *Story of the Count of Monte Cristo, The* (French/
    Claude Autant-Lara) Louis Jourdan.
1975: (ITC/David Greene) Richard Chamberlain.

The Count of Monte Cristo (**1934**): Robert **Donat.**

Courage of Black Beauty
  See *Black Beauty.*

Cowboy Quarterback, The
  See *Fast Company.*

Craig's Wife
  —from a play by George Kelly.
1928: (Pathé/William DeMille) Irene Rich.
1934: (Col/Dorothy Arzner) Rosalind Russell.
1950: *Harriet Craig* (Col/Vincent Sherman) Joan Crawford.

Creation Can't Be Bought
See *Martin Eden.*

Cricket on the Hearth, The
—from the story by Charles Dickens.
1909: (Bio/D. W. Griffith) Owen Moore.
1914: (Bio) Alan Hale.
1915: (Russian).
1923: (Selznick/Lorimer Johnston) Josef Swickard.

Crime and Punishment
—from a novel by Fyodor Dostoyevsky.
1913: (Russian).
1917: (Pathé) Derwent Hall Caine.
1922: (Russian).
1923: *Raskolnikov* (German/Robert Wiene) Grigori Khmara.
1926: (Russian).
1929: (M. J. Gourland).
1935: (France/Pierre Chenal) Harry Baur.
1935: (Col/Josef von Sternberg) Peter Lorre.
1946: *Fear* (Mon/Alfred Zeisler) Peter Cookson.
1948: (Swedish/Hampe Faustman) Hampe Faustman.
1958: *Most Dangerous Sin, The* (French/Georges Lampin) Jean Gabin.
1959: *Crime and Punishment USA* (AA/Denis Sanders) George Hamilton.

Crime and Punishment USA
See *Crime and Punishment.*

Crime School
See *Mayor of Hell, The.*

Criminal Code, The
—from a play by Martin Flavin.
1931: (Col/Howard Hawks) Walter Huston.
1938: *Penitentiary* (Col/John Brahm) Walter Connolly.
1950: *Convicted* (Col/Henry Levin) Broderick Crawford.

Crowd Roars, The (1)
1932: (WB/Howard Hawks) James Cagney.
1939: *Indianapolis Speedway* (WB/Lloyd Bacon) Ann Sheridan.

Crowd Roars, The (2)
1938: (MGM/Richard Thorpe) Robert Taylor.
1947: *Killer McCoy* (MGM/Roy Rowland) Mickey Rooney.

Curse of Frankenstein, The
See *Frankenstein.*

Cyrano de Bergerac
See *Cyrano de Bergerac's Adventures.*

Cyrano de Bergerac's Adventures
—from the play by Edmond Rostand.

1909: (French)
1925: *Cyrano de Bergerac* (Italian/Agusto Genina) Pierre Magnier.
1946: *Cyrano de Bergerac* (French).
1950: *Cyrano de Bergerac* (UA/Michael Gordon) Jose Ferrer.
1976: *Cyrano de Bergerac* (Italian) Remake announced.

Daddy Long Legs
—from a play by Jean Webster.
1919: (FN/Marshall Neilan) Mary Pickford.
1931: (Fox/Alfred Santell) Janet Gaynor.
1955: (Fox/Jean Negulesco) Fred Astaire.

Dama de las Camelias, La
See *Lady with the Camellias, The.*

Dame aux Camilias, La
See *Lady with the Camellias, The.*

Damnation of Faust, The
See *Faust and Mephistopheles.*

Dance, Charlie, Dance
See *Butter and Egg Man, The.*

Dance of Life, The
—from *Burlesque*, a play by George Manker and Arthur Hopkins.
1929: (Par/John Cromwell, Edward Sutherland) Nancy Carroll.
1937: *Swing High, Swing Low* (Par/Mitchell Leisen) Carole Lombard.
1948: *When My Baby Smiles at Me* (Fox/Walter Lang) Betty Grable.

Dangerous
1935: (WB/Alfred E. Green) Bette Davis.
1941: *Singapore Woman* (WB/Jean Negulesco) Brenda Marshall.

Dangerous Paradise
See *Victory.*

Dante's Inferno
—inspired by Dante's epic poem.
1911: (Italian).
1924: (Fox/Henry Otto) Ralph Lewis.
1935: (Fox/Harry Lachman) Spencer Tracy.

Dark Hazard
—from a novel by W. R. Burnett.
1934: (FN/Alfred E. Green) Edward G. Robinson.
1937: *Wine, Women, and Horses* (WB/Louis King) Barton MacLane.

Dark Past, The
See *Blind Alley.*

Dark Victory (1939): George Brent, Geraldine Fitzgerald, and Bette Davis.

Dark Victory
 —from a play by George Brewer, Jr., and Bertram
  Bloch.
1939: (FN/Edmund Goulding) Bette Davis.
1963: *Stolen Hours* (UA/Daniel Petrie) Susan Hayward.

D'Artagnan
 See *Three Musketeers, The.*

Daughters Courageous
 —from *Fly Away Home*, a play by Dorothy Bennett and
  Irving White.
1939: (FN/Michael Curtiz) John Garfield.
1942: *Always in My Heart* (WB/Joe Graham) Walter Huston.

David and Goliath
1908: (Kalem).
1961: (Italian/Richard Pottier) Orson Welles.

Stolen Hours (1963): Edward Judd and Susan Hayward.

David Copperfield
 —from the novel by Charles Dickens.
1911: (Thanhouser).

The Dawn Patrol (1930): **James Finlayson and Richard Barthelmess.**

The Dawn Patrol (1938): **Errol Flynn.**

1912: (French).
1913: (British/Thomas Bentley) Eric Desmond.
1935: (MGM/George Cukor) W. C. Fields.
1969: (British/Daniel Mann) Ralph Richardson.

David Harum
—from a novel by Edward Noyes.
1915: (Famous Players) William H. Crane.
1934: (Fox/James Cruze) Will Rogers.

Dawn Patrol, The
1930: (FN/Howard Hawks) Richard Barthelmess.
1938: (WB/Edmund Goulding) Errol Flynn.

Decameron Nights
—from the stories by Giovanni Boccaccio.
1924: (British/Herbert Wilcox) Lionel Barrymore.
1928: (German).
1953: (RKO/Hugo Fregonese) Joan Fontaine.

Deerslayer, The
—from the novel by James Fenimore Cooper.
1913: (Vit) Wallace Reid.
1923: (Cameo).
1943: (Rep/Lew Landers) Bruce Kellogg.
1957: (Fox/Kurt Neumann) Lex Barker.

Desert Song, The
—from the operetta by Lawrence Schwab, Otto Harbach, Frank Mandel, Oscar Hammerstein II, and Sigmund Romberg.
1929: (WB/Roy Del Ruth) John Boles.
1932: *Red Shadow, The* (WB short/Alf Goulding) Alexander Gray.
1943: (WB/Robert Florey) Dennis Morgan.
1953: (WB/Bruce Humberstone) Gordon MacRae.

Dillinger
1945: (Mon/Max Nosseck) Lawrence Tierney.
1973: (AIP/John Milius) Warren Oates.

Disraeli
—from the play by Louis N. Parker.
1916: (British/Percy Nash, Charles Calvert) Dennis Eadie.
1921: (UA/Henry Volker) George Arliss.
1929: (WB/Alfred E. Green) George Arliss.

D. O. A.
1949: (UA/Rudolph Mate) Edmond O'Brien.
1969: *Color Me Dead* (CW/Eddie Davis) Tom Tryon.

Dog of Flanders, A
See *Boy of Flanders, A.*

Dolls House, A
—from a play by Henrick Ibsen.
1911: (Thanhouser).

1917: (U).
1917: *Her Sacrifice* (Russian).
1918: (Par/Maurice Tourneur) Elsie Ferguson.
1922: (UA/Charles Bryant) Alla Nazimova.
1944: *Nora* (German).
1973: (Par/Patrick Garland) Claire Bloom.
1973: (British/Joseph Losey) Jane Fonda.

Don Juan
1926: (WB/Alan Crosland) John Barrymore.
1949: *Adventures of Don Juan* (WB/Vincent Sherman) Errol Flynn.

Donovan's Brain
See *Lady and the Monster, The.*

Don Quixote
—from the novel by Cervantes.
1908: (French/George Méliés).
1909: (French).
1915: (Triangle/Edward Dillon) De Wolf Hopper.
1923: (British/Maurice Elvey) Jerrold Robertshaw.
1933: (British/G. W. Pabst) Feodor Chaliapin.
1947: (Spanish/Rafael Gil) Rafael Rivelles.
1957: (Russian/Kozintsev) Nikolai Cherkassov.
1962: *Dulcinea* (Spanish).
1972: *Man of La Mancha* (UA/Arthur Hiller) Peter O'Toole.
1973: (Continental/Rudolph Nureyev, Robert Helpmann) Ballet.

Dorian Gray
See *Picture of Dorian Gray, The.*

Dracula
See *Nosferatu.*

Dream of Butterfly, The
See *Madame Butterfly.*

Dream Woman, The
See *Woman in White, The.*

Dreigroschenoper, Die
—from *The Beggar's Opera,* a play by John Gay.
1930: (German/G. W. Pabst) Rudolph Forster.
1953: *Beggar's Opera, The* (WB/Peter Brook) Laurence Olivier.
1963: *Threepenny Opera, The.* (German/Wolfgang Staudte) Curt Jurgens.

Dr. Faustus
See *Faust and Mephistopheles.*

Dr. Praetorius
—from a play by Curt Goetz.
1950: (German).

1951: *People Will Talk* (Fox/Joseph L. Mankiewicz) Cary Grant.

Dr. Socrates
   —from a story by W. R. Burnett.
1935: (WB/William Dieterle) Paul Muni.
1939: *King of the Underworld* (WB/Lewis Seiler) Kay Francis.

Dr. Syn
   —from a novel by Russell Thorndike.
1937: (British/Roy William Neill) George Arliss.
1962: *Night Creatures* (British/Peter Graham Scott) Peter Cushing.
1963: *Dr. Syn—Alias the Scarecrow* (Disney/James Neilson) Patrick McGoohan.

Dr. Syn—Alias the Scarecrow
   See *Dr. Syn.*

Dulcinea
   See *Don Quixote.*

Dulcy
   —from a play by George S. Kaufman and Marc Connelly.
1923: (FN/Sidney Franklin) Constance Talmadge.
1930: *Not so Dumb* (MGM/King Vidor) Marion Davies.
1940: (MGM/Sylvan Simon) Ann Sothern.

Dummy, The
   —from a play by Harvey J. O'Higgins and Harriet Ford.
1917: (Par/Francis J. Grandon) Jack Pickford.
1929: (Par/Robert Milton) Fredric March.

Durand of the Badlands
1917: (Fox/Richard Stanton) Tom Mix.
1925: (Fox/Lynn Reynolds) Buck Jones.

Dust Be My Destiny
   —from a novel by Jerome Odlum.
1939: (FN/Lewis Seiler) John Garfield.
1942: *I Was Framed* (WB/D. Ross Lederman) Michael Ames.

East Is West
   —from a play by Samuel Shipman and John B. Hymer.
1922: (FN/Sidney Franklin) Constance Talmadge.
1930: (U/Monta Bell) Lupe Velez.

East Lynne
   —from a novel and play by Mrs. Henry Wood.
1902: (British/Dicky Winslow) A. W. Fitzgerald.
1908: (Vit).
1910: (British).
1913: (British/Bert Haldane) Blanche Forsythe.
1913: (British/Arthur Charrington) Nell Emerald.
1915: (Bio).

1916: (Fox/Bertram Bracken) Theda Bara.
1921: (HOD/Hugo Ballin) Edward Earle.
1922: (British) Iris Hoey.
1925: (Fox/Emmett Flynn) Edmund Lowe.
1930: *Ex-Flame* (Liberty/Victor Halperin) Neil Hamilton.
1931: (Fox/Frank Lloyd) Ann Harding.

East Side, West Side
   —from a novel by Felix Riesenberg.
1927: (Fox/Allan Dwan) George O'Brien.
1931: *Skyline* (Fox/Sam Taylor) Myrna Loy.

Easy To Wed
   See *Libeled Lady.*

Ebb Tide
   —from a story by Robert Louis Stevenson and Lloyd Osbourne.
1915: (Selig/Colin Campbell).
1922: (Par/George Melford) Jacqueline Logan.
1937: (Par/James Hogan) Ray Milland.
1947: *Adventure Island* (Par/Peter Stewart) Rory Calhoun.

Elmer the Great
   See *Fast Company.*

Elusive Pimpernel, The
   See *Scarlet Pimpernel, The.*

Emergency Wedding
   See *You Belong to Me.*

Enchanted Cottage, The
   —from the play by Arthur Wing Pinero.
1924: (FN/J. S. Robertson) Richard Barthelmess.
1945: (RKO/John Cromwell) Robert Young.

Enoch Arden
   See *After Many Years.*

L'equipage
   —from a novel by Joseph Kessel.
1927: (French) M. Georges Charlia.
1935: (French/Anatole Litvak) Annabella.
1937: *Woman I Love, The* (RKO/Anatole Litvak) Paul Muni.

Escape
   —from a play by John Galsworthy.
1930: (RKO/Basil Dean) Gerald du Maurier.
1948: (Fox/Joseph L. Mankiewicz) Rex Harrison.

Escape from Crime
   See *Picture Snatcher, The.*

Escape in the Desert
   See *Petrified Forest, The.*

Escape Me Never
—from a play by Margaret Kennedy.
1935: (British/Paul Czinner) Elisabeth Bergner.
1947: (WB/Peter Godfrey) Ida Lupino.

Evelyn Prentice
—from a novel by W. E. Woodward.
1934: (MGM/William K. Howard) Myrna Loy.
1939: *Stronger Than Desire* (MGM/Leslie Fenton) Virginia Bruce.

Everybody Does It
See *Wife, Husband, Friend.*

Ex-Flame
See *East Lynne.*

Falcon Takes Over, The
—from *Farewell My Lovely,* a novel by Raymond Chandler.
1942: (RKO/Irving Reis) George Sanders.
1944: *Murder, My Sweet* (RKO/Edward Dmytryk) Dick Powell.

1975: *Farewell My Lovely* Remake announced to star Robert Mitchum.

Fall of the House of Usher, The
—from the story by Edgar Allan Poe.
1927: (French/Jean Epstein) Jean Debucourt.
1928: (Webber/John S. Watson, Jr.) Melville Webber.
1950: (British/George Ivan Barnett) Kay Tendeter.
1960: *House of Usher, The* (AIP/Roger Corman) Vincent Price.

Fancy Pants
See *Ruggles of Red Gap.*

Fan-Fan
—from *The Mikado,* an opera by Gilbert and Sullivan.
1918: (Fox/C. M. Franklin, S. A. Franklin).
1939: *Mikado, The* (British/Victor Schertzinger) Kenny Baker.
1963: *Cool Mikado, The* (British/Michael Winner) Frankie Howard.
1967: *Mikado, The* (British/Stuart Burge) Donald Adams.

A Farewell to Arms (**1932**): **Gary Cooper and Helen Hayes.**

Fanny
—from the play by Marcel Pagnol.
1932: (French).
1938: *Port of Seven Seas* (MGM/James Whale) Wallace Beery.
1961: (WB/Joshua Logan) Leslie Caron.

Farewell My Lovely
See *Falcon Takes Over, The*.

Farewell to Arms, A
—from the novel by Ernest Hemingway.
1932: (Par/Frank Borzage) Gary Cooper.
1957: Fox/Charles Vidor) Rock Hudson.

Far From the Madding Crowd
—from the novel by Thomas Hardy.
1915: (British/Larry Trimble) Florence Turner.
1967: (MGM/John Schlesinger) Julie Christie.

Farmer Takes a Wife, The
—from *Rome Haul*, a novel by Walter E. Edmonds.
1935: (Fox/Victor Fleming) Janet Gaynor.
1953: (Fox/Henry Levin) Betty Grable.

Fast Company
—from *Elmer the Great*, a play by Ring Lardner and George M. Cohan.
1929: (Par/A. Edward Sutherland) Jack Oakie.

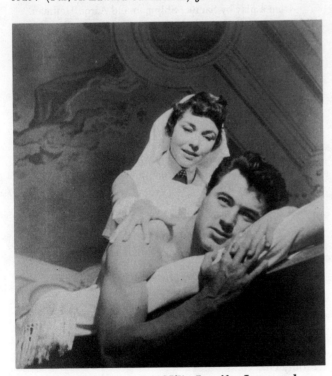

A Farewell to Arms (1957): Jennifer Jones and Rock Hudson.

1933: *Elmer the Great* (FN/Mervyn LeRoy) Joe E. Brown.
1939: *Cowboy Quarterback, The* (FN/Noel Smith) Bert Wheeler.

Faust
See *Faust and Mephistopheles*.

Faust and Mephistopheles
1898: (British/A. A. Smith).
1903: *Damnation of Faust, The* (French).
1909: *Faust* (French/George Méliés).
1909: *Faust* (Edison).
1911: *Faust* (French/Georges Eagot, M. Andreani).
1916: *Faust* (Italian).
1922: *Faust* (British/Challis Sanderson) Dick Webb.
1926: *Faust* (German/F. W. Murnau) Emil Jannings.
1927: *Faust* (British/H. B. Parkinson) Herbert Langley.
1932: *Walpurgis Night* (Edu/Howard Higgin).
1936: *Faust* (British/Albert Hopkins) Webster Booth.
1950: *Faust and the Devil* (Italian/Carmine Gallone) Gino Mattera.
1963: *Faust* (German/Peter Gorski) Will Quadflieg.
1968: *Dr. Faustus* (British/Richard Burton, Nevill Coghill) Richard Burton.

Faust and the Devil
See *Faust and Mephistopheles*.

Fear
See *Crime and Punishment*.

Fiddler on the Roof
See *Tevya*.

Fiend Who Walked the West, The
See *Kiss of Death*.

Fighting Coward, The
—from *Magnolia*, a play by Booth Tarkington.
1924: (Par/James Cruze) Ernest Torrence.
1927: *River of Romance* (Par/Richard Wallace) Charles "Buddy" Rogers.
1935: *Mississippi* (Par/A. Edward Sutherland) Bing Crosby.

Five Came Back
1939: (RKO/John Farrow) Chester Morris.
1956: *Back from Eternity* (RKO/John Farrow) Robert Ryan.

Five Star Final
—from a play by Louis Weitzenkorn.
1931: (WB/Mervyn LeRoy) Edward G. Robinson.
1936: *Two Against the World* (FN/William McGann) Humphrey Bogart.

Flaming Forties, The
See *Tennessee's Pardner*.

Flowing Gold
—from a story by Rex Beach.
1924: (FN/Joseph De Grasse) Anna Q. Nilsson.
1940: (WB/Alfred Green) John Garfield.

Fog Over Frisco
—from "The Five Fragments," a story by George Dyer.
1934: (WB/William Dieterle) Bette Davis.
1942: *Spy Ship* (WB/B. Reeves Eason) Craig Stevens.

Folies Bergere
—from a play by Rudolph Lothar and Hans Adler.
1935: (UA/Roy Del Ruth) Maurice Chevalier.
1941: *That Night in Rio* (Fox/Irving Cummings) Alice Faye.
1951: *On the Riviera* (Fox/Walter Lang) Danny Kaye.

Follow the Fleet
See *Shore Leave.*

Fool's Paradise
—from *Laurels and the Lady*, a novel by Leonard Merrick.
1921: (Par/Cecil B. DeMille) Dorothy Dalton.
1931: *Magnificent Lie, The* (Par/Berthold Viertel) Ruth Chatterton.

Forever
See *Peter Ibbetson.*

Forgotten Faces
See *Heliotrope.*

Fortunes of Captain Blood
See *Captain Blood.*

Forty Little Mothers
—from a story by Jean Guitton.
1938: (French).
1940: (MGM/Busby Berkeley) Eddie Cantor.

Four Feathers, The
—from the novel by A. E. W. Mason.
1921: (British/Rene Plaissetty) Harry Ham.
1929: (Par/Merian C. Cooper, Ernest B. Schoedsack, Lothar Mendes) Richard Arlen.
1939: (British/Zoltan Korda) Ralph Richardson.
1956: *Storm Over the Nile* (Col/Zoltan Korda, Terence Young) Anthony Steel.

Four Horsemen of the Apocalypse, The
—from the novel by Vicente Blasco-Ibanez.
1921: (MGM/Rex Ingram) Rudolph Valentino.
1962: (MGM/Vincente Minnelli) Glenn Ford.

Four Jacks and a Jill
See *Street Girl.*

Four Musketeers, The
See *Three Musketeers, The.*

Four Sons
—from "Grandmother Bernle Learns Her Letters," a story by Ida Alexa Ross Wylie.
1928: (Fox/John Ford) James Hall.
1940: (Fox/Archie Mayo) Don Ameche.

Frankenstein
—from the novel by Mary Shelley.
1910: (Edison) Charles Ogle.
1931: (U/James Whale) Boris Karloff.
1957: *Curse of Frankenstein, The* (British/Terence Fisher) Peter Cushing.

Frau Cheney's Ende
See *Last of Mrs. Cheyney, The.*

Free Soul, A
—from a novel by Adela Rogers St. John.
1931: (MGM/Clarence Brown) Norma Shearer.
1953: *Girl Who Had Everything, The.* (MGM/Richard Thorpe) Elizabeth Taylor.

Freshman Love
See *College Widow, The.*

Friendly Enemies
—from a play by Samuel Shipman and Aaron Hoffman.
1925: (PDC/George Melford) Lew Fields.
1942: (UA/Allan Dwan) Charles Winninger.

From the Manger to the Cross
See *Life of Christ, The.*

Frontier Marshal
—from *Wyatt Earp—Frontier Marshal*, a novel by Stuart N. Lake.
1934: (Fox/Lew Seiler) George O'Brien.
1939: (Fox/Allan Dwan) Randolph Scott.
1946: *My Darling Clementine* (Fox/John Ford) Henry Fonda.

Front Page, The
—from the play by Ben Hecht and Charles MacArthur.
1931: (UA/Lewis Milestone) Pat O'Brien.
1940: *His Girl Friday* (Col/Howard Hawks) Cary Grant.
1974: (U/Billy Wilder) Jack Lemmon.

Fun and Fancy Free
See *Jack and the Beanstalk.*

Funny Girl
See *Rose of Washington Square.*

Gaby
See *Waterloo Bridge.*

Game of Death, A
See *Most Dangerous Game, The.*

Garden of Allah, The
—from a novel by Robert Hichens.
1916: (Selig/Colin Campbell) Tom Santschi.
1927: (MGM/Rex Ingram) Alice Terry.
1936: (UA/Richard Boleslawski) Charles Boyer.

Gaslight
See *Angel Street.*

Gentleman After Dark, A
See *Heliotrope.*

Gentlemen Prefer Blondes
—from the novel by Anita Loos.
1928: (Par/Malcolm St. Clair) Ruth Taylor.
1953: (Fox/Howard Hawks) Marilyn Monroe.

Getting Gertie's Garter
—from a play by Avery Hopwood and Wilson Collison.
1927: (PDC/E. Mason Hopper) Marie Prevost.
1933: *Night of the Garter, A* (British/Jack Raymond) Sydney Howard.
1945: (UA/Allan Dwan) Dennis O'Keefe.

Ghost Breaker, The
—from a play by Paul Dickey and Charles W. Goddard.
1914: (Par) H. B. Warner.
1922: (Par/Alfred E. Green) Wallace Reid.
1940: *Ghost Breakers, The* (Par/George Marshall) Bob Hope.
1953: *Scared Stiff* (Par/George Marshall) Martin and Lewis.

Ghost Breakers, The
See *Ghost Breaker, The.*

Gift of Love, The
See *Sentimental Journey.*

Gigi
—from the novel by Colette.
1950: (French/Jacqueline Audry) Daniele Delorme.
1958: (MGM/Vincente Minnelli) Leslie Caron.

Girl Most Likely, The
See *Tom, Dick, and Harry.*

Girl of the Golden West, The
—from the play by David Belasco.
1915: (Par/Cecil B. DeMille) Mabel Van Buren.
1923: (FN/Edwin Carewe) Sylvia Breamer.
1930: (FN/John Francis Dillon) Ann Harding.

1938: (MGM/Robert Z. Leonard) Jeanette MacDonald.

Girl Who Had Everything, The
See *Free Soul, A.*

Girl Who Ran Wild, The
See *M'liss.*

Glass Key, The
—from a novel by Dashiell Hammett.
1935: (Par/Frank Tuttle) George Raft.
1942: (Par/Stuart Heisler) Alan Ladd.

Glass Slipper, The
See *Cinderella and the Fairy Godmother.*

Glorious Betsy
—from a play by Rita Johnson Young.
1928: (WB/Alan Crosland) Dolores Costello.
1936: *Hearts Divided* (FN/Frank Borzage) Marion Davies.

God's Country
See *God's Country and the Woman.*

God's Country and the Woman
—from a novel by James Oliver Curwood.
1916: (Vit/Rollin S. Sturgeon).
1920: (Vit/Rollin S. Sturgeon).
1937: (WB/William Keighley) George Brent.
1946: *God's Country* (SG/Robert E. Tansey) Buster Keaton.

Going Places
See *Hottentot, The.*

Gold Diggers, The
—from a play by Avery Hopwood.
1923: (WB/Harry Beaumont) Hope Hampton.
1929: *Gold Diggers of Broadway* (WB/Roy Del Ruth) Nancy Welford.
1933: *Gold Diggers of 1933* (WB/Mervyn LeRoy) Warren William.
1951: *Painting the Clouds with Sunshine* (WB/David Butler) Dennis Morgan.

Gold Diggers of Broadway
See *Gold Diggers, The.*

Gold Diggers of 1933
See *Gold Diggers, The.*

Goodbye Again
—from a play by George Haight and Allan Scott
1933: (WB/Michael Curtiz) Warren William.
1941: *Honeymoon for Three* (WB/Lloyd Bacon) Ann Sheridan.

The Girl of the Golden West (1938): Jeanette MacDonald and Nelson Eddy.

Goodbye Broadway
   See *Shannons of Broadway, The.*

Good News
   —from the play by Laurence Schwab, Lew Brown, Frank
      Mandel, and B. G. DeSylva.
1930: (MGM/Nick Grinde) Bessie Love.
1947: (MGM/Charles Walters) June Allyson.

Gorilla, The
   —from a play by Ralph Spence.
1927: (FN/Alfred Santell) Charlie Murray.
1931: (FN/Bryan Foy) Joe Frisco.
1939: (Fox/Allan Dwan) The Ritz Brothers.

Grand Hotel
   —from the novel by Vicki Baum.
1932: (MGM/Edmund Goulding) Greta Garbo.
1945: *Weekend at the Waldorf* (MGM/Robert Z. Leonard)
      Ginger Rogers.

Great Adventure, The
   —from *Buried Alive,* a novel by Arnold Bennett.
1915: (British/Larry Trimble) Henry Ainley.
1921: (FN/Kenneth Webb) Lionel Barrymore.
1933: *His Double Life* (Par/Arthur Hopkins) Roland Young.
1943: *Holy Matrimony* (Fox/John M. Stahl) Monty Woolley.

Great Divide, The
   —from a play by William Vaughn Moody.
1915: (Lubin/Edgar Lewis) Ethel Clayton.
1925: (MGM/Reginald Barker) Alice Terry.
1929: (FN/Reginald Barker) Dorothy Mackaill.
1930: *Woman Hungry* (FN/Clarence Badger) Lila Lee.

Greatest Story Ever Told, The
   See *Life of Christ, The.*

Great Expectations
   —from the novel by Charles Dickens.
1917: (Par) Jack Pickford.
1934: (U/Stuart Walker) Phillips Holmes.

1947: (British/David Lean) John Mills.
1974: (British/Joseph Hardy) Michael York.

Great Gatsby, The
—from the novel by F. Scott Fitzgerald.
1926: (Par/Herbert Brenon) Warner Baxter.
1949: (Par/Elliott Nugent) Alan Ladd.
1974: (Par/Jack Clayton) Robert Redford.

Great Impersonation, The
—from the novel by Edward Phillips Oppenheim.
1921: (Par/George Melford) James Kirkwood.
1935: (U/Alan Crosland) Edmund Lowe.
1942: (U/John Rawlins) Ralph Bellamy.

Great O'Malley, The
See *Making of O'Malley, The.*

Great Waltz, The
1938: (MGM/Julien Duvivier) Luise Rainer.
1972: (MGM/Andrew L. Stone) Horst Bucholz.

Great White Way, The
—from "Cain and Mabel," a story by H. C. Witwer.
1924: (Goldwyn/E. Mason Hopper) Anita Stewart.
1936: *Cain and Mabel* (WB/Lloyd Bacon) Clark Gable.

Greeks Had a Word for Them, The
—from *The Greeks Had a Word For It*, a play by Zoe Adkins.
1932: (UA/Lowell Sherman) Joan Blondell.
1953: *How To Marry a Millionaire* (Fox/Jean Negulesco) Marilyn Monroe.

Greene Murder Case, The
—from a novel by S. S. Van Dine.
1929: (Par/Frank Tuttle) William Powell.
1937: *Night of Mystery* (Par/E. A. Dupont) Grant Richards.

Green Goddess, The
—from a play by William Archer.
1923: (Goldwyn/Sidney Olcott) George Arliss.
1930: (WB/Alfred E. Green) George Arliss.
1943: *Adventure in Iraq* (WB/D. Ross Lederman) John Loder.

Greyfriars Bobby
See *Challenge of Lassie.*

Guardsman, The
—from the play by Ferenc Molnar.
1931: (MGM/Sidney Franklin) Alfred Lunt.
1941: *Chocolate Soldier, The* (2) (MGM/Roy Del Ruth) Nelson Eddy.

Gulliver's Travels
—from the novel by Jonathan Swift.
1903: (Lubin).

1934: *New Gulliver, The* (Russian/Alexander Ptuschko) V. Konstantinov.
1939: (Par/Animation).
1960: *Three Worlds of Gulliver, The* (Col/Jack Sher) Kerwin Matthews.

Gunfight at Comanche Creek
See *Last of the Badmen.*

Gunga Din
—from a poem by Rudyard Kipling.
1939: (RKO/George Stevens) Cary Grant.
1962: *Sergeants Three* (UA/John Sturges) Frank Sinatra.

Gun Runners, The
See *To Have and Have Not.*

Gypsy Blood
See *Carmen.*

Half a Sixpence
See *Kipps.*

Hamlet
—from the play by William Shakespeare.
1900: (French) Sarah Bernhardt.
1907: (French/Georges Méliés).
1909: (Italian).
1910: (French).
1911: (Danish) Alwin Neuss.
1912: (British/Charles Raymond) Charles Raymond.
1913: (British/Hay Plumb) Johnston Forbes-Robertson
1914: (Vit/James Young) James Young.
1920: (German/Svend Gade) Asta Nielsen.
1948: (British/Laurence Olivier) Laurence Olivier.
1959: *Rest is Silence, The.* (German).
1960: (German/Franz Wirth) Maximilian Schell.
1963: *Ophelia* (French/Claude Chabrol) Andre Jocelyn.
1964: (Russian/Grigori Kozintsev) Innokenti Smoktunovsky.
1964: (WB/John Gielgud) Richard Burton.
1969: (British/Tony Richardson) Nicol Williamson.

Hands of Orlac, The
—from the novel by Maurice Renard.
1924: (Austria/Robert Wiene) Conrad Veidt.
1935: *Mad Love* (MGM/Karl Freund) Peter Lorre.
1960: (British/Edmond T. Greville) Mel Ferrer.

Harriet Craig
See *Craig's Wife.*

Headless Horseman, The
—from "The Legend of Sleepy Hollow," a story by Washington Irving.
1922: (HOD/Edward Venturini) Will Rogers.

Hamlet (1948): Laurence Olivier and Jean Simmons.

Hamlet (1960): Maximilian Schell and Dunja Movar.

Hamlet: (1964): Richard Burton and Eileen Herlie.

Hamlet: (1969): Judy Parfitt and Nicol Williamson.

1949: *Ichabod and Mr. Toad* (Disney/Animation).

Heart of Paris
—from a story by Marcel Achard.
1939: (French/Marc Allegret) Raimu.
1940: *Lady in Question, The* (Col/Charles Vidor) Brian Aherne.

Hearts Divided
See *Glorious Betsy.*

Heidi
—from the novel by Johanna Spyri.
1937: (Fox/Allan Dwan) Shirley Temple.
1953: (Swiss/Luigi Comencini) Elsbeth Sigmund.
1968: (WB/Werner Jacobs) Eva Maria Singhammer.

Helen of Troy
1927: (FN/Alexander Korda) Maria Corda.
1955: (WB/Robert Wise) Rossana Podesta.

Heliotrope
—from "Whiff of Heliotrope," a story by Richard Washburn Child.
1920: (Cos/George D. Baker) Fred Burton.
1928: *Forgotten Faces* (Par/Victor Schertzinger) Clive Brook.
1936: *Forgotten Faces* (Par/E. A. Dupont) Herbert Marshall.
1942: *Gentleman After Dark, A* (UA/Edwin L. Marin) Brian Donlevy.

Hellgate
See *Prisoner of Shark Island, The.*

Hello, Dolly
See *Matchmaker, The.*

Hello, Frisco, Hello
See *King of Burlesque.*

Hell's Heroes
See *Broncho Billy and the Baby.*

Hell's Kitchen
See *Mayor of Hell, The.*

Her Cardboard Lover
See *Cardboard Lover, The.*

Her Sacrifice
See *Doll's House, A.*

He Who Gets Slapped
—from a play by Leonid Andreyev.
1916: (Russian).
1924: (MGM/Victor Seastrom) Lon Chaney.

Hi, Nellie
—from a story by Roy Chanslor.

1934: (WB/Mervyn LeRoy) Paul Muni.
1937: *Love Is on the Air* (FN/Nick Grinde) Ronald Reagan.
1942: *You Can't Escape Forever* (WB/Jo Graham) George Brent.
1949: *House Across the Street, The* (WB/Richard Bare) Wayne Morris.

His Double Life
See *Great Adventure, The.*

His Girl Friday
See *Front Page, The.*

His Glorious Night
—from *Olympia,* a play by Ferenc Molnar.
1929: (MGM/Lionel Barrymore) John Gilbert.
1960: *Breath of Scandal, A* (Par/Michael Curtiz) Sophia Loren.

His Woman
See *Sal of Singapore.*

Hit the Deck
See *Shore Leave.*

Holiday
—from a play by Philip Barry.
1930: (Pathé/Edward H. Griffith) Mary Astor.
1938: (Col/George Cukor) Cary Grant.

Holiday for Henrietta
—from a story by Julien Duvivier and Henri Jeanson.
1955: (French/Julien Duvivier) Hildegarde Neff.
1964: *Paris When It Sizzles* (Par/Richard Quine) Audrey Hepburn.

Holy Matrimony
See *Great Adventure, The.*

Holy Terror, A
See *Trailin'.*

Home in Indiana
—from "The Phantom Filly," a story by George Agnew Chamberlain.
1944: (Fox/Henry Hathaway) Jeanne Crain.
1957: *April Love* (Fox/Henry Levin) Pat Boone.

Home on the Range
See *Code of the West.*

Home Towners, The
—from a play by George M. Cohan.
1928: (WB/Bryan Foy) Richard Bennett.
1936: *Times Square Playboy* (WB/William McGann) Warren William.

Honeymoon for Three
See *Goodbye Again.*

Honeymoon's Over, The
  See *Six-Cylinder Love.*

Honourable Murder, An
  See *Julius Caesar.*

Hoop-La
  See *Barker, The.*

Horror of Dracula
  See *Nosferatu.*

Hotel Imperial
  —from a play by Lajos Biro.
1927: (Par/Mauritz Stiller) Pola Negri.
1939: (Par/Robert Florey) Ray Milland.

Hottentot, The
  —from a play by Victor Mapes and William Collier.
1923: (FN/J. W. Horne, Del Andrews) Douglas MacLean.
1929: (WB/Roy Del Ruth) Edward Everett Horton.
1938: *Going Places* (FN/Ray Enright) Dick Powell.

Hound of the Baskervilles, The
  —from the novel by Arthur Conan Doyle.
1915: (French).
1917: (German/Richard Oswald).
1921: (British/Maurice Elvey) Ellie Norwood.
1929: (German) Carlyle Blackwell.
1931: (British/V. Gareth Gundrey) Robert Rendel.
1937: *Murder at the Baskervilles* (British/Thomas Bentley) Arthur Wontner.

1939: (Fox/Sidney Lanfield) Basil Rathbone.
1959: (British/Terence Fisher) Peter Cushing.

House Across the Street, The
  See *Hi, Nellie.*

House of Bamboo
  See *Street with No Name, The.*

House of Usher, The
  See *Fall of the House of Usher, The.*

House of Wax
  See *Mystery of the Wax Museum.*

House of Women
  See *Caged.*

How To Marry a Millionaire
  See *Greeks Had a Word for Them, The.*

Huckleberry Finn
  —from the novel by Mark Twain.
1920: (Par/William D. Taylor) Lewis Sargent.
1931: (Par/Norman Taurog) Junior Durkin.
1939: *Adventures of Huckleberry Finn, The* (MGM/Richard Thorpe) Mickey Rooney.
1960: *Adventures of Huckelberry Finn, The* (MGM/Michael Curtiz) Eddie Hodges.
1974: (UA/J. Lee Thompson) Jeff East.

Human Beast, The
  —from the novel by Emile Zola.
1940: (French/Jean Renoir) Jean Gabin.
1954: *Human Desire* (Col/Fritz Lang) Broderick Crawford.

Human Desire
  See *Human Beast, The.*

Humoresque
  —from the story by Fannie Hurst.
1920: (Par/Frank Borzage) Alma Rubens.
1947: (WB/Jean Negulesco) Joan Crawford.

I Am a Camera
  —from a play by John Van Druten.
1955: (British/Henry Cornelius) Julie Harris.
1972: *Cabaret* (AA/Robert Fosse) Liza Minnelli.

Ichabod and Mr. Toad
  See *Headless Horseman, The.*

Idle Rich
  —from *White Collars*, a play by Edith Ellis.
1929: (MGM/William C. DeMille) Conrad Nagel.
1938: *Rich Man, Poor Girl* (MGM/Reinhold Schunzel) Robert Young.

The Adventures of Huckleberry Finn (1939): Mickey Rooney starred in the most popular filming of the Mark Twain classic.

244 MAKE IT AGAIN, SAM

Idol of Seville, The
See *Carmen.*

I'd Rather Be Rich
See *It Started with Eve.*

If I Were King
—from a novel by Justin McCarthy.
1920: (Fox/J. Gordon Edwards) William Farnum.
1930: *Vagabond King, The* (Par/Ludwig Berger) Dennis King.
1938: (Par/Frank Lloyd) Ronald Colman.
1956: *Vagabond King, The* (Par/Michael Curtiz) Oreste.

I Like Money
See *Topaze.*

Illegal
See *Mouthpiece, The.*

I'll Get By
See *Tin Pan Alley.*

I'll Never Forget You
See *Berkeley Square.*

I Married a Doctor
See *Main Street.*

Imitation of Life
—from the novel by Fannie Hurst.
1934: (U/John M. Stahl) Claudette Colbert.
1959: (U/Douglas Sirk) Lana Turner.

Indianapolis Speedway
See *Crowd Roars, The* (1).

Informer, The
—from the novel by Liam O'Flaherty.
1929: (British/Arthur Robinson) Lars Hansen.
1935: (RKO/John Ford) Victor McLaglen.
1968: *Uptight* (Par/Jules Dassin) Raymond St. Jacques.

In Old Kentucky
—from a play by Charles T. Dazey.
1920: (FN/Marshall Neilan) Anita Stewart.
1927: (MGM/John M. Stahl) James Murray.
1935: (Fox/George Marshall) Will Rogers.

Inspector General, The
See *Revizor.*

Intermezzo
1936: (Swedish/Gustav Molander) Ingrid Bergman.
1939: (UA/Gregory Ratoff) Ingrid Bergman.

International Squadron
See *Ceiling Zero.*

In the Good Old Summertime
See *Shop Around the Corner, The.*

Irene
—from the musical play by James Montgomery, Joseph McCarthy, and Harry Tierney.
1926: (FN/Alfred E. Green) Colleen Moore.
1940: (RKO/Herbert Wilcox) Anna Neagle.

Iron Man, The
—from a novel by W. R. Burnett.
1931: (U/Tod Browning) Lew Ayres.
1951: (U/Joseph Pevney) Jeff Chandler.

Iron Mask, The
See *Man in the Iron Mask, The.*

Island of Lost Souls
—from "The Island of Dr. Moreau," a story by H. G. Wells.
1932: (Par/Erle C. Kenton) Charles Laughton.
1959: *Terror is a Man* (Valiant/Gerardo de Leon) Francis Lederer.
1976: (Fox) Remake announced.

Isle of Fury
See *Narrow Corner, The.*

Istanbul
See *Singapore.*

Is Zat So?
—from a play by James Gleason and Richard Taber.
1927: (Fox/Alfred E. Green) George O'Brien.
1935: *Two Fisted* (Par/James Cruze) Lee Tracy.

It Ain't Hay
See *Princess O'Hara.*

It Happened One Night
—from "Night Bus," a story by Samuel Hopkins Adams.
1934: (Col/Frank Capra) Clark Gable.
1956: *You Can't Run Away from It* (Col/Dick Powell) Jack Lemmon.

It's a Dog's Life
See *Almost Human.*

It Started with Eve
1941: (U/Henry Koster) Deanna Durbin.
1964: *I'd Rather Be Rich* (U/Jack Smight) Sandra Dee.

Ivanhoe
—from the novel by Sir Walter Scott.
1911: (Vit).
1913: (British/Herbert Brenon) King Baggot.
1913: (British/Leedham Bantock) Lauerdale Maitland.
1952: (MGM/Richard Thorpe) Robert Taylor.

I Wake Up Screaming
—from the novel by Steve Fisher.
1941: (Fox/Bruce Humberstone) Betty Grable.
1953: *Vickie* (Fox/Harry Horner) Jeanne Crain.

I Was Framed
See *Dust Be My Destiny.*

Jackals, The
See *Yellow Sky.*

Jack and the Beanstalk
1902: (Edison/Edwin S. Porter).
1903: (Lubin).
1904: (Edwin S. Porter).
1912: (Kine) Thomas Carnahan, Jr.
1917: (Fox/C. M. and S. A. Franklin) Francis Carpenter.
1924: (U/Alf Goulding) Baby Peggy.
1947: *Fun and Fancy Free* (Disney/Animation).
1952: (WB/Jean Yarbrough) Abbott and Costello.

Jailbreak
—from "Murder in Sing Sing," a story by Jonathan Finn.
1936: (WB/Nick Grinde) Craig Reynolds.
1939: *Smashing the Money Ring* (FN/Terry Morse) Ronald Reagan.

You Can't Run Away from It (1956): **June Allyson and Jack Lemmon.**

Jane Eyre
—from the novel by Charlotte Bronte.
1909: (Italian).
1910: (Thanhouser).
1914: (Imp) Ethel Grandin.
1915: (Bio) Louise Vale.
1918: *Woman and Wife* (Select/Edward Jose) Alice Brady.
1921: (HOD/Hugo Ballin) Mabel Ballin.
1934: (Mon/Christy Cabanne) Virginia Bruce.
1944: (Fox/Robert Stevenson) Joan Fontaine.
1970: (British/Delbert Mann) Susannah York.

Jazz Singer, The
—from the play by Samson Raphaelson.
1927: (WB/Alan Crosland) Al Jolson.
1953: (WB/Michael Curtiz) Danny Thomas.

Jesus
See *Life of Christ, The.*

Jigsaw
See *Mirage.*

Joan of Arc
1909: (French).
1913: (Italian/Nino Oxilia) Maria Jacobini Savoia.
1917: *Joan the Woman* (Par/Cecil B. DeMille) Geraldine Farrar.
1927: *Passion of Joan of Arc, The* (French/Carl Dreyer) Mlle. Falconetti.
1949: (RKO/Victor Fleming) Ingrid Bergman.
1957: *Saint Joan* (UA/Otto Preminger) Jean Seberg.

It Happened One Night (1934): **Clark Gable and Claudette Colbert.**

1962: *Trial of Joan of Arc, The* (French/Robert Bresson) Florence Carrez.

Joan the Woman
   See *Joan of Arc.*

Joe Smith, American
   —from a story by Paul Gallico.
1942: (MGM/Richard Thorpe) Robert Young.
1959: *Big Operator, The* (MGM/Charles Haas) Mickey Rooney.

Johnny Allegro
   See *Most Dangerous Game, The.*

Journey into Fear
   —from the novel by Eric Ambler.
1942: (RKO/Norman Foster) Joseph Cotten.
1975: (New World/Daniel Mann) Sam Waterston.

Judge Priest
   —from stories by Irwin S. Cobb.
1934: (Fox/John Ford) Will Rogers.
1953: *Sun Shines Bright, The* (Rep/John Ford) Charles Winninger.

Julius Caesar
   —from the play by William Shakespeare.
1908: (Lubin).
1908: (Vit).
1911: (British) Frank Benson.
1914: (Italian/Enrico Guazzoni) Amleto Novelli.
1918: (Kleine).
1950: (Avon/David Bradley) Charlton Heston.
1953: (MGM/Joseph L. Mankiewicz) Marlon Brando.
1960: *Honourable Murder, An* (British/Godfrey Grayson) Norman Wooland.
1971: (AIP/Stuart Burge) Charlton Heston.

Jumping Frog, The
   —from "The Celebrated Jumping Frog of Calaveras County," a story by Mark Twain.
1922: (U. S./Arthur Barringer).
1948: *Best Man Wins, The* (Col/John Sturges) Edgar Buchanan.

June Moon
   —from a play by Ring Lardner and George S. Kaufman.
1931: (Par/A. Edward Sutherland) Jack Oakie.
1937: *Blonde Trouble* (Par/George Archainbaud) Johnny Downs.

Jungle Book, The
   —from the stories by Rudyard Kipling.
1942: (UA/Zoltan Korda) Sabu.
1967: (Disney/Animation).

Karamazov
   —from the novel by Fyodor Dostoyevsky.
1921: (German/Robert Wiene) Emil Jannings.
1930: (German/Fedor Ozep) Fritz Kortner.
1957: *Brothers Karamazov, The* (MGM/Richard Brooks) Yul Brynner.
1967: (Russian/Pyriev).

Kathleen Mavoureen
   —from a play by Dion Boucicault.
1911: (Yankee).
1913: (Imp/Herbert Brenon).
1919: (Fox/Charles J. Brabin) Theda Bara.
1930: (Tif/Albert Ray) Sally O'Neil.

Keeper of the Bees
   —from a novel by Gene Stratton Porter.
1925: (FBO/James Leo Meehan) Robert Frazer.
1935: (Mon/Christy Cabanne) Neil Hamilton.
1947: (Col/John Sturges) Michael Duane.

Kennel Murder Case, The
   —from the novel by S. S. Van Dine.
1933: (WB/Michael Curtiz) William Powell.
1940: *Calling Philo Vance* (WB/William Clemens) James Stephenson.

Kid from Brooklyn, The
   See *Milky Way, The.*

Kid Galahad
   —from a story by Francis Wallace.
1937: (WB/Michael Curtiz) Edward G. Robinso·
1941: *Wagons Roll at Night, The* (FN/Ray Enright) Humphrey Bogart.
1962: (UA/Phil Karlson) Elvis Presley.

Kidnapped
   —from the novel by Robert Louis Stevenson.
1917: (Edison/Alan Crosland) Raymond McKee.
1938: (Fox/Alfred L. Werker) Warner Baxter.
1948: (Mon/William Beaudine) Dan O'Herlihy.
1960: (Disney/Robert Stevenson) Peter Finch.
1971: (AIP/Delbert Mann) Michael Caine.

Kiki
   —from the play by André Picard, as adapted by David Belasco.
1926: (FN/Clarence Brown) Ronald Colman.
1931: (UA/Sam Taylor) Mary Pickford.

Killer McCoy
   See *Crowd Roars, The* (2).

Killers, The
   —from the story by Ernest Hemingway.

1946: (U/Robert Siodmak) Burt Lancaster.
1964: (U/Don Siegel) Lee Marvin.

Kill or Be Killed
  See *Most Dangerous Game, The.*

Kind Lady
  —from a play by Edward Chodorov.
1935: (MGM/George B. Seitz) Aline MacMahon.
1951: (MGM/John Sturges) Ethel Barrymore.

King and I, The
  See *Anna and the King of Siam.*

King Lear
  —from the play by William Shakespeare.
1909: (Vit).
1970: (British/Peter Brook) Paul Scofield.
1970: (Russian/Grigori Kozintsev) Yuri Jarvet.

King of Burlesque
1936: (Fox/Sidney Lanfield) Alice Faye.
1943: *Hello, Frisco, Hello* (Fox/Bruce Humberstone) Alice Faye.

King of Kings
  See *Life of Christ, The.*

King of the Khyber Rifles
  See *Black Watch, The.*

King of the Underworld
  See *Dr. Socrates.*

King Richard and the Crusaders
  See *Richard, The Lion-Hearted.*

King Solomon's Mines
  —from a novel by H. Rider Haggard.

Kismet (1931): Otis Skinner (left), who also starred in the 1920 version.

1937: (British/Robert Stevenson) Cedric Hardwicke.
1950: (MGM/Compton Bennett, Andrew Marton) Stewart Granger.

Kings Pirate, The
See *Against All Flags.*

Kipps
—from the novel by H. G. Wells.
1921: (British/Harold Shaw) George K. Arthur.
1941: (British/Carol Reed) Michael Redgrave.
1967: *Half a Sixpence* (Par/George Sidney) Tommy Steele.

Kismet
—from a play by Edward Knoblock.
1914: (British/Leedham Bantock) Oscar Asche.
1920: (RC/Louis Gesnier) Otis Skinner.
1931: (FN/John Francis Dillon) Otis Skinner.
1944: (MGM/William Dieterle) Ronald Colman.
1955: (MGM/Vincente Minnelli) Howard Keel.

Kismet **(1944): James Craig and Ronald Colman.**

Kiss Me Kate
See *Taming of the Shrew, The.*

Kiss of Death
—from a story by Eleazar Lipsky.
1947: (Fox/Henry Hathaway) Victor Mature.
1958: *Fiend Who Walked the West, The* (Fox/Gordon Douglas) Hugh O'Brian.

Kongo
See *West of Zanzibar.*

Ladies in Retirement
—from a play by Reginald Denham and Edward Percy.
1941: (Col/Charles Victor) Ida Lupino.
1969: *Mad Room, The* (Col/Bernard Girard) Stella Stevens.

Lady and the Monster, The
—from *Donovan's Brain,* a novel by Curt Siodmak.
1944: (Rep/George Sherman) Erich von Stroheim.
1953: *Donovan's Brain* (UA/Felix Feist) Lew Ayres.
1962: *Brain, The* (British/Freddie Francis) Peter Van Eyck.

Lady Eve, The
1941: (Par/Preston Sturges) Henry Fonda.
1956: *Birds and the Bees, The* (Par/Norman Taurog) George Gobel.

Lady for a Day
—from the story by Damon Runyon.
1933: (Col/Frank Capra) May Robson.
1961: *Pocketful of Miracles* (Col/Frank Capra) Bette Davis.

Lady in Question, The
See *Heart of Paris.*

Lady in the Iron Mask, The
See *Man in the Iron Mask, The.*

Lady with the Camellias, The
—from a novel by Alexandre Dumas, fils.
1907: (Danish) Oda Alstrup.
1909: *Camille* (French).
1912: *Camille* (Champion) Gertrude Shipman.
1912: *Dame Aux Camilas, La* (French/André Calmettes) Sarah Bernhardt.
1915: *Camille* (World/Albert Capellani) Clara Kimball Young.
1917: *Camille* (Fox/J. Gordon Edwards) Theda Bara.
1921: *Camille* (Metro/Ray C. Smallwood) Nazimova.
1927: *Camille* (FN/Fred Niblo) Norma Talmadge.
1934: *Dame Aux Camelias, La* (French/Ferdinand Rivers) Yvonne Printemps.
1936: *Camille* (MGM/George Cukor) Greta Garbo.
1944: *Dama de las Camelias, La* (Mexican/Gabriel Soria) Lina Montes.
1948: *Lost One, The* (Col/Carmine Callone) Massimo Serato.
1952: *Traviata, La* (Italian).
1953: *Mujer de las Camellias, La* (Argentinan).
1969: *Camille 2000* (Aud/Radley Metzger) Daniele Gaubert.

Lady To Love, A
See *Secret Hour, The.*

Last Days of Pompeii, The
—from the book by Bulwer-Lytton.
1908: (Italian).

Kismet (1955): **Howard Keel, Dolores Gray, Ann Blyth and Vic Damone.**

1913: (Italian).
1913: (Italian).
1913: (Kleine).
1918: (Italian).
1926: (Italian/Carmine Gallone) Maria Corda.
1935: (RKO/Ernest B. Schoedsack) Preston Foster.
1960: (Italian/Mario Bonnard) Steve Reeves.

Last Man on Earth, The
 —from *I Am Legend,* a novel by Richard Matheson.
1964: (AIP/Sidney Salkow) Vincent Price.
1971: *Omega Man, The* (WB/Boris Sagal) Charlton Heston.

Last Mile, The
 —from the play by John Wexley.
1932: (WW/Sam Bischoff) Preston Foster.
1959: (UA/Howard W. Koch) Mickey Rooney.

Last of Mrs. Cheyney, The
 —from a play by Frederick Lonsdale.
1929: (MGM/Sidney Franklin) Norma Shearer.
1937: (MGM/Richard Boleslawski) Joan Crawford.
1951: *Law and the Lady, The* (MGM/Edwin H. Knoph)
 Greer Garson.
1962: *Frau Cheney's Ende* (German).

Last of the Badmen
1957: (AA/Paul Landres) George Montgomery.
1964: *Gunfight at Comanche Creek* (AA/Frank McDonald)
 Audie Murphy.

Last of the Comanches
See *Thirteen, The.*

Last of the Duanes, The
—from the novel by Zane Grey.
1919: (Fox/J. Gordon Edwards) William Farnum.
1924: (Fox/Lynn Reynolds) Tom Mix.
1930: (Fox/Alfred L. Werker) George O'Brien.
1941: (Fox/James Tinling) George Montgomery.

Last of the Mohicans, The
—from the novel by James Fenimore Cooper.
1911: (Powers).
1911: (Thanhouser).
1920: (AP/Maurice Tourneur, Clarence L. Brown) Wallace Beery.
1922: (Germany) Bela Lugosi.
1936: (UA/George B. Seitz) Randolph Scott.
1947: *Last of the Redmen, The* (Col/George Sherman) Jon Hall.
1976: (de Laurentiis/Michael Winner) Charles Bronson. Remake announced.

Last of the Redmen, The
See *Last of the Mohicans, The.*

Last Round-Up, The
See *Border Legion, The.*

Last Trail, The
—from the novel by Zane Grey.
1921: (Fox/Emmett J. Flynn) Maurice B. Flynn.
1927: (Fox/Lewis Seiler) Tom Mix.
1933: (Fox/James Tinling) George O'Brien.

Laughing Lady, The
See *Society Scandal, A.*

Law and the Lady, The
See *Last of Mrs. Cheyney, The.*

Law of the Tropics
See *Oil for the Lamps of China.*

Lemon Drop Kid, The
—from a story by Damon Runyon.
1934: (Par/Marshall Neilan) Lee Tracy.
1951: (Par/Sidney Lanfield) Bob Hope.

Let's Do It Again
See *Awful Truth, The.*

Letter, The
—from the play by W. Somerset Maugham.
1929: (Par/Jean De Limur) Jeanne Eagels.
1940: (WB/William Wyler) Bette Davis.
1947: *Unfaithful, The* (WB/Vincent Sherman) Ann Sheridan.

Libeled Lady
1936: (MGM/Jack Conway) William Powell.
1946: *Easy To Wed* (MGM/Edward Buzzell) Van Johnson.

Life Begins
—from a play by Mary McDougal Axelson.
1932: (FN/James Flood) Loretta Young.
1940: *Child Is Born, A* (WB/Lloyd Bacon) Geraldine Fitzgerald.

Life of Christ, The
1910: (French).
1911: *Jesus* (French).
1911: *From the Manger to the Cross* (Kalem/Sidney Olcott) Robert Henderson Bland.
1914: *Life of Our Saviour, The* (French) M. Normand.
1927: *King of Kings* (Pathé/Cecil B. DeMille) H. R. Warner.
1961: *King of Kings* (MGM/Nicholas Ray) Jeffrey Hunter.
1965: *Greatest Story Ever Told, The* (UA/George Stevens) Max Von Sydow.

Life of Jimmy Dolan, The
—from a novel by Bertram Milhauser and Beulah Marie Dix.
1933: (WB/Archie Mayo) Douglas Fairbanks, Jr.
1939: *They Made Me a Criminal* (WB/Busby Berkeley) John Garfield.

Life of Our Saviour, The
See *Life of Christ, The.*

Lightnin'
—from the play by Winchell Smith and Frank Bacon.
1925: (Fox/John Ford) Jay Hunt.
1930: (Fox/Henry King) Will Rogers.

Light of the Western Stars, The
—from a novel by Zane Grey.
1918: (SHU) Dustin Farnum.
1925: (Par/William K. Howard) Jack Holt.
1930: (Par/Otto Brower) Richard Arlen.
1940: (Par/Lesley Selander) Victor Jory.

Light That Failed, The
—from the novel by Rudyard Kipling.
1916: (Pathé) Robert Edeson.
1923: (Par/George Melford) Jacqueline Logan.
1939: (Par/William Wellman) Ronald Colman.

Liliom
See *Trip to Paradise, A.*

Little Johnny Jones
—from the play by George M. Cohan.
1923: (WB/Arthur Rosson, Johnny Hines) Johnny Hines.
1929: (FN/Mervyn LeRoy) Eddie Buzzell.

Little Miss Marker (1934): **Adolphe Menjou and Shirley Temple.**

Little Lord Fauntleroy
  —from the novel by Frances Hodgson Burnett.
1914: (British/F. Martin Thornton) Gerald Royston.
1921: (UA/Alfred E. Green, Jack Pickford) Mary Pickford.
1936: (Selznick/John Cromwell) Freddie Bartholomew.

Little Men
  —from the novel by Louisa May Alcott.
1935: (Mascot/Phil Rosen) Ralph Morgan.
1940: (RKO/Norman Z. McLeod) Jack Oakie.

Little Minister, The
  See *Story of the Little Minister, The.*

Little Miss Marker
  —from a story by Damon Runyon.

Sorrowful Jones (1949): **Bob Hope and Mary Jane Saunders.**

1934: (Par/Alexander Hall) Adolphe Menjou.
1949: *Sorrowful Jones* (Par/Sidney Lanfield) Bob Hope.

Little Old New York
  —from the play by Rida Johnson Young.
1923: (Goldwyn/Sidney Olcott) Marion Davies.
1940: (Fox/Henry King) Alice Faye.

Little Shepherd of Kingdom Come, The
  —from the novel by John Fox, Jr.
1920: (Goldwyn/Wallace Worsley) Jack Pickford.
1928: (FN/Alfred Santell) Richard Barthelmess.
1961: (Fox/Andrew V. McLaglen) Jimmie Rodgers.

Little Women
  —from the novel by Louisa May Alcott.
1917: (British/G. B. Samuelson, Alexander Butler) Daisy Burrell.
1918: (Par/Harley Knowles) Lillian Hall.
1933: (RKO/George Cukor) Katharine Hepburn.
1949: (MGM/Mervyn LeRoy) June Allyson.

Living Dead, The
  —from "The Black Cat," a story by Edgar Allan Poe.
1932: (German/Richard Oswald) Paul Wegener.
1934: *Black Cat, The* (U/Edgar G. Ulmer) Boris Karloff.
1941: *Black Cat, The* (U/Albert S. Rogell) Basil Rathbone.
1962: *Tales of Terror* (AIP/Roger Corman) Vincent Price.
1966: *Black Cat, The* (HEH/Harold Hoffman) Robyn Baker.

Living It Up
  See *Nothing Sacred.*

Lodger The
  —from a novel by Marie Belloc Lowndes.
1926: (British/Alfred Hitchcock) Ivor Novello.
1933: (British/Maurice Elvey) Ivor Novello.
1944: (Fox/John Brahm) Laird Cregar.
1953: *Man in the Attic* (Fox/Hugo Fregonese) Jack Palance.

London After Midnight
1927: (MGM/Tod Browning) Lon Chaney.
1935: *Mark of the Vampire* (MGM/Tod Browning) Lionel Barrymore.

Lone Star Ranger, The
  —from the novel by Zane Grey.
1919: (Fox/J. Gordon Edwards) William Farnum.
1923: (Fox/Lambert Hillyer) Tom Mix.
1930: (Fox/A. F. Erickson) George O'Brien.
1942: (Fox/James Tinling) John Kimbrough.

Lord Jim
  —from the novel by Joseph Conrad.

1927: (Par/Victor Fleming) Percy Marmont.
1967: (Col/Richard Brooks) Peter O'Toole.

Lorna Doone
   —from the novel by Richard Doddridge Blackmore.
1911: (Thanhouser).
1912: (British/Wilfred Noy) Dorothy Bellew.
1915: (Bio).
1920: (British/H. Lisle Lucoque) Bertie Gordon.
1922: (Ince/Maurice Tourneur) Madge Bellamy.
1935: (British/Basil Dean) Victoria Hopper.
1951: (Col/Phil Karlson) Barbara Hale.

Lost Horizon
   —from the novel by James Hilton.
1937: (Col/Frank Capra) Ronald Colman.
1973: (Col/Charles Jarrott) Peter Finch.

Lost Lady, A
   —from a story by Willa Cather.
1925: (WB/Harry Beaumont) Irene Rich.
1934: (WB/Alfred E. Green) Barbara Stanwyck.

Lost Man, The
   See *Odd Man Out.*

Lost One, The
   See *Lady with the Camellias, The.*

Lost Patrol, The
   —from "Patrol," a story by Philip MacDonald.
1929: (British/Walter Summers) Cyril McLaglen.
1934: (RKO/John Ford) Victor McLaglen.

Lost World, The
   —from the novel by Conan Doyle.
1925: (FN/Harry Hoyt) Wallace Beery.
1960: (Fox/Irwin Allen) Claude Rains.

Love
   See *Anna Karenina.*

Love Affair
1939: (RKO/Leo McCarey) Charles Boyer.
1957: *Affair To Remember, An* (Fox/Leo McCarey) Cary Grant.

Love From a Stranger
   —from the play by Frank Vosper,
      based on "Philomel Cottage," a story by Agatha Christie.
1937: (UA/Rowland V. Lee) Basil Rathbone.
1947: (EL/Richard Whorf) John Hodiak.

Love in a Wood
   See *As You Like It.*

Love Is News
1937: (Fox/Tay Garnett) Tyrone Power.
1943: *Sweet Rosie O'Grady* (Fox/Irving Cummings) Betty Grable.
1948: *That Wonderful Urge* (Fox/Robert B. Sinclair) Tyrone Power.

Love Is on the Air
   See *Hi, Nellie.*

Lovely To Look At
   See *Roberta.*

Loves of Carmen, The
   See *Carmen.*

Love That Brute
   See *Tall, Dark and Handsome.*

Lt. Robin Crusoe, U.S.N.
   See *Robinson Crusoe.*

Lure of the Wilderness
   See *Swamp Water.*

M
1931: (German/Fritz Lang) Peter Lorre.
1951: (Col/Joseph Losey) David Wayne.

Mad about Music
1938: (U/Norman Taurog) Deanna Durbin.
1956: *Toy Tiger, The* (U/Jerry Hopper) Jeff Chandler.

Madame Bovary
   See *Unholy Love.*

Madame Butterfly
   —from the opera by Puccini.
1915: (Par) Mary Pickford.
1932: (Par/Marion Gering) Sylvia Sidney.
1941: *Dream of Butterfly, The* (Italian/Carmine Gallone) Maria Cebotari.
1956: (Italian/S. Gallone) Kauru Yachigusa.

Mad Love
   See *Hands of Orlac, The.*

Mad Room, The
   See *Ladies in Retirement.*

Magnificent Ambersons, The
   See *Pampered Youth.*

Magnificent Lie, The
   See *Fool's Paradise.*

Magnificent Obsession
—from a novel by Lloyd C. Douglas.
1935: (U/John M. Stahl) Irene Dunne.
1954: (U/Douglas Sirk) Jane Wyman.

Magnificent Seven, The
See *Seven Samurai, The.*

Main Street
—from the story by Sinclair Lewis.
1923: (WB/Harry Beaumont) Florence Vidor.
1936: *I Married a Doctor* (FN/Archie Mayo) Pat O'Brien.

Major and the Minor, The
—from *Connie Goes Home,* a play by Edward Childs Carpenter and "Sunny Goes Home," a story by Fannie Kilbourne.
1942: (Par/Billy Wilder) Ray Milland.
1955: *You're Never Too Young* (Par/Norman Taurog) Martin and Lewis.

Make Me a Star
See *Merton of the Movies.*

Making of O'Malley, The
1925: (FN/Lambert Hillyer) Milton Sills.
1937: *Great O'Malley, The* (WB/William Dieterle) Pat O'Brien.

Male and Female
See *Admirable Crichton, The.*

Male Animal, The
—from a play by Elliott Nugent and James Thurber.
1942: (WB/Elliott Nugent) Hendy Fonda.
1952: *She's Working Her Way Through College* (WB/H. Bruce Humberstone) Virginia Mayo.

Mame
See *Auntie Mame.*

Man Called Gannon, A
See *Man Without a Star.*

Man Friday
See *Robinson Crusoe.*

Man in Half-Moon Street, The
—from a play by Barre Lyndon.
1944: (Par/Ralph Murphy) Nils Asther.
1959: *Man Who Could Cheat Death, The* (British/Terence Fisher) Anton Diffring.

Man in the Attic
See *Lodger, The.*

Man in the Iron Mask, The
—from the novel by Alexandre Dumas.
1928: (British/George J. Banfield) G. H. Mulcaster.
1929: *Iron Mask, The* (UA/Allan Dwan) Douglas Fairbanks.
1939: (UA/James Whale) Louis Hayward.
1952: *Lady in the Iron Mask, The* (Fox/Ralph Murphy) Patricia Medina.
1962: *Prisoner of the Iron Mask, The* (Italian/Francesco De Feo) Michel Lemoine.

Man of La Mancha
See *Don Quixote.*

Man of the Forest
—from the novel by Zane Grey.
1921: (HOD) Carl Gantvoort.
1926: (Par/John Waters) Jack Holt.
1933: (Par/Henry Hathaway) Randolph Scott.

Manslaughter
—from a story by Alice Duer Miller.
1922: (Par/Cecil B. DeMille) Thomas Meighan.
1930: (Par/George Abbott) Fredric March.

Man Who Could Cheat Death, The
See *Man in Half-Moon Street, The.*

Man Who Knew Too Much, The
1934: (British/Alfred Hitchcock) Leslie Banks.
1956: (Par/Alfred Hitchcock) James Stewart.

Man Who Played God, The
—from *The Silent Voice,* a play by Jules Eckert Goodman.
1922: (UA/Harmon Weight) George Arliss.
1932: (WB/John G. Adolfi) George Arliss.
1955: *Sincerely Yours* (WB/Gordon Douglas) Liberace.

Man Who Talked Too Much, The
See *Mouthpiece, The.*

Man Who Wouldn't Talk, The
See *Valiant, The.*

Man without a Country, The
—from a story by Edward Everett Hale.
1909: (Edison).
1917: (Jewel/Ernest C. Warde).
1925: *As No Man Has Loved* (Fox/Rowland V. Lee) Edward Hearn.
1938: (Vitaphone short/Crane Wilbur).

Man without a Star
—from a novel by Dee Linford.
1955: (U/King Vidor) Kirk Douglas.
1969: *Man Called Gannon, A* (U/James Goldstone) Tony Franciosa.

Marked Men
  See *Broncho Billy and the Baby.*

Mark of the Vampire
  See *London after Midnight.*

Mark of Zorro, The
  —from *The Curse of Capistrano,* a novel by Johnston Mc-
    Culley.
1920: (UA/Fred Niblo) Douglas Fairbanks.
1940: (Fox/Rouben Mamoulian) Tyrone Power.
1975: *Zorro* (Italian/Duccio Tessari) Alain Delon.

Martin Eden
  —from a novel by Jack London.
1914: (Par).
1918: *Creation Can't Be Bought* (Russian).
1942: *Adventures of Martin Eden, The* (Col/Sidney Salkow)
    Glenn Ford.

Masquerader, The
  —from a novel by Katherine Cecil Thurston and a play
    by John Hunter Booth.
1922: (FN/James Young) Guy Bates Post.
1933: (UA/Richard Wallace) Ronald Colman.

Mata Hari
  See *Mata Hari: The Red Dancer.*

Mata Hari Agent H-21
  See *Mata Hari: The Red Dancer.*

Mata Hari: The Red Dancer
1928: (BRI/Friedrich Fehr) Magda Sonja.

The Matchmaker (1958): **Anthony Perkins and Shirley
Booth.**

1932: *Mata Hari* (MGM/George Fitzmaurice) Greta Garbo.
1964: *Mata Hari Agent H-21* (French/Jean-Louis Richard)
    Jeanne Moreau.

Matchmaker, The
  —from the play by Thornton Wilder.
1958: (Par/Joseph Anthony) Shirley Booth.
1969: *Hello, Dolly* (Fox/Gene Kelly) Barbra Streisand.

Maybe It's Love
  See *Saturday's Children.*

Mayerling
  —from *Idyl's End,* a novel by Claude Anet.
1915: (Russian).
1937: (French/Anatole Litvak) Charles Boyer.
1968: (British/Terence Young) Omar Sharif.

Mayor of Hell, The
1933: (WB/Archie Mayo) James Cagney.
1938: *Crime School* (FN/Lewis Seiler) Humphrey Bogart.
1939: *Hell's Kitchen* (WB/Lewis Seiler, E. A. Dupont)
    Ronald Reagan.

Maytime
  —from a play by Rida Johnson Young and Sigmund
    Romberg.
1923: (Preferred/Louis Gannier) Ethel Shannon.
1937: (MGM/Robert Z. Leonard) Jeanette MacDonald.

Men Are Like That
  See *Show-Off, The.*

Men of Sherwood Forest
  See *Robin Hood and His Merry Men.*

Merry Widow, The
  —from the operetta by Franz Lehar; libretto by Victor
    Leon and Leo Stein.
1913: (French).
1925: (MGM/Erich von Stroheim) Mae Murray.
1934: (MGM/Ernst Lubitsch) Jeanette MacDonald.
1952: (MGM/Curtis Bernhardt) Lana Turner.

Merton of the Movies
  —from the book by Harry Leon Wilson and the play
    by George S. Kaufman and Marc Connelly.
1924: (Par/James Cruze) Glenn Hunter.
1932: *Make Me A Star* (Par/William Beaudine) Stuart Er-
    win.
1947: (MGM/Robert Alton) Red Skelton.

Michigan Kid, The
  —from a story by Rex Beach.
1928: (U/Irvin Willat) Renée Adorée.
1947: (U/Ray Taylor) Jon Hall.

Hello, Dolly (1969): **Walter Matthau and Barbra Streisand.**

Midsummer Night's Dream, A
—from the play by William Shakespeare.
1909: (Vit).
1914: (German/Werner Krauss).
1935: (WB/Max Reinhardt, William Dieterle) James Cagney.
1959: (Czech/Puppets).
1967: (Col/Dan Eriksen) Ballet.
1968: (British/Peter Hall) Paul Rogers.

Mikado, The
See *Fan-Fan.*

Milky Way, The
—from a play by Lynn Root and Harry Clork.
1936: (Par/Leo McCarey) Harold Lloyd.
1946: *Kid from Brooklyn, The* (RKO/Norman Z. McLeod) Danny Kaye.

Millionaire, The
—from "Idle Hands," a story by Earl Derr Biggers.
1931: (WB/John G. Adolfi) George Arliss.
1947: *That Way with Women* (WB/Frederick DeCordova) Dane Clark.

Mill on the Floss, The
—from the novel by George Eliot.
1915: (Mutual).
1937: (British/Tim Whelan) Frank Lawton.

Miracle Man, The
—from a novel by Frank L. Packard and a play by George M. Cohan.
1919: (Par/George Loane Tucker) Thomas Meighan.
1932: (Par/Norman Z. McLeod) Chester Morris.

Miracle of Morgan's Creek, The
1944: (Par/Preston Sturges) Eddie Bracken.
1958: *Rock-a-Bye Baby* (Par/Frank Tashlin) Jerry Lewis.

Mirage
 —from *Fallen Angel,* a novel by Walter Ericson.
1965: (U/Edward Dmytryk) Gregory Peck.
1968: *Jigsaw* (U/James Goldstone) Harry Guardino.

Miss Brewster's Millions
 See *Brewster's Millions.*

Mississippi
 See *Fighting Coward, The.*

Miss Robin Crusoe
 See *Robinson Crusoe.*

M'Liss
 —from a story by Bret Harte.
1915: (World).
1918: (Par/Marshall Neilan) Mary Pickford.
1922: *Girl Who Ran Wild, The* (U/Rupert Julian) Gladys
      Walton.
1936: (RKO/George Nicholls, Jr.) Anne Shirley.

Monkey's Paw, The
 —from the story by W. W. Jacobs.
1915: (British/Sidney Northcote) John Lawson.
1923: (British/Manning Haynes) Moore Marriott.
1933: (RKO/Wesley Ruggles) C. Aubrey Smith.
1948: (British/Norman Lee) Milton Rosmer.

Monsieur Beaucaire
 —from the novel by Booth Tarkington.
1924: (Par/Sidney Olcott) Rudolph Valentino.
1946: (Par/George Marshall) Bob Hope.

Monte Cristo
 See *Count of Monte Cristo, The.*

Moon Over Miami
 See *Three Blind Mice.*

More the Merrier, The
1943: (Col/George Stevens) Jean Arthur.
1966: *Walk, Don't Run* (Col/Charles Walters) Cary Grant.

Morning Glory
 —from a play by Zoe Akins.
1933: (RKO/Lowell Sherman) Katharine Hepburn.
1958: *Stage Struck* (BV/Sidney Lumet) Henry Fonda.

Most Dangerous Game, The
 —from a story by Richard Connell.
1932: (RKO/Ernest Schoedsack, ·Irving Pichel) Joel Mc-
      Crea.

The Most Dangerous Game (1932): **Fay Wray and Joel McCrea.**

1946: *Game of Death, A* (RKO/Robert Wise) John Loder.
1949: *Johnny Allegro* (Col/Ted Tetzlaff) George Raft.
1950: *Kill or Be Killed* (EL/Max Nosseck) Lawrence Tier-
      ney.
1956: *Run for the Sun* (UA/Roy Boulting) Richard Wid-
      mark.

Most Dangerous Sin, The
 See *Crime and Punishment.*

Run for the Sun (1956): **Richard Widmark and Jane Greer.**

Mother Carey's Chickens
—from a novel by Kate Douglass Wiggin.
1938: (RKO/Rowland V. Lee) Fay Bainter.
1963: *Summer Magic* (Disney/James Neilson) Hayley Mills.

Mouthpiece, The
—from a play by Frank J. Collins.
1932: (WB/James Flood, Elliott Nugent) Warren William.
1940: *Man Who Talked Too Much, The* (FN/Vincent Sherman) George Brent.
1955: *Illegal* (WB/Lewis Allen) Edward G. Robinson.

Move Over, Darling
See *My Favorite Wife.*

Mr. Music
See *Accent on Youth.*

Mr. Robinson Crusoe
See *Robinson Crusoe.*

Mrs. Wiggs of the Cabbage Patch
—from the novel by Alice Hegan Rice.
1914: (CMPC).
1919: (Par/Hugh Ford) Marguerite Clark.
1934: (Par/Norman Taurog) W. C. Fields.
1942: (Par/Ralph Murphy) Hugh Herbert.

Mr. Wu
—from the novel by Louise Jordan Miln.
1919: (British/Maurice Elvey) Matheson Lang.
1927: (MGM/William Nigh) Lon Chaney.

Mujer de las Camellias, La
See *Lady with the Camellias, The.*

Murder at the Baskervilles
See *Hound of the Baskervilles, The.*

Murder, My Sweet
See *Falcon Takes Over, The.*

Murders in the Rue Morgue
—from the story by Edgar Allan Poe.
1914: (Sol A. Rosenberg)
1932: (U/Robert Florey) Bela Lugosi.
1954: *Phantom of the Rue Morgue* (WB/Roy Del Ruth) Karl Malden.
1972: (AIP/Gordon Hessler) Jason Robards.

My Darling Clementine
See *Frontier Marshal.*

My Fair Lady
See *Pygmalion.*

My Favorite Wife
1940: (RKO/Garson Kanin) Cary Grant.
1963: *Move Over, Darling* (Fox/Michael Gordon) Doris Day.

My Man Godfrey
—from *Ten Eleven Fifth,* a novel by Eric Hatch.
1936: (U/Gregory LaCava) William Powell.
1957: (U/Henry Koster) David Niven.

My Sister Eileen
—from a play by Joseph Fields and Jerome Chodorov.
1942: (Col/Alexander Hall) Rosalind Russell.
1955: (Col/Richard Quine) Betty Garrett.

Mysterious Island, The
—from the novel by Jules Verne.
1929: (MGM/Lucien Hubbard) Lionel Barrymore.
1941: (Russian/E. Penzline, B. Chelintzev) M. V. Commisarov.
1951: (Col. serial/Spencer G. Bennet) Richard Crane.
1961: (Col/Cy Endfield) Michael Craig.
1974: *Mysterious Island of Captain Nemo, The* (Cinerama/Henri Colpi, Juan Antonio Bardem) Omar Sharif.

Mysterious Island of Captain Nemo, The
See *Mysterious Island, The.*

Mysterious Rider, The
—from the novel by Zane Grey.
1921: (HOD/Benjamin B. Hampton) Robert McKim.
1927: (Par/John Waters) Jack Holt.
1933: (Par/Fred Allen) Kent Taylor.
1938: (Par/Lesley Selander) Douglass Dumbrille.

Mystery of the 13th Guest
See *Thirteenth Guest, The.*

Mystery of the Wax Museum **(1933): Lionel Atwill.**

House of Wax (1953): Paul Cavanagh and Vincent Price.

Mystery of the Wax Museum
—from a play by Charles S. Belden.
1933: (WB/Michael Curtiz) Lionel Atwill.
1953: *House of Wax* (WB/Andre De Toth) Vincent Price.

Nana
—from the novel by Emile Zola.
1913: (Italian).
1926: (French/Jean Renoir) Catherine Hessling.
1934: (UA/Dorothy Arzner) Anna Sten.
1957: (French/Christian Jaque) Martine Carol.
1971: (Swedish/Mac Ahlberg) Anna Gael.

Narrow Corner, The
—from a story by Somerset Maugham.
1933: (WB/Alfred E. Green) Douglas Fairbanks, Jr.
1936: *Isle of Fury* (WB/Frank McDonald) Humphrey Bogart.

Nervous Wreck, The
—from a play by Owen Davis.
1926: (PDC/Scott Sidney) Harrison Ford.
1930: *Whoopie* (UA/Thornton Freeland) Eddie Cantor.

1944: *Up in Arms* (RKO/Elliott Nugent) Danny Kaye.

Nevada
—from the novel by Zane Grey.
1927: (Par/John Waters) Gary Cooper.
1936: (Par/Charles Barton) Buster Crabbe.
1944: (RKO/Edward Killy) Robert Mitchum.

New Gulliver, The
See *Gulliver's Travels.*

New Moon
—from the operetta by Sigmund Romberg, Oscar Hammerstein II, Frank Mandel, and Lawrence Schwab.
1930: (MGM/Jack Conway) Grace Moore.
1940: (MGM/Robert Z. Leonard) Nelson Eddy.

Nicholas Nickelby
—from the novel by Charles Dickens.
1903: (Bio).
1912: (Thanhouser).
1947: (British/Cavalcanti) Cedric Hardwicke.

Night Creatures
See *Dr. Syn.*

Night Must Fall
—from a play by Emlyn Williams.
1937: (MGM/Richard Thorpe) Robert Montgomery.
1964: (MGM/Karel Reisz) Albert Finney.

Night of Mystery
See *Greene Murder Case, The.*

Night of the Garter, A
See *Getting Gertie's Garter.*

Nights of Cabiria
1957: (Italian/Federico Fellini) Giulietta Masina.
1969: *Sweet Charity* (U/Bob Fosse) Shirley MacLaine.

Nikki, Wild Dog of the North
See *Nomads of the North.*

Ninotchka
1939: (MGM/Ernst Lubitsch) Greta Garbo.
1957: *Silk Stockings* (MGM/Rouben Mamoulian) Fred Astaire.

Nomads of the North
—from the novel by James Oliver Curwood.
1920: (FN/David M. Hartford) Lon Chaney.
1954: *Northern Patrol* (AA/Rex Bailey) Kirby Grant.
1961: *Nikki, Wild Dog of the North* (Disney/Jack Couffer) Jean Coutu.

No, No, Nanette
—from the play by Otto Harbach and Frank Mandel.
1930: (FN/Clarence Badger) Alexander Gray.
1940: (RKO/Herbert Wilcox) Anna Neagle.
1950: *Tea for Two* (WB/David Butler) Doris Day.

Nora
See *Doll's House, A.*

Northern Patrol
See *Nomads of the North.*

Nosferatu
—from *Dracula,* a novel by Bram Stoker.
1922: (German/F. W. Murnau) Max Schreck.
1931: *Dracula* (U/Tod Browning) Bela Lugosi.
1958: *Horror of Dracula* (British/Terence Fisher) Christopher Lee.
1971: *Count Dracula* (German-Spanish/Jesus Franco) Christopher Lee.

Nothing Sacred
—from a story by James H. Street.
1937: (UA/William Wellman) Fredric March.
1954: *Living It Up* (Par/Norman Taurog) Martin and Lewis.

Not So Dumb
See *Dulcy.*

Odd Man Out
—from a novel by F. L. Green.
1947: (British/Carol Reed) James Mason.
1969: *Lost Man, The* (U/Robert Alan Arthur) Sidney Poitier.

Of Human Bondage
—from a novel by Somerset Maugham.
1934: (RKO/John Cromwell) Bette Davis.
1946: (WB/Edmund Goulding) Eleanor Parker.
1964: (MGM/Ken Hughes, Henry Hathaway) Kim Novak.

Oh, Doctor!
—from a novel by Harry Leon Wilson.
1925: (U/Harry A. Pollard) Reginald Denny.
1937: (U/Raymond B. McCarey) Edward Everett Horton.

Oil for the Lamps of China
—from the novel by Alice Tisdale Hobart.
1935: (WB/Mervyn LeRoy) Pat O'Brien.
1941: *Law of the Tropics* (WB/Ray Enright) Constance Bennett.

Old Curiosity Shop, The
—from the novel by Charles Dickens.

Nosferatu (1922): **Max Schreck.**

Dracula (1931): **Bela Lugosi and Dwight Frye.**

Horror of Dracula (1958): **Christopher Lee.**

1911: (Thanhouser).

1912: (British/Frank Powell).

1913: (British/Thomas Bentley) E. Felton.

1921: (British/Thomas Bentley) Pino Conti.

1934: (British/Thomas Bentley) Hay Petrie.

1975: *Quilp* (British/Michael Tuchner) Anthony Newley.

Old Dark House, The
—from the novel by J. B. Priestly.

1932: (U/James Whale) Boris Karloff.

1963: (Col/William Castle) Tom Poston.

Oliver!
See *Oliver Twist.*

Oliver Twist
—from the novel by Charles Dickens.

1909: (Vit) Elita Otis.

1910: (French).

1912: (GPSC) Nat C. Goodwin.

1912: (British/Thomas Bentley) John McMahon.

1916: (Par) Tully Marshall.

1921: *Oliver Twist, Jr.* (Fox/Millard Webb) Wilson Hummell.

1922: (FN/Frank Lloyd) Lon Chaney.

1933: (Mon/William J. Cowen) Irving Pichel.

1948: (British/David Lean) Alec Guinness.

1968: *Oliver!* (Col/Carol Reed) Ron Moody.

Oliver Twist, Jr.
See *Oliver Twist.*

Omega Man, The
See *Last Man on Earth, The.*

On a Deserted Island
See *Victory.*

Once a Lady
See *Three Sinners.*

Once You Kiss a Stranger
See *Strangers on a Train.*

One Million B.C.

1940: (UA/Hal Roach, Hal Roach, Jr.) Victor Mature.

1966: *One Million Years B. C.* (Fox/Don Chaffey) Raquel Welch.

One Million Years B.C.
See *One Million B. C.*

One More Tomorrow
See *Animal Kingdom, The.*

One Romanic Night
See *Swan, The.*

One Stolen Night
—from "The Arab," a story by D. D. Calhoun.

1923: (Vit/Robert Ensminger) Alice Calhoun.

1929: (WB/Scott R. Dunlap) Betty Bronson.

One Way Passage
—from "S. S. Atlantic," a story by Robert Lord.

1932: (WB/Tay Garnett) Kay Francis.

1940: *'Til We Meet Again* (WB/Edmund Goulding) Merle Oberon.

Only Way, The
See *Tale of Two Cities, A.*

On the Riviera
See *Folies Bergere.*

Ophelia
See *Hamlet.*

Opposite Sex, The
See *Women, The.*

Othello
—from the play by William Shakespeare.

1914: (Italy).

1922: (German/Dimitri Buchowetzki) Emil·Jannings.

1955: (UA/Orson Welles) Orson Welles.

1955: (Russian/Sergeli Yutkevich) Sergei Bondarchuk.

1965: (British/Stuart Burge) Laurence Olivier.

Outcasts of Poker Flat, The
—from a story by Bret Harte.

1919: (U/John Ford) Harry Carey.

1937: (RKO/Christy Cabanne) Preston Foster.

1952: (Fox/Joseph M. Newman) Anne Baxter.

Outrage, The
See *Rashomon.*

Outward Bound
—from a play by Sutton Vane.

1930: (WB/Robert Milton) Leslie Howard.

1944: *Between Two Worlds* (WB/Edward A. Blatt) John Garfield.

Pacific Rendezvous
See *Rendezvous.*

Paid
See *Within the Law.*

Painted Veil, The
—from the novel by W. Somerset Maugham.

1934: (MGM/Richard Boleslawski) Greta Garbo.

1957: *Seventh Sin, The* (MGM/Ronald Neame) Eleanor Parker.

Painting the Clouds with Sunshine
See *Gold Diggers, The.*

Paleface The
1948: (Par/Norman Z. McLeod) Bob Hope.
1968: *Shakiest Gun in the West, The* (U/Alan Rafkin) Don Knotts.

Pampered Youth
—from *The Magnificent Ambersons*, a novel by Booth Tarkington.
1925: (Vit/David Smith) Cullen Landis.
1942: *Magnificent Ambersons, The* (RKO/Orson Welles) Joseph Cotten.

Paradise Lagoon
See *Admirable Crichton, The.*

Pardners
See *Rhythm on the Range.*

Paris When It Sizzles
See *Holiday for Henrietta.*

Passionate Plumber, The
See *Cardboard Lover, The.*

Passion of Joan of Arc, The
See *Joan of Arc.*

Peg O' My Heart
—from the play by J. Hartley Manners.
1922: (Metro/King Vidor) Laurette Taylor.
1933: (MGM/Robert Z. Leonard) Marion Davies.

Peking Express
See *Shanghai Express.*

Penitentiary
See *Criminal Code, The.*

Penrod and Sam
—from the story by Booth Tarkington.
1923: (FN/William Beaudine) Ben Alexander.
1931: (FN/William Beaudine) Leon Janney.
1937: (FN/William McGann) Billy Mauch.

Penthouse
—from a story by Arthur Somers Roche.
1933: (MGM/W. S. Van Dyke) Warner Baxter.
1939: *Society Lawyer* (MGM/Edwin L. Marin) Walter Pidgeon.

People Will Talk
See *Dr. Praetorius.*

Pepé Le Moko
—from the novel by D'Ashelbe.
1937: (French/Julien Duvivier) Jean Gabin.
1938: *Algiers* (UA/John Cromwell) Charles Boyer.
1948: *Casbah* (U/John Berry) Tony Martin.

Perils of the Wild (Serial)
—from *The Swiss Family Robinson*, a novel by Johann David Wyss.
1925: (U/Francis Ford) Joe Bonomo.
1940: *Swiss Family Robinson, The* (RKO/Edward Ludwig) Thomas Mitchell.
1961: *Swiss Family Robinson, The.* (Disney/Ken Annakin) John Mills.

Peter Ibbetson
—from a novel by George Du Maurier.
1914: (Par).
1921: *Forever* (Par/George Fitzmaurice) Wallace Reid.
1935: (Par/Henry Hathaway) Gary Cooper.

Peter Pan
—from the play by James M. Barrie.
1924: (Par/Herbert Brenon) Betty Bronson.
1953: (Disney/Animation).

Petrified Forest, The
—from a play by Robert E. Sherwood.
1936: (WB/Archie Mayo) Leslie Howard.
1945: *Escape in the Desert* (WB/Edward A. Blatt) Philip Dorn.

Pettigrew's Girl
—from a story by Dana Burnet.
1919: (Par/George Melford) Ethel Clayton.
1929: *Shopworn Angel, The* (Par/Richard Wallace) Nancy Carroll.
1938: *Shopworn Angel, The* (MGM/H. C. Potter) Margaret Sullivan.

Phantom of the Rue Morgue
See *Murders in the Rue Morgue.*

Pickwick Papers, The
—from the novel by Charles Dickens.
1913: (Vit/Larry Trimble) John Bunny.
1952: (British/Noel Langley) Nigel Patrick.

Picture of Dorian Gray, The
—from the novel by Oscar Wilde.
1913: (Phillips Smalley) Wallace Reid.
1915: (Thanhouser) Harris Gordon.
1915: (Russian/Meyerhold).
1916: (British/Fred W. Durrant) Henry Victor.
1917: (Hungarian/Alfred Deesy) Bela Lugosi.

1945: (MGM/Albert Lewin) George Sanders.
1970: *Dorian Gray* (AIP/Massimo Dallamano) Helmut Berger.

Picture Snatcher, The
—from a story by Danny Ahern.
1933: (WB/Lloyd Bacon) James Cagney.
1942: *Escape from Crime* (WB/D. Ross Lederman) Richard Travis.

Pit and the Pendulum, The
—from the story by Edgar Allan Poe.
1910: (Warwick/Henri Desfontaines).
1913: (Solax/Alice Guy) Darwin Karr.
1961: (AIP/Roger Corman) Vincent Price.

Plainsman, The
—from *Wild Bill Hickock*, a novel by Frank J. Wilstach.
1936: (Par/Cecil B. DeMille) Gary Cooper.
1966: (U/David Lowell Rich) Don Murray.

Platinum High School
See *Bad Day at Black Rock*.

Pleasure Seekers, The
See *Three Coins in the Fountain*.

Pocketful of Miracles
See *Lady for a Day*.

Pollyana
—from a novel by Eleanor H. Porter.
1920: (UA/Paul Powell) Mary Pickford.
1960: (Disney/David Swift) Hayley Mills.

Polly of the Circus
—from the play by Margaret Mayo.
1917: (Goldwyn/Charles Thomas Horan, Edwin L. Hollywood) Mae Marsh.
1932: (MGM/Alfred Santell) Marion Davies.

Port of Seven Seas
See *Fanny*.

Prince and the Pauper, The
—from the novel by Mark Twain.
1909: (Edison) Cecil Spooner.

The Prince and the Pauper (1937): **Bobby Mauch and Errol Flynn.**

Quo Vadis (1925): **Emil Jannings.**

Quo Vadis (1951): **Peter Ustinov.**

1915: (Famous Players) Marguerite Clark.
1923: (Austrian/Alexander Kardo) Tibi Lubin.
1937: (FN/William Keighley) Errol Flynn.
1962: (Disney/Don Chaffey) Guy Williams.

Prince of Thieves
See *Robin Hood and His Merry Men.*

Princess O'Hara
—from a story by Damon Runyon.
1935: (U/David Burton) Jean Parker.
1943: *It Ain't Hay* (U/Erle C. Kenton) Abbott and Costello.

Prisoner of Shark Island, The
1936: (Fox/John Ford) Warner Baxter.
1953: *Hellgate* (Lip/Charles Marquis Warren) Sterling Hayden.

Prisoner of the Iron Mask, The
See *Man in the Iron Mask, The.*

Private Affairs of Bel Ami, The
See *Bel Ami.*

Private Number
See *Common Clay.*

Public Enemy's Wife
—from a story by P. J. Wolfson and David O. Selznick.
1936: (WB/Nick Grinde) Pat O'Brien.
1941: *Bullets for O'Hara* (WB/William K. Howard) Joan Perry.

Pygmalian
—from the play by G. B. Shaw.
1935: (German/Erich Engel) Jenny Jugo.
1938: (British/Anthony Asquith, Leslie Howard) Leslie Howard.
1964: *My Fair Lady* (WB/George Cukor) Rex Harrison.

Quality Street
—from a play by James M. Barrie.
1927: (MGM/Sidney Franklin) Marion Davies.
1937: (RKO/George Stevens) Katharine Hepburn.

Quilp
See *Old Curiosity Shop, The.*

Quo Vadis
—from the novel by Henryk Sienkiewicz.
1912: (Italian/Enrico Guazzoni) G. Serena.
1925: (Italian/Arturo Ambrosio) Emil Jannings.
1951: (MGM/Mervyn LeRoy) Robert Taylor.

The Racket (1928): Thomas Meighan and Lucien Prival.

Rachel and the Stranger
—from a story by Howard Fast.
1948: (RKO/Norman Foster) Loretta Young.
1976: Remake announced to star Julie Andrews.

Racket, The
—from the play by Bartlett Cormack.
1928: (Par/Lewis Milestone) Thomas Meighan.
1951: (RKO/John Cromwell) Robert Mitchum.

The Racket (1951): Robert Mitchum, William Talman, and William Conrad.

Raffles
See *Raffles, The Amateur Cracksman.*

Raffles, Ladra Gentiluomo
See *Raffles, The Amateur Cracksman.*

Raffles, the Amateur Cracksman
  —from the stories by E. W. Hornung.
1905: (Vit/G. M. Anderson) J. Barney Sherry.
1917: (Hyclass/George Irving) John Barrymore.
1920: *Raffles, Ladra Gentiluomo* (Italian).
1925: (U/King Baggot) House Peters.
1930: *Raffles* (UA/Harry D'Abbadie D'Arrast, George Fitzmaurice) Ronald Colman.
1940: *Raffles* (UA/Sam Wood) David Niven.

Rainbow Trail
  —from a novel by Zane Grey.
1918: (Fox/Frank Lloyd) Buck Jones.
1925: (Fox/Lynn Reynolds) Tom Mix.
1932: (Fox/David Howard) George O'Brien.

Rains Came, The
  —from the novel by Louis Bromfield.
1939: (Fox/Clarence Brown) Myrna Loy.
1955: *Rains of Ranchipur, The* (Fox/Jean Negulesco) Lana Turner.

Rains of Ranchipur, The
  See *Rains Came, The*

Ramona
  —from a novel by Helen Hunt Jackson.
1910: (Bio/D. W. Griffith) Mary Pickford.
1916: (Clune/Donald Crisp) Adda Gleason.
1928: (UA/Edwin Carewe) Dolores del Rio.
1936: (Fox/Henry King) Loretta Young.

Rashomon
  —from *In the Forest*, a novel by Ryunosuke Akutagawa.
1951: (Japanese/Akira Kurosawa) Toshiro Mifune.
1964: *Outrage, The* (MGM/Martin Ritt) Paul Newman.

Raskolnikov
  See *Crime and Punishment*.

Rebecca of Sunnybrook Farm
  —from the book by Kate Douglas Wiggin.
1917: (Par/Marshall Neilan) Mary Pickford.
1932: (Fox/Alfred Santell) Marian Nixon.
1938: (Fox/Allan Dwan) Shirley Temple.

Red Shadow, The
  See *Desert Song, The*.

Rendezvous
  —from *American Black Chamber*, a novel by Major Herbert O. Yardley.
1935: (MGM/William K. Howard) William Powell.
1942: *Pacific Rendezvous* (MGM/George Sidney) Lee Bowman.

Rest Is Silence, The
  See *Hamlet*.

Resurrection
  —from the novel by Leo Tolstoy.
1907: (French).
1909: (Russian).
1909: (Bio/D. W. Griffith) Florence Lawrence.
1912: (Masko) Blanche Walsh.
1915: *Woman's Resurrection, A* (Fox/J. Gordon Edwards).
1918: (Par/Edward Jose) Pauline Frederick.
1927: (UA/Edwin Carewe) Dolores del Rio.
1931: (U/Edwin Carewe) Lupe Velez.
1934: *We Live Again* (UA/Rouben Mamoulian) Anna Sten.
1961: (Russian/Mikhail Schweitzer) Tamara Syomina.

Return of Peter Grimm, The
  —from the play by David Belasco.
1926: (Fox/Victor Schertzinger) Alec B. Francis.
1935: (RKO/George Nicholls, Jr.) Lionel Barrymore.

Revizor
  —from a play by Nikolai Gogol.
1915: (Russian).
1937: *Inspector General, The* (Czech/Mac Fric) Viasta Burian.
1949: *Inspector General, The* (WB/Henry Koster) Danny Kaye.
1954: *Inspector General, The* (Russian/Vladimir Petrov) I. Gorbachev.

Rhythm on the Range
1936: (Par/Norman Taurog) Bing Crosby.
1956: *Pardners* (Par/Norman Taurog) Martin and Lewis.

Richard, the Lion-Hearted
  —from *The Talisman*, a novel by Sir Walter Scott.
1923: (APD/Chet Withey) Wallace Beery.
1954: *King Richard and the Crusaders* (WB/David Butler) Rex Harrison.

Richard III
  —from the play by William Shakespeare.
1908: (Vit) Thomas H. Ince.
1911: (British) Frank Benson.
1913: (Sterling/M. B. Dudley) Frederick Warde.
1956: (British/Laurence Olivier, Anthony Bushell) Laurence Olivier.

Richelieu
  —from a play by Bulwer-Lytton.
1909: (Vit).
1911: *Cardinal's Edict, The* (Edison).
1914: (Bison) Lon Chaney.
1935: *Cardinal Richelieu* (UA/Rowland V. Lee) George Arliss.

Rich Man, Poor Girl
  See *Idle Rich*.

Riders of the Purple Sage
—from the novel by Zane Grey.
1918: (Fox/Frank Lloyd) Buck Jones.
1925: (Fox/Lynn Reynolds) Tom Mix.
1931: (Fox/Hamilton MacFadden) George O'Brien.
1941: (Fox/James Tinling) George Montgomery.

Riding High
See *Broadway Bill*.

Right To Be Happy, The
See *Scrooge*.

Rip Van Winkle
—from the story by Washington Irving.
1903: (British/Alf Collins) Alf Collins.
1903: (Bio) Joseph Jefferson.
1908: (Selig).
1910: (Thanhouser).
1912: (Vit/Charles Kent) Robert McWade.
1914: (British/Stuart Kinder) Fred Storey.
1914: (Alco) Thomas Jefferson.
1921: (HOD/Warde Lascelle) Thomas Jefferson.

River of Romance
See *Fighting Coward, The*.

River's End
—from a story by James Oliver Curwood.
1930: (WB/Michael Curtiz) Charles Bickford.
1940: (WB/Ray Enright) Dennis Morgan.

Robber's Roost
—from a story by Zane Grey.
1932: (Fox/Louis King) George O'Brien.
1955: (UA/Sidney Salkow) George Montgomery.

Roberta
—from the musical play by Otto Harbach and Jerome Kern.
1935: (RKO/William A. Seiter) Fred Astaire.
1952: *Lovely To Look At* (MGM/Mervyn LeRoy) Howard Keel.

Robin Hood
See *Robin Hood and His Merry Men*.

Robin Hood and His Merry Men
1908: (British/Percy Stow).
1912: *Robin Hood Outlawed* (British/Charles Raymond) Brian Plant.
1912: *Robin Hood* (U. S./Etienne Arnaud) Alec B. Francis.
1922: *Robin Hood* (UA/Allan Dwan) Douglas Fairbanks.
1938: *Adventures of Robin Hood, The* (WB/Michael Curtiz, William Keighley) Errol Flynn.
1948: *Prince of Thieves* (Col/Howard Bretherton) Jon Hall.
1952: *Story of Robin Hood, The* (RKO/Ken Annakin) Richard Todd.

1954: *Men of Sherwood Forest* (British/Val Guest) Don Taylor.
1961: *Sword of Sherwood Forest* (British/Terence Fisher) Richard Greene.
1973: *Robin Hood* (Disney/Animation).
1976: Remake announced to star Sean Connery.

Robin Hood Outlawed
See *Robin Hood and His Merry Men*.

Robinson Crusoe
—from the novel by Daniel Defoe.
1902: (French).
1903: (Lubin).
1910: (Danish).
1913: (Rex/Otis Turner) Robert Leonard.
1916: (Henry Savage).
1917: (U).
1924: (U short) Harry C. Myers.
1927: (British/M. A. Wetherell) M. A. Wetherell.
1932: *Mr. Robinson Crusoe* (UA/Edward Sutherland) Douglas Fairbanks.
1946: (Russian).
1954: *Adventures of Robinson Crusoe* (UA/Luis Buñuel) Dan O'Herlihy.
1954: *Miss Robin Crusoe* (Fox/Eugene Frenke) Amanda Blake.
1964: *Robinson Crusoe on Mars* (Par/Byron Haskin) Paul Mantee.
1966: *Lt. Robin Crusoe, U.S.N.* (Disney/Byron Paul) Dick Van Dyke.
1975: *Man Friday* (ITC/Jack Gold) Peter O'Toole.

Robinson Crusoe on Mars
See *Robinson Crusoe*.

Rob Roy
—from the novel by Sir Walter Scott.
1911: (British/Arthur Vivian) John Clyde.
1913: (Eclair) Robert Frazer.
1922: (British/W. P. Kellino) David Hawthorne.
1953: (Disney/Harold French) Richard Todd.

Rock-a-Bye Baby
See *Miracle of Morgan's Creek, The*.

Romance
—from the play by Edward Brewster Sheldon.
1920: (UA) Doris Keane.
1930: (MGM/Clarence Brown) Greta Garbo.

Romance of the Rio Grande
—from *Conquistador*, a novel by Katharine Fullerton Gerould.
1929: (Fox/Alfred Santell) Warner Baxter.
1941: (Fox/Herbert I. Leeds) Cesar Romero.

Romeo and Juliet
  —from a play by William Shakespeare.
1908: (Vit) Florence Lawrence.
1908: (British) Godfrey Tearle.
1911: (Thanhouser) Irma Taylor.
1912: (French).
1914: (Bio).
1916: (MGM/Maxwell Karger) Beverly Bayne.
1916: (Fox/J. Gordon Edwards) Theda Bara.
1936: (MGM/George Cukor) Norma Shearer.
1954: (UA/Renato Castellani) Laurence Harvey.
1956: *Ballet of Romeo and Juliet, The* (British/Lev Arnshtam) Yuri Zhdanov.
1961: *West Side Story* (UA/Robert Wise, Jerome Robbins) Natalie Wood.
1968: (Italian/Ricardo Freda) Gerald Meynier.
1968: (Par/Franco Zeffirelli) Leonard Whiting.

Room Service
  —from a play by John Murray and Allen Boretz.
1938: (RKO/William A. Seiter) The Marx Brothers.
1944: *Step Lively* (RKO/Tim Whelan) Frank Sinatra.

Rose Marie
  —from the operetta by Otto Harbach, Oscar Hammerstein II, and Rudolph Friml.
1928: (MGM/Lucien Hubbard) Joan Crawford.
1936: (MGM/W. S. Van Dyke II) Jeanette MacDonald.
1954: (MGM/Mervyn LeRoy) Ann Blyth.

Rose of the Rancho
  —from the play by Richard Walton Tully and David Belasco.
1914: (Par/Cecil B. DeMille) Bessie Barriscale.
1936: (Par/Marion Gering) John Boles.

Rose of Washington Square
1939: (Fox/Gregory Ratoff) Alice Faye.
1968: *Funny Girl* (Col/William Wyler) Barbra Streisand.

Roxie Hart
  See *Chicago.*

Ruggles of Red Gap
  —from the novel by Harry Leon Wilson.
1918: (Ess/L. C. Windom) Taylor Holmes.
1923: (Par/James Cruze) Edward Everett Horton.
1935: (Par/Leo McCarey) Charles Laughton.
1950: *Fancy Pants* (Par/George Marshall) Bob Hope.

Run for the Sun
  See *Most Dangerous Game, The.*

Rupert of Hentzau
  —from the novel by Anthony Hope.
1915: (British/George Loane Tucker) Henry Ainley.
1923: (Selznick/Victor Heerman) Bert Lytell.

Rose Marie (1936): **Jeanette MacDonald and Nelson Eddy.**

Sahara
  See *Thirteen, The.*

Saint Joan
  See *Joan of Arc.*

Sally
  —from the musical play by Guy Bolton and Jerome Kern.
1925: (FN/Alfred E. Green) Colleen Moore.
1929: (FN/John Francis Dillon) Marilyn Miller.

Sally, Irene, and Mary
  —from a play by Edward Dowling and Cyrus Wood.
1925: (MGM/Edmund Goulding) Joan Crawford.
1938: (Fox/William A. Seiter) Alice Faye.

Sal of Singapore
  —from *The Sentimentalist*, a novel by Dale Collins.
1929: (Pathé/Howard Higgin) Phyllis Haver.
1931: *His Woman* (Par/Edward Sloman) Gary Cooper.

Sanctuary
  See *Story of Temple Drake, The.*

Rose Marie (1954): Ann Blyth and Howard Keel.

Saturday's Children
— from a play by Maxwell Anderson.
1929: (FN/Gregory LaCava) Corinne Griffith.
1934: *Maybe It's Love* (FN/William McGann) Gloria Stuart.
1940: (WB/Vincent Sherman) John Garfield.

Scaramouche
— from the novel by Rafael Sabatini.
1923: (Metro/Rex Ingram) Ramon Novarro.
1952: (MGM/George Sidney) Stewart Granger.
1964: *Adventures of Scaramouche, The* (French/Antonio Isamendi) Gerard Barray.

Scared Stiff
See *Ghost Breaker, The.*

Scarlet Daredevil, The
See *Scarlet Pimpernel, The.*

Scarlet Letter, The
— from the novel by Nathaniel Hawthorne.
1917: (Fox/Carl Harbaugh) Mary Martin.
1926: (MGM/Victor Seastrom) Lillian Gish.
1934: (Majestic/Robert G. Vignola) Colleen Moore.

Scarlet Pimpernel, The
— from the novel by Baroness Orczy.
1917: (Fox/Richard Stanton) Dustin Farnum.
1919: *Elusive Pimpernel, The* (British/Maurice Elvey) Cecil Humphreys.
1929: *Scarlet Daredevil, The* (British/T. Hayes Hunter) Matheson Lang.
1935: (British/Harold Young) Leslie Howard.
1950: *Elusive Pimpernel, The* (British/Michael Powell) David Niven.

School for Scandal, The
— from the play by Richard Brinsley Sheridan.
1914: (Kalem/Kenean Buel) Alice Joyce.
1923: (British/Edwin Greenwood) Russell Thorndike.
1923: (British/Bertram Phillips) Basil Rathbone.
1930: (British/Maurice Elvey) Basil Gill.

Scrooge (1970): Albert Finney starred in this musical version of the Dickens classic.

Scrooge
—from "A Christmas Carol," a story by Charles Dickens.
1901: (British/W. R. Booth).
1908: *Christmas Carol, A* (Ess).
1910: *Christmas Carol, A* (Edison).
1913: (British/Leedham Bantock) Seymour Hicks.
1914: *Christmas Carol, A* (British/Harold Shaw) Charles Rock.
1916: *Right To Be Happy, The* (U/Rupert Julien).
1935: (British/Henry Edwards) Seymour Hicks.
1938: *Christmas Carol, A* (MGM/Edwin L. Marin) Reginald Owen.
1951: *Christmas Carol, A* (British/Brian Desmond Hurst) Alastair Sim.
1960: *Christmas Carol, A* (British short/Robert Hartford-Davis) John Hayter.
1970: (British/Ronald Neame) Albert Finney.

Secret Garden, The
—from the book by Frances Hodgson Burnett.
1919: (Par/G. Butler Clonebaugh) Lila Lee.
1949: (MGM/Frank M. Wilcox) Margaret O'Brien.

Secret Hour, The
—from *They Knew What They Wanted*, a play by Sidney Howard.
1928: (Par/Rowland V. Lee) Pola Negri.
1930: *Lady To Love, A* (MGM/Victor Seastrom) Vilma Banky.
1940: *They Knew What They Wanted* (RKO/Garson Kanin) Carole Lombard.

Secrets
—from the play by Rudolf Besier and May Edginton.
1924: (FN/Frank Borzage) Norma Talmadge.
1933: (UA/Frank Borzage) Mary Pickford.

Secret Service
—from the play by William Gillette.
1919: (Par/Hugh Ford) Robert Warwick.
1931: (RKO/J. Walter Ruben) Richard Dix.

Sentimental Journey
—from "The Little Horse," a story by Nelia Gardner White.
1946: (Fox/Walter Lang) Maureen O'Hara.
1958: *Gift of Love, The* (Fox/Jean Negulesco) Lauren Bacall.

Sergeants Three
See *Gunga Din.*

Seven Keys to Baldpate
—from the novel by Earl Derr Biggers and the play by George M. Cohan.
1917: (Par/Hugh Ford) George M. Cohan.
1925: (Par/Fred Newmeyer) Douglas MacLean.
1929: (RKO/Reginald Barker) Richard Dix.
1935: (RKO/William Hamilton, Edward Kelly) Gene Raymond.
1947: (RKO/Lew Landers) Philip Terry.

Seven Samurai, The
1954: (Japanese/Akira Kurosawa) Toshiro Mifune.
1960: *Magnificent Seven, The* (UA/John Sturges) Yul Brynner.

Seventh Heaven
—from a play by Austin Strong.
1927: (Fox/Frank Borzage) Janet Gaynor.
1937: (Fox/Henry King) James Stewart.

Seventh Sin, The
See *Painted Veil, The.*

Shadow of a Doubt
1943: (U/Alfred Hitchcock) Joseph Cotten.
1958: *Step Down to Terror* (U/Harry Keller) Charles Drake.

Shakiest Gun in the West, The
See *Paleface, The.*

Shanghai Express
—from a story by Harry Hervey.
1932: (Par/Josef von Sternberg) Marlene Dietrich.
1951: *Peking Express* (Par/William Dieterle) Joseph Cotten.

Shannons of Broadway, The
—from the play by James Gleason.
1929: (U/Emmett J. Flynn) James Gleason.
1938: *Goodbye Broadway* (U/Ray McCarey) Charles Winninger.

She
—from the novel by H. Rider Haggard.
1908: (Edison).
1911: (Thanhouser) James Cruze.
1916: (British/Will Barker, H. Lisle Lucoque) Henry Victor.
1917: (Fox/Kenear Buel) Valesha Suratt.
1925: (British/Leander de Cordova) Betty Blythe.
1935: (RKO/Irving Pichell, Lansing Holden) Randolph Scott.
1965: (British/Robert Day) Ursula Andress.

Shepherd of the Hills
—from the novel by Harold Bell Wright.
1919: (Wright) Catherine Curtis.
1928: (FN/Albert Rogell) John Boles.
1941: (Par/Henry Hathaway) John Wayne.
1963: (Howco/Ben Parker) Richard Arlen.

She's Working Her Way Through College
See *Male Animal, The.*

Shop Around the Corner, The
—from *Perfumerie*, a play by Nikolaus Laszlo.
1940: (MGM/Ernst Lubitsch) James Stewart.
1949: *In the Good Old Summertime* (MGM/Robert Z. Leonard) Judy Garland.

Shopworn Angel, The
See *Pettigrew's Girl.*

Shore Leave
—from a play by Hubert Osborne.
1925: (FN/J. S. Robertson) Richard Barthelmess.
1936: *Follow the Fleet* (RKO/Mark Sandrich) Fred Astaire.
1955: *Hit the Deck* (MGM/Roy Rowland) Jane Powell.

Short Cut to Hell
See *This Gun for Hire.*

Show-Off, The
—from a play by George Kelly.
1926: (Par/Malcolm St. Clair) Ford Sterling.
1930: *Men Are Like That* (Par/Frank Tuttle) Hal Skelly.
1934: (MGM/Charles F. Riesner) Spencer Tracy.
1946: (MGM/Harry Beaumont) Red Skelton.

Sign of the Cross, The
—from the play by Wilson Barrett.
1904: (British/William Haggar) Will Haggar, Jr.
1914: (Par) William Farnum.
1932: (Par/Cecil B. DeMille) Fredric March.

Silk Stockings
See *Ninotchka.*

Sincerely Yours
See *Man Who Played God, The.*

Singapore
1947: (U/John Brahm) Fred MacMurray.
1957: *Istanbul* (U/Joseph Pevney) Errol Flynn.

Singapore Woman
See *Dangerous.*

Six-Cylinder Love
—from a play by William Anthony McGuire.
1931: (Fox/Thornton Freeland) Spencer Tracy.
1939: *Honeymoon's Over, The* (Fox/Eugene Forde) Stuart Erwin.

Skyline
See *East Side, West Side.*

Slight Case of Murder, A
—from a play by Damon Runyon and Howard Lindsay.
1938: (WB/Lloyd Bacon) Edward G. Robinson.
1952: *Stop, You're Killing Me* (WB/Roy Del Ruth) Broderick Crawford.

Smashing the Money Ring
See *Jailbreak.*

Smiling Lieutenant, The
See *Waltz Dream, A.*

Smilin' Through
—from the play by Jane Cowl and Jane Murfin.
1922: (FN/S. A. Franklin) Norma Talmadge.
1932: (MGM/Sidney Franklin) Norma Shearer.
1941: (MGM/Frank Borzage) Jeanette MacDonald.

Smoky
—from the novel by Will James.
1946: (Fox/Louis King) Fred MacMurray.
1966: (Fox/George Sherman) Fess Parker.

So Big
—from the novel by Edna Ferber.
1924: (FN/Charles Brabin) Colleen Moore.
1932: (WB/William Wellman) Barbara Stanwyck.
1953: (WB/Robert Wise) Jane Wyman.

Society Lawyer
See *Penthouse.*

Society Scandal, A
—from *The Laughing Lady*, a play by Alfred Sutro.
1924: (Par/Allan Dwan) Gloria Swanson.
1929: *Laughing Lady, The* (Par/Victor Schertzinger) Ruth Chatterton.

So Big (1932): **Barbara Stanwyck and Dick Winslow.**

So Big (1953): **Jane Wyman.**

Song Is Born, A
  See *Ball of Fire*.

Son of Fury
  —from *Benjamin Blake,* a novel by Edison Marshall.
  1942: (Fox/John Cromwell) Tyrone Power.
  1953: *Treasure of the Golden Condor* (Fox/Delmer Daves)
  Cornel Wilde.

Sorrell and Son
  —from the novel by George Warwick Deeping.
  1927: (UA/Herbert Brenon) H. B. Warner.
  1934: (British/Jack Raymond) H. B. Warner.

Sorrowful Jones
  See *Little Miss Marker*.

So This Is London
  —from the play by Arthur Goodrich.
  1930: (Fox/John Blystone) Will Rogers.
  1939: (British/Thornton Freeland) Robertson Hare.

Spartacus
  1914: (Italian).
  1960: (U/Stanley Kubrick) Kirk Douglas.

Spawn of the North
  —from a novel by Barrett Willoughby.
  1938: (Par/Henry Hathaway) George Raft.
  1954: *Alaska Seas* (Par/Jerry Hopper) Robert Ryan.

Spiral Staircase, The
  —from *Some Must Watch,* a novel by Ethel Lina White.
  1946: (RKO/Robert Siodmak) Dorothy McGuire.
  1975: (WB/Peter Collinson) Jacqueline Bisset.

Spy Ship
  See *Fog Over Frisco*.

Squaw Man, The
  —from a play by Edwin Milton Royle.
  1914: (Par/Cecil B. DeMille) Dustin Farnum.
  1918: (Par/Cecil B. DeMille) Jack Holt.
  1931: (Par/Cecil B. DeMille) Warner Baxter.

Stage Struck
  See *Morning Glory*.

Star Is Born, A
  See *What Price Hollywood*.

State Fair
  —from the novel by Philip Stong.
  1933: (Fox/Henry King) Will Rogers.
  1945: (Fox/Walter Lang) Jeanne Crain.
  1961: (Fox/Jose Ferrer) Alice Faye.

Stella Dallas
  —from the novel by Olive Higgins Prouty.
  1925: (UA/Henry King) Ronald Colman.
  1937: (UA/King Vidor) Barbara Stanwyck.

Step Down to Terror
  See *Shadow of a Doubt*.

Step Lively
  See *Room Service*.

Stolen Hours
  See *Dark Victory*.

Stolen Life, A
  —from a novel by Karel J. Benes.
  1939: (British/Paul Czinner) Elisabeth Bergner.
  1946: (WB/Curtis Bernhardt) Bette Davis.

Stop, You're Killing Me
  See *Slight Case of Murder, A*.

Storm, The
  —from the play by Langdon McCormick.
  1922: (U/Reginald Barker) Matt Moore.
  1930: (U/William Wyler) Lupe Velez.

Storm Over the Nile
  See *Four Feathers, The*.

Story of Robin Hood, The
  See *Robin Hood and His Merry Men*.

Story of Temple Drake, The
  —from the novel by William Faulkner.
  1933: (Par/Stephen Roberts) Miriam Hopkins.
  1961: *Sanctuary* (Fox/Tony Richardson) Lee Remick.

Story of the Count of Monte Cristo, The
  See *Count of Monte Cristo, The*.

Story of the Little Minister, The
  —from the novel by James M. Barrie.
  1912: (Vit) Clara Kimball Young.
  1915: *Little Minister, The* (British/Percy Nash) Joan Ritz.
  1921: *Little Minister, The* (Par/Penrhyn Stanlaws) Betty
  Compson.
  1922: *Little Minister, The* (Vit/David Smith) Alice Calhoun.
  1934: *Little Minister, The* (RKO/Richard Wallace) Katharine Hepburn.

Strangers of the Night
  —from *Captain Applejack,* a play by Walter Hackett.
  1923: (Metro/Fred Niblo) Matt Moore.
  1931: *Captain Applejack* (WB/Hobart Henley) Mary Brian.

The Story of Temple Drake (1933): **Miriam Hopkins and Florence Eldridge.**

Strangers on a Train
—from the novel by Patricia Highsmith.
1951: (WB/Alfred Hitchcock) Robert Walker.
1970: *Once You Kiss a Stranger* (WB/Robert Sparr) Carol Lynley.

Street Girl
—from "The Viennese Charmer," a story by William Carey Wonderly.
1929: (RKO/Wesley Ruggles) Betty Compson.
1937: *That Girl from Paris* (RKO/Leigh Jason) Lily Pons.
1941: *Four Jacks and a Jill* (RKO/Jack Hively) Ray Bolger.

Sanctuary (1961): **Bradford Dillman and Lee Remick.**

Streets of Laredo
See *Texas Rangers, The.*

Street with No Name, The
1948: (Fox/William Keighley) Richard Widmark.
1955: *House of Bamboo* (Fox/Samuel Fuller) Robert Ryan.

Stronger Than Desire
See *Evelyn Prentice.*

Student Prince, The
—from the operetta by Sigmund Romberg and Dorothy Donnelly.
1923: (German).
1927: (MGM/Ernst Lubitsch) Norma Shearer.
1954: (MGM/Richard Thorpe) Ann Blyth.

Study in Scarlet, A
—from the novel by Conan Doyle.
1914: (British/George Pearson) James Braginton.
1933: (Fox/Edwin L. Marin) Reginald Owen.

Summer Holiday
See *Ah, Wilderness.*

Summer Magic
See *Mother Carey's Chickens.*

Sunny
—from the musical play by Otto Harbach, Oscar Hammerstein II, and Jerome Kern.
1930: (FN/William Seiter) Marilyn Miller.
1941: (RKO/Herbert Wilcox) Anna Neagle.

Sunset Pass
—from the novel by Zane Grey.
1929: (Par/Otto Brower) Jack Holt.
1933: (Par/Henry Hathaway) Randolph Scott.
1946: (RKO/William Berke) James Warren.

Sun Shines Bright, The
See *Judge Priest.*

Svengali
See *Trilby.*

Swamp Water
—from a novel by Vereen Bell.
1941: (Fox/Jean Renoir) Walter Brennan.
1952: *Lure of the Wilderness* (Fox/Jean Negulesco) Walter Brennan.

Swan, The
—from the play by Ferenc Molnar.
1925: (Par/Dimitri Buchowetzki) Frances Howard.
1930: *One Romantic Night* (UA/Paul L. Stein) Lillian Gish.
1956: (MGM/Charles Vidor) Grace Kelly.

Sweet Charity
   See *Nights of Cabiria.*

Sweet Rosie O'Grady
   See *Love Is News.*

Swing High, Swing Low
   See *Dance of Life, The.*

Swiss Family Robinson, The
   See *Perils of the Wild.*

Sword and the Rose, The
   See *When Knighthood Was in Flower.*

Sword of Sherwood Forest
   See *Robin Hood and His Merry Men.*

Tale of Two Cities, A
   —from the novel by Charles Dickens.
1911: (Vit/William Humphreys) Maurice Costello.
1917: (Fox/Frank Lloyd) William Farnum.
1922: (British/W. C. Rowden) Clive Brook.
1925: *Only Way, The* (British/Herbert Wilcox) John Martin Harvey.

A Tale of Two Cities (1935): **Ronald Colman and Donald Woods.**

1935: (MGM/Jack Conway) Ronald Colman.
1958: (British/Ralph Thomas) Dirk Bogarde.

Tales of Terror
   See *Living Dead, The.*

Tall, Dark, and Handsome
1941: (Fox/Bruce Humberstone) Cesar Romero.
1950: *Love That Brute* (Fox/Alexander Hall) Paul Douglas.

Taming of the Shrew, The
   —from the play by William Shakespeare.
1908: (Bio/D. W. Griffith) Florence Lawrence.
1911: (British/Frank Benson).
1914: (Norwegian).
1923: (British/Edwin J. Collins) Dacia Deane.
1929: (UA/Sam Taylor) Mary Pickford.
1953: *Kiss Me Kate* (MGM/George Sidney) Howard Keel.
1955: (French/Antonio Roman) Alberto Closas.
1961: (Russian/Sergei Kolosov) Alexei Popov.
1967: (Col/Franco Zeffirelli) Richard Burton.

Tangled Lives
   See *Woman in White, The.*

Tarzan of the Apes
   —from the story by Edgar Rice Burroughs.
1918: (FN/Scott Sidney) Elmo Lincoln.
1932: *Tarzan, the Ape Man* (MGM/W. S. Van Dyke) Johnny Weissmuller.
1959: *Tarzan, the Ape Man* (MGM/Joseph M. Newman) Dennis Miller.

Tarzan, the Ape Man
   See *Tarzan of the Apes.*

Tea for Two
   See *No, No, Nanette.*

Tell-Tale Heart, The
   See *Avenging Conscience, The.*

Tenderfoot, The
   See *Butter and Egg Man, The.*

Ten Little Indians
   See *And Then There Were None.*

Tennessee's Pardner
   —from a story by Bret Harte.
1916: (Lasky) Jack Dean.
1925: *Flaming Forties, The* (PDC/Tom Forman) Harry Carey.
1955: *Tennessee's Partner* (RKO/Allan Dwan) John Payne.

Tennessee's Partner
   See *Tennessee's Pardner.*

Kiss Me Kate (1953): Howard Keel and Kathryn Grayson starred in this modernization of Shakespeare's The Taming of the Shrew.

Ten Nights in a Barroom
  —from the novel by T. S. Arthur and the play by William
    W. Pratt.
1903: (Bio).
1903: (Lubin).
1909: (Ess).
1910: (Thanhouser).
1911: (Selig) Kathlyn Williams.
1913: (Photo Drama/Lee Beggs) Violet Homer.
1921: (Arrow/Oscar Apfel) John Lowell.
1926: (Colored) Charles Gilpin.
1931: (Kent/Willis Kent) William Farnum.

Terror Is a Man
  See *Island of Lost Souls.*

Tess of the Storm Country
  —from the novel by Grace Miller White.
1914: (Par/Edwin S. Porter) Mary Pickford.
1922: (UA/John S. Robertson) Mary Pickford.

1932: (Fox/Alfred Santell) Janet Gaynor.
1960: (Fox/Paul Guilfoyle) Diane Baker.

Tevya
  —from the play by Sholem Aleichem.
1939: (Maymam/Maurice Schwartz) Maurice Schwartz.
1971: *Fiddler on the Roof* (UA/Norman Jewison) Topol.

Texas Rangers, The
1936: (Par/King Vidor) Fred MacMurray.
1949: *Streets of Laredo* (Par/Leslie Fenton) William Holden.

That Girl from Paris
  See *Street Girl.*

That Night in Rio
  See *Folies Bergere.*

That Way with Women
  See *Millionaire, The.*

That Wonderful Urge
See *Love Is News.*

There's Always Tomorrow
—from a story by Ursula Parrott.
1934: (U/Edward Sloman) Frank Morgan.
1956: (U/Douglas Sirk) Barbara Stanwyck.

These Three
—from *The Children's Hour,* a play by Lillian Hellman.
1936: (UA/William Wyler) Miriam Hopkins.
1962: *Children's Hour, The* (UA/William Wyler) Audrey Hepburn.

They Drive by Night
See *Bordertown.*

They Knew What They Wanted
See *Secret Hour, The.*

They Made Me a Criminal
See *Life of Jimmy Dolan, The.*

Thief of Bagdad, The
1924: (UA/Raoul Walsh) Douglas Fairbanks.
1940: (UA/Ludwig Berger, Tim Whelan, Michael Powell) Sabu.
1961: (Italian/Arthur Lubin) Steve Reeves.

Thirteen, The
1937: (Russian/Mikhail Romm) Ivan Novoseltsei.
1943: *Sahara* (Col/Zoltan Korda) Humphrey Bogart.
1953: *Last of the Comanches* (Col/Andre de Toth) Broderick Crawford.

Last of the Comanches (1953): **Broderick Crawford and Barbara Hale.**

Thirteenth Chair, The
—from a play by Bayard Veiller.
1919: (Pathé/Leonce Perret) Creighton Hale.
1929: (MGM/Tod Browning) Conrad Nagel.
1937: (MGM/George Seitz) Lewis Stone.

Thirteenth Guest, The
—from a story by Armitage Trail.
1932: (Mon/Albert Ray) Ginger Rogers.
1943: *Mystery of the 13th Guest* (Mon/William Beaudine) Dick Purcell.

Thirteenth Letter, The
See *Corbeau, Le.*

Thirty-Nine Steps, The
from the novel by John Buchan.
1935: (British/Alfred Hitchcock) Robert Donat.
1960: (British/Ralph Thomas) Kenneth More.
1975: Remake announced to star Michael York.

This Gun for Hire
—from a novel by Graham Greene.
1942: (Par/Frank Tuttle) Alan Ladd.
1957: *Short Cut to Hell* (Par/James Cagney) Robert Ivers.

Those Who Dance
1924: (FN/Lambert Hillyer) Blanche Sweet.
1930: (WB/William Beaudine) Lila Lee.

Three Blind Mice
—from the play by Stephen Powys.
1938: (Fox/Walter A. Seiter) Loretta Young.
1941: *Moon over Miami* (Fox/Walter Lang) Betty Grable.
1946: *Three Little Girls in Blue* (Fox/Bruce Humberstone) June Haver.

Sahara (1943): **Bruce Bennett, Humphrey Bogart, and Dan Duryea.**

Three Coins in the Fountain
—from a novel by John H. Secondari.
1954: (Fox/Jean Negulesco) Clifton Webb.
1964: *Pleasure Seekers, The* (Fox/Jean Negulesco) Brian Keith.

Three Faces East
—from a play by Anthony Paul Kelly.
1926: (PDC/Rupert Julian) Jetta Goudal.
1930: (WB/Roy Del Ruth) Constance Bennett.
1940: *British Intelligence* (WB/Terry Morse) Boris Karloff.

Three for the Show
See *Too Many Husbands.*

Three Godfathers
See *Broncho Billy and the Baby.*

Three Hours
—from *Purple and Fine Linen,* a novel by May Edington.
1927: (FN/James Flood) Corinne Griffith.
1936: *Adventure in Manhattan* (Col/Edward Ludwig) Jean Arthur.

Three Little Girls in Blue
See *Three Blind Mice.*

Three Musketeers, The
—from the novel by Alexandre Dumas.
1908: (Italian).
1911: (Edison) Sydney Booth.
1913: (Edward Lurrillard).
1914: (France) M. Dehelly.
1916: *D'Artagnan* (Triangle/Thomas Ince) Orin Johnson.
1921: (UA/Fred Niblo) Douglas Fairbanks.
1935: (RKO/Rowland V. Lee) Walter Abel.
1939: (Fox/Allan Dwan) Don Ameche.
1948: (MGM/George Sidney) Gene Kelly.
1953: *Trois Mousqueteers, Le* (French/Andre Hunebelle) Georges Marchal.
1961: *Trois Mousqueteers, Le* (French/Bernard Borderie) Gerard Barry.
1974: (Fox/Richard Lester) Michael York.
1975: *Four Musketeers, The* (Fox/Richard Lester) Michael York.

Three on a Spree
See *Brewster's Millions.*

Threepenny Opera, The
See *Dreigroschenoper, Die.*

Three Sailors and a Girl
See *Butter and Egg Man, The.*

Three Sinners
—from *The Second Life,* a play by Rudolf Bernauer and Rudolf Oesterreicher.

1928: (Par/Rowland V. Lee) Pola Negri.
1931: *Once a Lady* (Par/Guthrie McClintic) Ruth Chatterton.

Three Worlds of Gulliver, The
See *Gulliver's Travels.*

Thundering Herd, The
—from the novel by Zane Grey.
1925: (Par/William K. Howard) Jack Holt.
1934: (Par/Henry Hathaway) Randolph Scott.

Tiger Rose
—from the play by David Belasco and Willard Mack.
1923: (WB/Sidney Franklin) Lenore Ulric.
1929: (WB/George Fitzmaurice) Lupe Velez.

'Til We Meet Again
See *One Way Passage.*

Times Square Playboy
See *Home Towners, The.*

Time To Kill
—from *The High Window,* a novel by Raymond Chandler.
1942: (Fox/Herbert I. Leeds) Lloyd Nolan.
1947: *Brasher Doubloon, The* (Fox/John Brahm) George Montgomery.

Tin Pan Alley
1940: (Fox/Walter Lang) Alice Faye.
1950: *I'll Get By* (Fox/Richard Sale) June Haver.

Toby Tyler
See *Circus Days.*

To Have and Have Not
—from a novel by Ernest Hemingway.
1944: (WB/Howard Hawks) Humphrey Bogart.
1950: *Breaking Point, The* (WB/Michael Curtiz) John Garfield.
1958: *Gun Runners, The* (UA/Don Siegel) Audie Murphy.

Tol'able David
—from the story by Joseph Hergesheimer.
1921: (FN/Henry King) Richard Barthelmess.
1930: (Col/John G. Blystone) Richard Cromwell.

Tom Brown's School Days
—from the novel by Thomas Hughes.
1914: (British/Rex Wilson) Jack Hobbs.
1940: (RKO/Robert Stevenson) Freddie Bartholomew.
1951: (British/Gordon Parry) John Howard Davies.

Tom, Dick, and Harry
1941: (RKO/Garson Kanin) Ginger Rogers.
1957: *Girl Most Likely, The* (RKO/Mitchell Leisen) Jane Powell.

Tom Jones
—from the novel by Henry Fielding.
1917: (British/Edwin J. Collins) Langhorne Burton.
1963: (British/Tony Richardson) Albert Finney.

Tom Sawyer
—from the novel by Mark Twain.
1917: (Par/Wm. Desmond Taylor) Jack Pickford.
1930: (Par/John Cromwell) Jackie Coogan.
1938: *Adventures of Tom Sawyer, The* (Selznick/Norman Taurog) Tommy Kelly.
1973: (UA/Don Taylor) Johnny Whitaker.

Too Many Husbands
—from a play by W. Somerset Maugham.
1940: (Col/Wesley Ruggles) Jean Arthur.
1955: *Three for the Show* (Col/H. C. Potter) Betty Grable.

Topaze
—from the play by Marcel Pagnol.
1933: (RKO/Harry D'Arrast) John Barrymore.
1935: (French/Louis Gasnier) Louis Jouvet.
1952: (French/Marcel Pagnol) Fernandel.
1962: *I Like Money* (British/Peter Sellers) Peter Sellers.

Tower of London
1939: (U/Rowland V. Lee) Basil Rathbone.
1962: (UA/Roger Corman) Vincent Price.

Toy Tiger, The
See *Mad about Music.*

Trader Horn
—from the book by Ethelreda Lewis.
1931: (MGM/W. S. Van Dyke) Harry Carey.
1972: (MGM/Reza S. Badiyi) Rod Taylor.

Trailin'
—from a novel by Max Brand.
1921: (Fox/Lynn F. Reynolds) Tom Mix.
1931: *Holy Terror, A* (Fox/Irving Cummings) George O'Brien.

Trail of the Lonesome Pine
—from the novel by John William Fox.
1916: (Par/Cecil B. DeMille) Thomas Meighan.
1923: (Par/Charles Maigne) Mary Miles Minter.
1936: (Par/Henry Hathaway) Henry Fonda.

Traviata, La
See *Lady with the Camellias, The.*

Treasure Island
—from the novel by Robert Louis Stevenson.
1908: (Vit).
1912: (Edison/J. Searle Dawley) Addison Rothermel.
1915: (Fox/C. M. Franklin, S. A. Franklin).
1920: (Par/Maurice Tourneur) Charles Ogle.

1934: (MGM/Victor Fleming) Wallace Beery.
1950: (Disney/Byron Haskin) Robert Newton.
1972: (British/John Hough) Orson Welles.

Treasure of the Golden Condor
See *Son of Fury.*

Trent's Last Case
—from the novel by Edmund Clerihew Bentley.
1920: (British/Richard Garrick) Gregory Scott.
1929: (Fox/Howard Hawks) Donald Crisp.
1952: (British/Herbert Wilcox) Orson Welles.

Trial of Joan of Arc, The
See *Joan of Arc.*

Trial of Mary Dugan, The
—from the play by Bayard Veiller.
1929: (MGM/Bayard Veiller) Norma Shearer.
1941: (MGM/Norman Z. McLeod) Laraine Day.

Trilby
—from the novel by George du Maurier.
1914: (British/Harold Shaw) Sir Herbert Tree.
1917: (World/Maurice Tourneur) Wilton Lackaye.
1923: (FN/James Young) Arthur Edmund Carewe.
1931: *Svengali* (WB/Archie Mayo) John Barrymore.
1953: *Svengali* (British/Noel Langley) Donald Wolfit.

Trip to Paradise, A
—from *Liliom,* a play by Ferenc Molnar.
1921: (Metro/Maxwell Karger) Bert Lytell.
1930: *Liliom* (Fox/Frank Borzage) Charles Farrell.
1935: *Liliom* (French/Fritz Lang) Charles Boyer.
1956: *Carousel* (Fox/Henry King) Gordon MacRae.

Trois Mousqueteers, Le
See *Three Musketeers, The.*

Tropennachte
See *Victory.*

Twenty-Thousand Leagues under the Sea
—from the novel by Jules Verne.
1907: (French).
1916: (U) Alan Holubar.
1954: (Disney/Richard Fleischer) James Mason.

Twenty-Thousand Years in Sing Sing
—from a book by Warden Lewis E. Lawes.
1933: (FN/Michael Curtiz) Spencer Tracy.
1940: *Castle on the Hudson* (WB/Anatole Litvak) John Garfield.

Two Against the World
See *Five Star Final.*

Two Fisted
See *Is Zat So?*

Twenty-Thousand Years in Sing Sing (1933): **Spencer Tracy and Arthur Byron.**

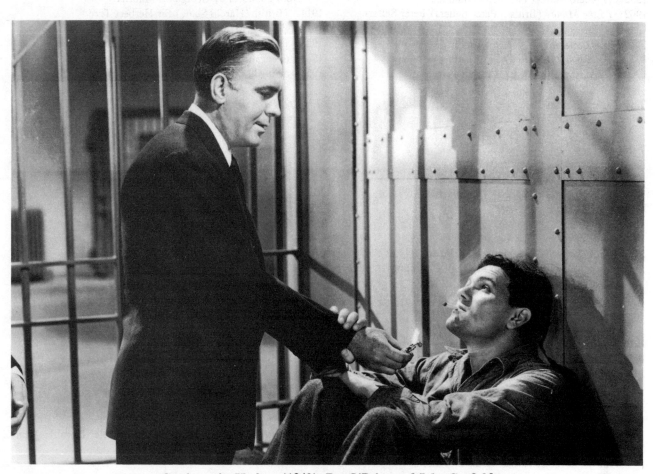

Castle on the Hudson (1940): **Pat O'Brien and John Garfield.**

Uncle Tom's Cabin
—from the novel by Harriet Beecher Stowe.
1903: (Edison/Edwin S. Porter).
1903: (Lubin).
1910: (French).
1910: (Thanhouser).
1913: (Imp) Harry Pollard.
1914: (World/William Robert Daly) Marie Eline.
1918: (Par/J. Searle Dawley) Marguerite Clark.
1927: (U/Harry Pollard) George Seigmann.
1965: (German/Geza von Radvanyi) Herbert Lom.

Under the Red Robe
—from the novel by Stanley Weyman and the play by Edward Rose.
1915: (British/Wilfred Noy) Owen Roughwood.
1923: (Goldwyn/Alan Crosland) Robert B. Mantell.
1937: (British/Victor Seastrom) Conrad Veidt.

Under the Tonto Rim
—from the novel by Zane Grey.
1928: (Par/Herman C. Raymaker) Richard Arlen.
1933: (Par/Henry Hathaway) Stuart Erwin.
1947: (RKO/Lew Landers) Tim Holt.

Under Two Flags
—from the novel by Ouida.
1916: (Fox/J. Gordon Edwards) Theda Bara.
1922: (U/Tod Browning) James Kirkwood.
1936: (Fox/Frank Lloyd) Ronald Colman.

Unfaithful, The
See *Letter, The.*

Unholy Love
—from *Madame Bovary,* a novel by Gustave Flaubert.
1932: (HOD/Albert Ray) Lila Lee.
1934: *Madame Bovary* (French/Jean Renoir) Valentine Tessier.
1937: *Madame Bovary* (German/Gerhard Lamprecht) Pola Negri.
1949: *Madame Bovary* (MGM/Vincente Minnelli) Jennifer Jones.

Unholy Three, The
—from the novel by Clarence A. Robbins.
1925: (MGM/Tod Browning) Lon Chaney.
1930: (MGM/Jack Conway) Lon Chaney.

Up in Arms
See *Nervous Wreck, The.*

Up in Mabel's Room
—from the play by Wilson Collison and Otto Harbach.
1926: (PDC/E. Mason Hopper) Marie Prevost.
1944: (UA/Allan Dwan) Marjorie Reynolds.

Up the River
1930: (Fox/John Ford) Spencer Tracy.
1938: (Fox/Alfred Werker) Preston Foster.

Uptight
See *Informer, The.*

Vagabond King, The
See *If I Were King.*

Valiant, The
—from the play by Robert Middlemass and Holworthy Hall.
1929: (Fox/William K. Howard) Paul Muni.
1940: *Man Who Wouldn't Talk, The* (Fox/David Burton) Lloyd Nolan.

Valley of the Giants
—from the story by Peter B. Kyne.
1919: (Par/James Cruze) Wallace Reid.
1927: (FN/Charles Brabin) Milton Sills.
1938: (WB/William Keighley) Wayne Morris.

Vanishing American, The
—from the novel by Zane Grey.
1926: (Par/George B. Seitz) Richard Dix.
1955: (Rep/Joseph Kane) Scott Brady.

Vanity Fair
—from a novel by William M. Thackeray.
1911: (Vit/Charles Kent) John Bunny.
1915: (Edison/Eugene Howland) Richard Tucker.
1923: (Goldwyn/Hugo Ballin) Eleanor Boardman.
1935: *Becky Sharp* (RKO/Rouben Mamoulian) Miriam Hopkins.

Verlorene Schuh, Der
See *Cinderella and the Fairy Godmother.*

Vickie
See *I Wake Up Screaming.*

Victory
—from the novel by Joseph Conrad.
1919: (Par/Maurice Tourneur) Jack Holt.
1930: *Dangerous Paradise* (Par/William Wellman) Richard Arlen.
1930: *On A Deserted Island* (French).
1930: *Tropennachte* (German).
1940: (Par/John Cromwell) Fredric March.

Virginian, The
—from the novel by Owen Wister.
1914: (Par) Dustin Farnum.
1923: (Preferred/Tom Forman) Kenneth Harlan.

1929: (Par/Victor Fleming) Gary Cooper.
1946: (Par/Stuart Gilmore) Joel McCrea.

Wabash Avenue
  See *Coney Island.*

Wagons Roll at Night, The
  See *Kid Galahad.*

Walk, Don't Run
  See *More the Merrier, The.*

Walpurgis Night
  See *Faust and Mephistopheles.*

Waltz Dream, A
  —from the operetta by Oscar Straus.
1926: (German/Ludwig Berger) Jacob Tiedtke.
1931: *Smiling Lieutenant, The* (Par/Ernst Lubitsch) Maurice Chevalier.

War and Peace
  —from the novel by Leo Tolstoy.
1916: (Russian).
1956: (Par/King Vidor) Audrey Hepburn.
1967: (Russian/Sergei Bondarchuk) Sergei Bondarchuk.

Warrens of Virginia, The
  —from the play by William C. DeMille.
1915: (Par/Cecil B. DeMille) Blanche Sweet.
1924: (Fox/Elmer Clifton) George Backus.

Watch the Birdie
  See *Cameraman, The.*

Waterloo Bridge
  —from a play by Robert E. Sherwood.
1931: (U/James Whale) Mae Clarke.
1940: (MGM/Mervyn LeRoy) Vivien Leigh.
1956: *Gaby* (MGM/Curtis Bernhardt) Leslie Caron.

Way Down East
  —from the play by Lottie Blair Parker.
1920: (UA/D. W. Griffith) Richard Barthelmess.
1935: (Fox/Henry King) Henry Fonda.

Way of All Flesh, The
  —from a story by Perley Poore Sheehan.
1927: (Par/Victor Fleming) Emil Jannings.
1940: (Par/Louis King) Akim Tamiroff.

Weekend at the Waldorf
  See *Grand Hotel.*

We Live Again
  See *Resurrection.*

We're Not Dressing
  See *Admirable Crichton, The.*

West of Shanghai
  See *Bad Man, The.*

West of the Pecos
  —from the novel by Zane Grey.
1935: (RKO/Phil Rosen) Richard Dix.
1945: (RKO/Edward Killy) Robert Mitchum.

West of Zanzibar
  —from the play by Chester DeVonde and Kilbourn Gordon.
1928: (MGM/Tod Browning) Lon Chaney.
1932: *Kongo* (MGM/William Cowen) Walter Huston.

West Side Story
  See *Romeo and Juliet.*

What Every Woman Knows
  —from the play by James M. Barrie.
1917: (British/Fred W. Durrant) Hilda Trevelyan.
1921: (Par/William C. DeMille) Lois Wilson.
1934: (MGM/Gregory La Cava) Helen Hayes.

What Price Glory
  —from the play by Maxwell Anderson and Laurence Stallings.
1926: (Fox/Raoul Walsh) Victor McLaglen.
1952: (Fox/John Ford) James Cagney.

What Price Hollywood
1932: (RKO/George Cukor) Constance Bennett.
1937: *Star Is Born, A* (UA/William Wellman) Janet Gaynor.
1954: *Star Is Born, A* (WB/George Cukor) Judy Garland.
1976: *Star Is Born, A* Remake announced to star Barbra Streisand.

When Knighthood Was in Flower
  —from the novel by Charles Major.
1922: (Par/Robert G. Vignola) Marion Davies.
1953: *Sword and the Rose, The* (Disney/Ken Annakin) Richard Todd.

When Ladies Meet
  —from a play by Rachel Crothers.
1932: (MGM/Harry Beaumont) Myrna Loy.
1941: (MGM/Robert Z. Leonard) Joan Crawford.

A Star Is Born (1937): **Fredric March** and **Janet Gaynor.**

A Star Is Born (1954): **James Mason** and **Judy Garland.**

When My Baby Smiles at Me
  See *Dance of Life, The.*

Where's Charley
  See *Charley's Aunt.*

Whistling in the Dark
  —from a play by Laurence Gross and Edward Carpenter.
1933: (MGM/Elliott Nugent) Ernest Truex.
1940: (MGM/S. Sylvan Simon) Red Skelton.

White Cargo
  —from a novel by Ida Vera Simonton.
1929: (British/J. B. Williams, Arthur Barnes) Gypsy Rhouma.
1942: (MGM/Richard Thorpe) Hedy Lamarr.

White Fang
  —from the novel by Jack London.
1925: (FBO/Lawrence Trimble) Theodore von Eltz.
1936: (Fox/David Butler) Michael Whalen.
1975: Remake announced.

White Sister, The
  —from the novel by F. Marion Crawford.
1915: (Ess) Viola Allen.
1923: (Metro/Henry King) Lillian Gish.
1933: (MGM/Victor Fleming) Helen Hayes.

Whoopee
  See *Nervous Wreck, The.*

Wife, Husband, and Friend
  —from *Career in C Major,* a novel by James M. Cain.
1939: (Fox/Gregory Ratoff) Warner Baxter.
1949: *Everybody Does It* (Fox/Edmund Goulding) Paul Douglas.

Wild Horse Mesa
  —from the novel by Zane Grey.
1925: (Par/George B. Seitz) Jack Holt.
1932: (Par/Henry Hathaway) Randolph Scott.
1947: (RKO/Wallace A. Grissell) Tim Holt.

Wine, Women, and Horses
  See *Dark Hazard.*

Within the Law
  —from a play by Bayard Veiller.
1917: (Vit/William P. S. Earle) Alice Joyce.
1923: (FN/Frank Lloyd) Norma Talmadge.
1931: *Paid* (MGM/Sam Wood) Joan Crawford.
1939: (MGM/Gustav Machaty) Ruth Hussey.

Wizard of Oz, The
  —from the book by Frank Baum.

1925: (Chadwick/Larry Semon) Dorothy Dawn.
1939: (MGM/Victor Fleming) Judy Garland.

Woman and Wife
  See *Jane Eyre.*

Woman Hungry
  See *Great Divide, The.*

Woman I Love, The
  See *L'Equipage.*

Woman in White, The
  —from the novel by Wilkie Collins.
1912: (Gem) Janet Salisbury.
1914: *Dream Woman, The* (Blaché/Alice Blaché) Claire Whitney.
1917: *Tangled Lives* (Fox/J. Gordon Edwards).
1929: (British/Herbert Wilcox) Blanche Sweet.
1948: (WB/Peter Godfrey) Eleanor Parker.

Woman's Face, A
  —from a play by Francis de Croisset.
1938: (Swedish/Gustav Molander) Ingrid Bergman.
1941: (MGM/George Cukor) Joan Crawford.

Woman's Resurrection, A
  See *Resurrection.*

Women, The
  —from a play by Clare Boothe.
1939: (MGM/George Cukor) Joan Crawford.
1956: *Opposite Sex, The* (MGM/David Miller) June Allyson.

Yellow Sky
  —from a story by W. R. Burnett.
1949: (Fox/William Wellman) Gregory Peck.
1967: *Jackals, The* (Fox/Robert D. Webb) Vincent Price.

You Belong to Me
1941: (Col/Wesley Ruggles) Henry Fonda.
1950: *Emergency Wedding* (Col/Edward Buzzell) Larry Parks.

You Can't Escape Forever
  See *Hi, Nellie.*

You Can't Run Away from It
  See *It Happened One Night.*

Young America
  —from a play by John Frederick Ballard.
1922: (Ess/Arthur Berthelet) Charles Frohman Everett.
1932: (Fox/Frank Borzage) Spencer Tracy.

The Woman in White (1948): **Eleanor Parker and Sydney Greenstreet.**

You're Never Too Young
  See *Major and the Minor, The.*

Your Obediant Servant
  See *Black Beauty.*

Zaza
  —from a play by Pierre Berton and Charles Simon.
1909: (Italian).

1915: (Par) Pauline Frederick.
1923: (Par/Allan Dwan) Gloria Swanson.
1939: (Par/George Cukor) Claudette Colbert.

Zorro
  See *Mark of Zorro, The.*